AF556500

UNDERSTANDING PATHOLOGY

By

Dr. Lata Bhattacharya

Professor
School of Studies in Zoology & Biotechnology
Vikram University
Ujjain (M.P.)
(India)

DISCOVERY PUBLISHING HOUSE PVT. LTD.
NEW DELHI-110 002

First Published - 2010

Reprinted - 2015

ISBN: 978-81-8356-526-4

Understanding Pathology

Published by:

DISCOVERY PUBLISHING HOUSE PVT. LTD.
4383/4B, Ansari Road, Darya Ganj
New Delhi-110 002 (India)
Phone: +91-11-23279245, 43596064-65
Fax: +91-11-23253475
E-mail: discoverypublishinghouse@gmail.com
sales@discoverypublishinggroup.com
web: www.discoverypublishinggroup.com

Printed at:
Infinity Imaging Systems
Delhi

Preface

The present title "Understanding Pathology" has been written for those students interested in careers in diverse fields of biological sciences. It provides a structured approach to learning by covering all the important topics in a uniform, systematic format. The book has been comprehensively designed incorporating recent advances in this fast moving field. It also provides accessible information on pathology in compact form for undergraduate students in biology and related life sciences. It is intelligible to the educated layman, though it deals with some complex ideas. It is an adequate text for all the requirements of students in this area. In addition, busy lecturers who require a quick reference compendium will find it useful, particularly for tutional planning. Simple, yet hopefully clear figures and tables are provided throughout the book.

The over-riding goal of this book, and indeed of the whole *Understanding series*, is to present the essential information concering pathology in a compact, readily accessible form which leads itself to student learning and revision. The convergence of various approaches has generated a rich panorama of detail, the significance of which we are still attempting to unraval. The present text has been written as an introduction to this rapidly growing field.

To make the work more comprehensive and informative, the author has consulted many authoritative books, research journals, abstracts, monographs etc., so there can be no claim to originality except in the manner of treatment.

The author expresses her thanks to her friends and colleagues whose continue inspirations have initiated her to bring out this book.

The author expresses her gratitude to Mr. Wasan and staff of M/s Discovery Publishing House Pvt. Ltd. for their whole hearted co-operation in the publication of this book.

In the mean time, the author will remain sincerely responsible for any shortcomings of the book and be grateful to the readers for their suggestions and constructive criticism for the continuous betterment of the book. She takes this opportunity to appeal to the readers to send their suggestions straightaway to his Publisher.

Author

Preface

Contents

1

INTRODUCTION

Pathology is the scientific study of disease. In clinical practice and medical education, pathology also has a wider meaning: pathology constitutes a large body of scientific knowledge and investigative methods essential for the understanding and practice of modern medicine.

Pathology embraces the *functional* and *structural* changes in disease, from the molecular level to the effects on the individual. Pathology is continually subject to change, revision and expansion as new scientific methods illuminate our knowledge of disease. The ultimate goal of pathology is the identification of the *causes* of disease, a fundamental objective leading to successful therapy and to disease prevention.

HISTORY OF PATHOLOGY

The evolution of concepts about the causes and nature of human disease reflects the prevailing ideas about the explanation for all worldly events and the techniques available for their investigation. Thus, the early dominance of *animism,* in the philosophies of Plato and Pythagoras, resulted in the attribution of disease to the adverse influences of immaterial or supernatural forces; it was therefore assumed that nothing could be learnt from the objective examination of the corpses of those who succumbed.

Even when the clinical significance of many abnormal physical signs and postmortem findings was established early in the long history of medicine, the nature of the underlying disease was thought to be due to an imbalance ('*isonomia*') of the various *humors* phlegm, black bile, and so on-as proposed by Empedocles and Hippocrates. These concepts are now firmly and irrevocably consigned to medical antiquity.

Morbid Anatomy

The first opportunity for the scientific study of disease came from the thorough internal examination of the body after death. *Autopsies* (necropsies or postmortem examinations) have been performed scientifically from about 300 Bc and have revealed much information that has helped to clarify the nature of many diseases.

As these examinations were confined initially to the gross (rather than microscopic) examination of the organs, this period is regarded as the era of morbid *anatomy*. During the 18th and 19th centuries in Europe, medical science was advanced by Baillie, Rokitansky and Aschoff, who meticulously performed and documented many thousands of autopsies and correlated their findings with the clinical signs and symptoms of the patients and with the natural history of a wide variety of diseases.

Microscopic and Cellular Pathology

Pathology, and indeed medicine as a whole, was revolutionised by the application *of microscopy* to the study of diseased tissues from about 1800. Before this, it was postulated that diseases arose by a process of *spontaneous generation;* that is, by metamorphosis independent of any external cause or other influence.

This notion seems ridiculous to us today, but 200 years ago nothing was known of bacteria, viruses, ionising radiation, carcinogenic chemicals, and so on. So Louis Pasteur's demonstration that micro-organisms in the environment could contaminate and impair the quality of wine was a major advance in our perception of the environment and our understanding of its possible adverse effects; it has had an enormous impact on medicine.

Rudolf Virchow, a German pathologist and ardent advocate of the microscope, recognised that the cell was the smallest viable constituent unit of the body and contrived a new and lasting set of ideas about disease-cellular *pathology*. The light miscroscope enabled him to see changes in diseased tissues at a cellular level and his observations, extended further by electron microscopy, have had a profound influence.

That does not mean to say that Virchow's cell pathology theory is immutable. Indeed, current advances in biochemistry are revolutionising our understanding of many diseases at a molecular level; we now have biochemical explanations for many of the cellular and clinical manifestations of disease.

Molecular Pathology

The impact of *molecular pathology* is exemplified by the advances

Table 1.1: Historical relationship between the hypothetical causes of disease and the dependence on techniques for their elucidation

Hypothetical cause of disease	*Techniques supporting causal hypothesis*	*Period*
Animism	None	Primitive, though the ideas persist in some cultures
Magic	None	Primitive, though the ideas persist in some cultures
Humors (excess or deficiency)	Early autopsies and clinical observations	c. 500 ac to c. 1500 AD
Spontaneous generation (abiogenesis)	Analogies with decomposing matter	Prior to 1800 AD
Environmental	Modern autopsp	1850 to present Cellular pathology (e.g. microscopy)
	Toxicology Microbiology Epidemiology	
Genetic	Molecular pathology (e.g. DNA analysis) and clinical observations on inherited defects	20th century to present

being made in our knowledge of the biochemical basis of congenital disorders and cancer. Techniques with relatively simple principles (less easy in practice) can reveal the change of a single nucleotide in genomic DNA resulting in the synthesis of the defective gene product that may be the fundamental lesion in a particular disease.

Cellular and Molecular Alterations in Disease

As a result of the application of modern scientific methods, we now have a clearer understanding of the ways in which diseases can be attributed to disturbances of normal cellular and molecular mechanisms.

SCOPE OF PATHOLOGY

Pathology is the foundation of medical science and practice. Without pathology, the practice of medicine would be reduced to myths and folklore.

Clinical and Experimental Pathology

Scientific knowledge about human diseases is derived from observations on patients or, by analogy, from experimental studies on animals and cell cultures. The greatest contribution comes from the detailed study of tissue and body fluids from patients.

Pathology has a key role in translational research by facilitating the transfer of knowledge derived from laboratory investigations into clinical practice.

Clinical Pathology

Clinical medicine is based on a longitudinal approach to a patient's illness-the patient's history, the examination and investigation, the diagnosis, and the treatment. Clinical pathology is more concerned with a cross-sectional. analysis at the level of the disease itself, studied in depth—the cause and mechanisms of the disease, and the effects of the disease upon the various organs and systems of the body.

These two perspectives are complementary and inseparable: clinical medicine cannot be practised without an understanding of pathology; pathology is meaningless if it is bereft of clinical implications.

Experimental Pathology

Experimental pathology is the observation of the effects of manipulations on experimental systems such as animal models of disease or cell cultures. Although advances in cell culture technology have reduced the usage of laboratory animals in medical research and experimental pathology, it is extremely difficult to mimic in cell cultures the physiological milieu that prevails in the intact human body.

Subdivisions of Clinical Pathology

Pathology is a vast subject with many ramifications. In practice, however, it has major subdivisions:

- *histopathology:* the investigation and diagnosis of disease from the examination of tissues
- *cytopathology:* the investigation and diagnosis of disease from the examination of isolated cells
- *haematology:* the study of disorders of the cellular and coagulable components of blood
- *microbiology:* the study of infectious diseases and the organisms responsible for them
- *immunology:* the study of the specific defence mechanisms of the body
- *chemical pathology:* the study and diagnosis of disease from the chemical changes in tissues and fluids
- *genetics:* the study of abnormal chromosomes and genes
- *toxicology:* the study of the effects of known or suspected poisons
- *forensic pathology:* the application of pathology to legal purposes (e.g. investigation of death in suspicious circumstances).

These subdivisions are more important professionally (because each requires its own team of expert specialists) than educationally at the undergraduate level.

The subject must be taught and learnt in an integrated manner, for the body and its diseases make no distinction between these professional subdivisions. This book, therefore, adopts a multidisciplinary approach to pathology.

In the systematic section, the normal structure and function of each organ is summarised, the pathological basis for clinical signs and symptoms is described, and the clinical implications of each disease are emphasised.

TECHNIQUES OF PATHOLOGY

Our knowledge of the nature and causation of disease has been disclosed by the continuing application of technology to its study.

Gross pathology

Before microscopy was applied to medical problems (c. 1800), observations were confined to those made with the unaided eye, and thus was accumulated much of our knowledge of the *morbid anatomy* of disease. Gross or macroscopic pathology is the modern nomenclature for this approach to the study of disease and, especially in the autopsy, it is still an important investigative method.

The gross pathology of many diseases is so characteristic that, when interpreted by the experienced pathologist, a fairly confident diagnosis can often be given before further investigation by, for example, light microscopy.

Light Microscopy

Advances in optics and the quality of lenses have resulted in a wealth of new information about the structure of tissues and cells in health and disease that can be gleaned from their examination by light microscopy.

If solid tissues are to be examined by light microscopy, the sample must first be thinly sectioned to permit the transmission of light and to minimise the superimposition of tissue components. These sections are routinely cut from tissue hardened by permeation with and embedding in wax or, less often, transparent plastic.

For some purposes (e.g. histochemistry, very urgent diagnosis) sections have to be cut from tissue that has been hardened rapidly by freezing. The sections are stained to help distinguish between different components of the tissue (e.g. nuclei, cytoplasm, collagen).

The microscope can also be used to examine cells from cysts, body cavities, sucked from solid lesions or scraped from body surfaces. This is *cytology* and is used widely in cancer diagnosis and screening.

Histochemistry

Histochemistry is the study of the chemistry of tissues, usually by microscopy of tissue sections after they have been treated with specific reagents so that the features of individual cells can be visualised.

Immunohistochemistry and Immunofluorescence

Immunohistochemistry and immunofluorescence employ antibodies (immunoglobulins with antigen specificity) to visualise substances in tissue sections or cell preparations; these techniques use antibodies linked chemically to enzymes or fluorescent dyes, respectively.

Immunofluorescence requires a microscope specially modified for ultraviolet illumination and the preparations are often not permanent (they fade). For these reasons, immunohistochemistry has become more popular; in this technique, the end product is a deposit of opaque or coloured material that can be seen with a conventional light microscope and does not deteriorate. The repertoire of substances detectable by

Table 1.2: Examples of the involvement of cellular and extra-cellular components in disease.

Component	*Normal function*	*Examples of alterations in disease*
Cellular		
Nucleus	Genes encoded in DNA	Inherited or spontaneous mutations (e.g. inherited, metabolic disorders, cancer) Site of viral replication
Mitochondria	Oxidative metabolism	Mutations of mitochondrial DNA Enzyme defects
Lysosomes	Enzymic degradation	Metabolic storage disorders Defects in microbial killing
Cell membrane	Functional envelope of cell	Defects in ion transfer (e.g. cystic fibrosis, hereditary spherocytosis)
Adhesion molecules	Cellular adhesion	increased expression in inflammation Decreased expression in neoplasia
HLA molecules	Immune recognition	Aberrant expression associated with autoimmune disease Haplotypes correlate with risk of some diseases
Receptors	Specific recognition	Hormone receptors cause cells to respond to physiological or pathological hormone levels Lymphocyte receptors enable immune responses to antigens

(Table Contd.)

(Table Contd.)

Component	*Normal function*	*Examples of alterations in disease*
Secreted products		
Collagen	Mechanical strength of tissues	Integrity of wounds Inherited defects (e.g. osteogenesis imperfecta)
Immunoglobulins	Antibody activity in immune reactions	Deficiency leads to increased infection risk Secreted by myeloma cells Specific antibody activity may be in response to infection or a marker of autoimmune disease
Nitric oxide	Endothelium-derived relaxing factor causing vasodilatation, inhibition of platelet aggregation and of proliferation	Increased levels in endotoxic shock and in asthma
Hormones	Control of specific target cells	Excess or deficiency due to disease of endocrine organs
Cytokines	Regulation of inflammatory and immune responses and of cell proliferation	Increased levels in inflammatory, immunological and reparative tissue reactions
Free radicals	Microbial killing	Inappropriate or excessive production causes tissue damage

these techniques has been greatly enlarged by the development of *monoclonal* antibodies.

Electron Microscopy

Electron microscopy has extended the range of pathology to the study of disorders at an organelle level, and to the demonstration of viruses in tissue samples from some diseases. The most common diagnostic use is for the interpretation of renal biopsies.

Biochemical Techniques

Biochemical techniques applied to the body's tissues and fluids in health and disease are now one of the dominant influences on our growing knowledge of pathological processes. The clinical role of biochemistry is exemplified by the importance of monitoring fluid and electrolyte homeostasis in many disorders. Serum enzyme assays are used to assess the integrity and vitality of various tissues; for example, raised levels of cardiac enzymes and troponin in the blood indicate damage to cardiac myocytes.

Haematological Techniques

Haematological techniques are used in the diagnosis and study of blood disorders. These techniques range from relatively simple cell counting, which can be performed electronically, to assays of blood coagulation factors.

Cell Cultures

Cell cultures are widely used in research and diagnosis. They are an attractive medium for research because of the ease with which the cellular environment can be modified and the responses to it monitored. Diagnostically, cell cultures are used to prepare chromosome spreads for *cytogenetic analysis*.

Medical Microbiology

Medical microbiology is the study of diseases caused by organisms such as bacteria, fungi, viruses and parasites. Techniques used include direct microscopy of appropriately stained material (e.g. pus), cultures to isolate and grow the organism, and methods to identify correctly the cause of the infection. In the case of bacterial infections, the most appropriate antibiotic can be selected by determining the sensitivity of the organism to a variety of agents.

Molecular Pathology

Many important advances are now coming from the science of molecular pathology revealing defects in the chemical structure of molecules arising from errors in the genome, the sequence of bases that directs amino acid synthesis. Using *in situ hybridisation* it is possible to render the presence of specific genes or their messenger RNA visible in tissue sections or cell preparations.

Minute quantities of nucleic acids can be amplified by the use of the *polymerase chain reaction* using oligonucleotide primers specific for the genes being studied.

DNA microarrays can be used to determine patterns of gene expression (mRNA). This powerful technique can reveal novel diagnostic and prognostic categories, indistinguishable by other methods.

Molecular pathology is manifested in various conditions, for example: abnormal haemoglobin molecules, such as in sickle cell disease; abnormal collagen molecules in osteogenesis imperfecta; and alterations in the genome governing the control of cell and tissue growth, playing an important part in the development of tumours.

LEARNING PATHOLOGY

Pathology is best learnt in two stages:

- *general pathology:* the mechanisms and characteristics of the principal types of disease process (e.g. inflammation, tumours, degenerations)
- *systematic pathology:* the descriptions of specific diseases as they affect individual organs or organ systems (e.g. appendicitis, lung cancer, atheroma).

General Pathology

General pathology is our current understanding of the causation, mechanisms and characteristics of the major categories of disease. These processes are covered in Part 2 of this textbook and many specific diseases are mentioned by way of illustration.

The principles of general pathology must be understood before an attempt is made to study systematic pathology. General pathology is the foundation of knowledge that has to be acquired before studying the systematic pathology of specific diseases.

Systematic Pathology

Systematic pathology is our current knowledge of specific diseases as they affect individual organs or systems. ('*Systematic*' should not be confused with '*systemic*' in this context. Systemic pathology would be characteristic of a disease that pervaded *all* body systems!) Each specific disease can usually be attributed to the operation of one or more categories of causation and mechanism featuring in general pathology.

Thus, acute appendicitis is acute inflammation affecting the appendix; carcinoma of the lung is the result of carcinogenesis acting upon cells in the lung, and the behaviour of the cancerous cells thus formed follows the pattern established for malignant tumours; and so on.

Building Knowledge and Understanding

There are two apparent difficulties facing the new student of pathology: *language* and *process*. Pathology, like most branches of science and medicine, has its own vocabulary of special terms: these need to be learnt and understood not just because they are the language of pathology; they are also a major part of the language of clinical medicine.

The student must not confuse the learning of the language with the learning of the mechanisms of disease and their effects on individual organs and patients. In this book, each important term will be clearly defined in the main text or the glossary or both.

A logical and orderly way of thinking about diseases and their characteristics must be cultivated; for each disease entity the student should be able to list the chief characteristics:

- epidemiology
- aetiology
- pathogenesis
- pathological and clinical features
- complications and sequelae
- prognosis
- treatment.

Our knowledge about many diseases is still incomplete, but at least such a list will prompt the memory and enable students to organise their knowledge. Pathology is learnt through a variety of media.

Even the bedside, operating theatre and outpatient clinic provide ample opportunities for further experience of pathology; hearing a diastolic cardiac murmur through a stethoscope should prompt the listening student to consider the pathological features of the narrowed mitral valve orifice (mitral stenosis) responsible for the murmur, and the effects of this stenosis on the lungs and the rest of the cardiovascular system.

Pathology in the Problem-oriented Integrated Medical Curriculum

Although medicine, surgery, pathology and other disciplines are still taught as separate subjects in some curricula, students must develop an integrated understanding of disease. To encourage this integrated attitude, in this textbook the pathological basis of common clinical signs is frequently emphasised so that students can relate their everyday clinical experiences to their knowledge of pathology.

In general, the development of a clinicopathological understanding of disease can be gained by two equally legitimate and complementary approaches:

- problem-oriented
- disease-oriented.

In learning pathology, the disease-oriented approach is more relevant because medical practitioners require knowledge of diseases (e.g. pneumonia, cancer, ischaemic heart disease) so that correct diagnoses can be made and the most appropriate treatment given.

The Problem-oriented Approach

The problem-oriented approach is the first step in the clinical diagnosis of a disease. In many illnesses, symptoms alone suffice for diagnosis. In other illnesses, the diagnosis has to be supported by clinical signs (e.g. abnormal heart sounds).

In some instances, the diagnosis can be made conclusively only by special investigations (e.g. laboratory analysis of blood or tissue samples, imaging techniques). The links between *diseases* and the *problems* they produce are emphasised in the systematic chapters and are exemplified here.

Justifications for the problem-oriented approach are that:

- Patients present with 'problems' rather than 'diagnoses'.
- Some clinical problems lack a known pathological basis (this is true particularly of psychiatric conditions such as depressive illness).
- Clinical treatment is often directed towards relieving the patient's problems rather than curing their disease (which may either remit spontaneously or be incurable).

The Disease-oriented Approach

Modern pathological understanding of illnesses is based on a disease-oriented approach; knowledge of diseases and their clinical manifestations is essential for good medical practice. The disease-oriented approach is also the most successful way of presenting pathological knowledge.

It would be possible to compose a textbook of pathology in which the chapters were entitled, for example, 'Cough', 'Weight loss', 'Headaches' and 'Pain' (these being problems), but the reader would be unlikely to come away with a clear understanding of the diseases.

Table 1.3: The problem-oriented approach: examples of combinations of clinical problems and their pathological basis

Problems	*Pathological basis (diagnosis)*	*Comment*
Weight loss and haemoptysis	*Lung cancer or tuberculosis*	Can be distinguished by finding either cancer cells or mycobacteria in sputum
Dyspnoea and ankle swelling	*Heart failure*	Due to, for example, valvular disease
Chest pain and hypotension	*Myocardial infarction*	Should be confirmed by ECG and serum assay of cardiac enzymes
Vomiting and diarrhoea	*Gastroenteritis*	Specific microbial cause can be determined
Headache, impaired vision and microscopic haematuria	*Hypertension*	May be due to various causes or, more commonly, without evident cause
Headache, vomiting and photophobia	*Subarachnoid haemorrhage or meningitis*	Can be distinguished by other clinical features and examination of cerebrospinal fluid

This is because one disease may cause a variety of problems-for example, cough, weight loss, headaches and pain-and may therefore crop up in several chapters. Consequently, this textbook, like most textbooks of pathology (and, indeed, of medicine) adopts a disease-oriented approach.

MAKING DIAGNOSES

Diagnosis is the act of naming a disease in an individual patient. The diagnosis is important because it enables the patient to benefit from treatment that is known, or is at least likely, to be effective from having observed its effects on other patients with the same disease.

The process of making diagnoses involves:

- taking a clinical history to document *symptoms*

- examining the patient for *clinical signs*
- if necessary, performing *investigations* guided by the provisional diagnosis based on signs and symptoms.

Although experienced clinicians can diagnose many patients' diseases quite rapidly (and usually reliably), the student will find that it is helpful to adopt a formal strategy based on a series of logical steps leading to the gradual exclusion of various possibilities and the emergence of a single diagnosis. For example:

- First decide which organ or body system seems to be affected by the disease.
- From the signs and symptoms, decide which general category of disease (inflammation, neoplasia, etc.) is likely to be present.
- Then, using other factors (age, gender, previous medical history, etc.), infer a diagnosis or a small number of possibilities for investigation.
- Investigations should be performed only if the outcome of each one can be expected to resolve the diagnosis, or influence management if the diagnosis is already known.

This strategy can be refined and presented in the form of decision trees or diagnostic algorithms, but these details are outside the scope of this book.

Diagnostic Pathology

In living patients we often investigate and diagnose their illness by applying pathological methods to the examination of *tissue biopsies* and *body fluids. If* there are clinical indications to do so, it may be possible to obtain a series of samples from which the course of the disease can be monitored.

The applications of pathology in clinical diagnosis and patient management are described in Chapter 4.

Autopsies

Autopsy (necropsy and postmortem examination are synonymous) means to 'see for oneself'. In other words, rather than relying on clinical signs and symptoms and the results of diagnostic investigations during life, here is an opportunity for direct inspection and analysis of the organs.

Autopsies are useful for:

- determining the *cause of death*

- *audit* of the accuracy of clinical diagnosis
- *education* of undergraduates and postgraduates
- *research* into the causes and mechanisms of disease
- gathering accurate *statistics* about disease incidence.

The clinical use of information from autopsies is described in other chapter of this book.

For the medical undergraduate and postgraduate, the autopsy is an important medium for the learning of pathology. It is an unrivalled opportunity to correlate clinical signs with their underlying pathological explanation.

PATHOLOGY AND POPULATIONS

Although pathology, as practised professionally, is a laboratory-based clinical discipline focused on the care of individual patients and the advancement of medical knowledge, our ideas about the causes of disease, disability and death have wide implications for society.

Causes and Agents of Disease

There is socially (and politically) relevant controversy about what actually constitutes the *cause* of a disease. Critics argue that the science of pathology leads to the identification of merely the *agents of* some diseases rather than their underlying causes.

For example, the bacterium *Mycobacterium tuberculosis* is the infective agent resulting in tuberculosis but, because many people exposed to the bacterium alone do not develop the disease, social deprivation and malnutrition (both of which are epidemiologically associated with the risk of tuberculosis) might be regarded by some as the actual causes.

Without doubt, the marked fall in the incidence of many serious infectious diseases during the 20th century has been achieved at least as much through improvements in housing, hygiene, nutrition and sewage treatment as by specific immunisation and antibiotic treatment directed at the causative organisms.

The Health of a Nation

Because the methods used in pathology enable reliable diagnoses to be made, either during life by, for example, biopsy or after death by autopsy, the discipline has an important role in documenting the incidence of disease in a population.

Cancer registration data are most reliable when based on histologically proven diagnoses; this happens in most cases. Epidemiological data derived from death certificates are notorio-usly unreliable unless verified by autopsy. The information thus obtained can be used to determine the true incidence of a disease in a population and the resources for its prevention and treatment can be deployed where they will achieve the greatest benefit.

Preventing Disability and Premature Death

Laboratory methods are used increasingly for the detection of early disease by population screening. The prospects of cure are invariably better the earlier a disease is detected.

For example, the incidence of death from cancer of the cervix is lowered by screening programmes; in many countries, women have their cervix scraped at regular intervals and the exfoliated cells are examined microscopically to detect the earliest changes associated with development of cancer.

Screening for breast cancer is primarily by mammography (X-ray imaging of the breast); any abnormalities are further investigated either by examining cells aspirated from the suspicious area or by histological examination of the tissue itself.

2

Clinical Diagnosis

Laboratory techniques play an important part in the diagnosis and treatment of disease in patients. Many of the tests performed in pathology laboratories are diagnostic, quantitative measurements or prognostic, but these are complemented by expert advice on the interpretation of the results.

Microbiologists are also involved in formulating policies designed to prevent spread of infection in hospitals; haematologists have clinical responsibilities for treating patients with haematological malignancies and other disorders.

In this chapter the general principles of diagnostic tests, quantitative measurements and prognostic tests are given and these are then related to the specific roles of clinical chemistry, cytogenetics, cytopathology, haematology, histopathology, immunology, microbiology and autopsies.

TYPES OF LABORATORY TESTS

Diagnostic Tests

Diagnostic tests are those which are made on a sample from a patient, the result allocating the case to a diagnostic grouping; an example would be a needle core biopsy of a lesion of the breast which is sent for histopathological examination and classified into a benign or malignant (i.e. cancer) category.

Quantitative measurements, such as haemoglobin concentration or arterial blood oxygen tension, may be used in the clinician's diagnostic process but they do not by themselves assign a patient to a particular diagnostic category. A diagnostic test may be based on:

- *quantitative measurement,* such as the level of (3 human

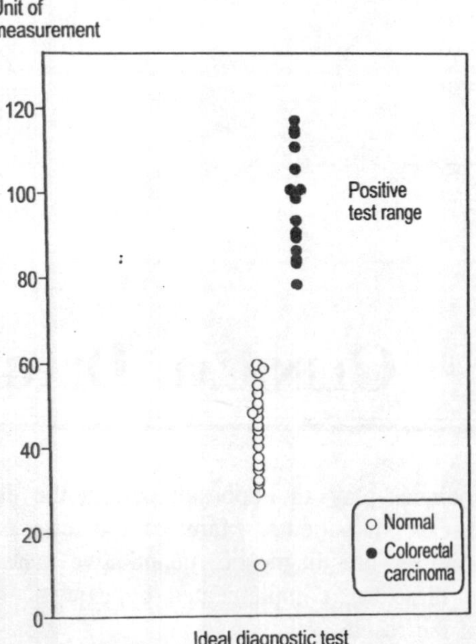

Figure 2.1: Distribution graph for an ideal diagnostic test.

chorionic gonadotrophin in the diagnosis of trophoblastic disease

- *subjective assessment,* based on past experience such as a histop athologist's assessment of a needle core biopsy or fine needle aspirate of the breast.

The ideal diagnostic test would produce complete separation between two diagnostic categories; usually, however, there is some overlap. This problem can be illustrated by taking as an example a screening test for colorectal carcinoma which makes measurements on a sample of faeces (many attempts have been made to devise such a test using measurements of blood contained in the faeces and other parameters).

An ideal diagnostic test would produce complete separation of patients with and without colorectal carcinoma. The majority of real diagnostic tests do not provide complete separation between diagnostic categories and there is overlap.

The effectiveness of a diagnostic test can be expressed using a number of different parameters:

- *A true positive* result (TP) is a positive result from the test under consideration which is confirmed by the real outcome of the situation (e.g. a needle core biopsy of the breast (NCB)

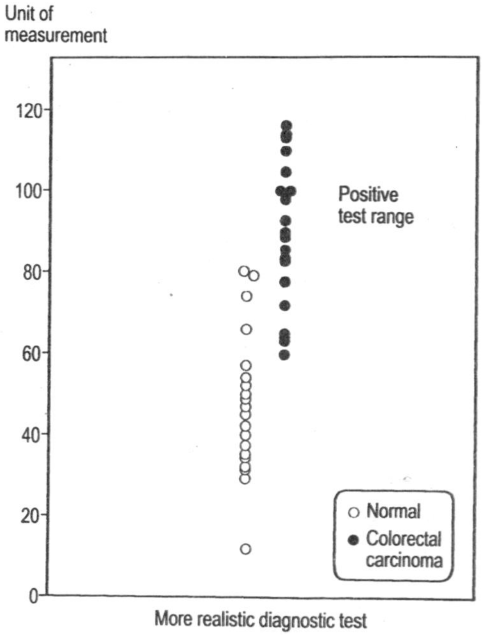

Figure 2.2: Distribution graph of a more realistic diagnostic test.

which is reported as malignant and the subsequently excised breast tissue contains invasive carcinoma).

- *A true negative* result (TN) is a negative test result confirmed by a negative real outcome.
- A *false positive* result (FP) is a positive test result which has a negative real outcome (e.g. an NCB which is reported as malignant but the subsequently excised breast tissue shows no evidence of malignancy).
- *A false negative* result (FN) is the reverse of this.

These can be combined into the following measures:

$$\text{Accuracy} = \frac{(\text{TN}+\text{TP})}{(\text{TN}+\text{TP}+\text{FN}+\text{FP})}.100$$

$$\text{Sensitivity} = \frac{(\text{TP})}{(\text{TP}+\text{FN})}.100$$

$$\text{Specificity} = \frac{(\text{TN})}{(\text{TN}+\text{FP})}.100$$

Table 4.1 True and false test results in needle core biopsy of the breast (NCB)

Actual outcome	*Test result from NCB*	
	Benign	***Malignant***
Benign	True negative	False positive
Malignant	False negative	True positive

$$\text{Prdictive value of positive result} = \frac{(\text{TP})}{(\text{TP} + \text{FP})}.100$$

$$\text{Predictive value of negative result} = \frac{(\text{TN})}{(\text{TN} + \text{FN})}.100$$

The desired values of these for a particular test will vary according to the action taken on the result. A malignant NCB result can result in a surgeon excising the breast (mastectomy), so the specificity and predictive value of a positive result must be as close to 100% as possible.

In contrast, if a disease has a relatively safe, non-toxic treatment (such as a course of antibiotics) but the consequences of not detecting the disease can be fatal (e.g. bacterial meningitis), the sensitivity and predictive value of a negative result should be as high as possible.

In most situations there is a direct 'trade-off' between sensitivity and specificity and a suitable threshold has to be set that will give the best overall performance. In many medical situations a continuous biological spectrum is arbitrarily divided into a number of discrete categories which will always lead to some apparent misclassification but is necessary to give information on which clinicians can base their management decisions (e.g. division of intraepithelial neoplasia of the uterine cervix into three categories).

A laboratory's performance in diagnostic tests should be monitored by a formal *audit process* and by use of appropriate positive and negative controls in tests.

Quantitative Measurements

Many tests in pathology do not categorise results into discrete groups but give a quantitative result which is interpreted in relation to a 'normal' range of values. Examples of such tests include measurement of haemoglobin concentration, electrolyte concentrations and blood oxygen and carbon dioxide levels.

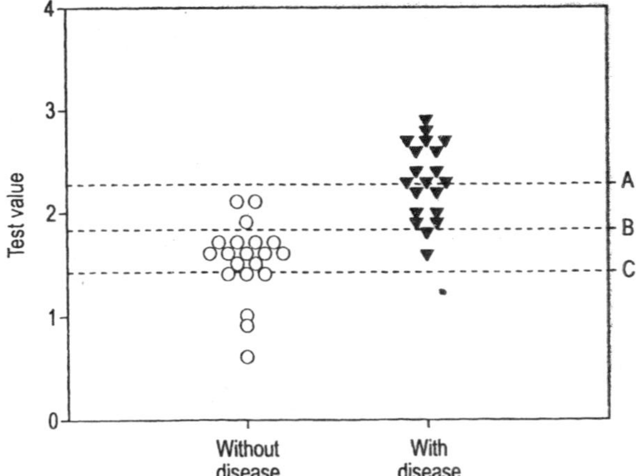

Figure 2.3: A graph showing the effect of moving the threshold value for a test on its sensitivity and specificity.

The measures of performance for such tests differ from diagnostic grouping tests. In quantitative tests the *accuracy* of the measurement (how close the measured value is to the 'true' value determined by a more accurate or absolute method) and the *reproducibility* of the measurement (what variation there is when measuring the same sample many times) are important parameters.

These can be assessed by using reference samples with 'known' values and putting these through the measurement system at regular intervals; most laboratories will have their own reference samples which are used frequently (internal quality assurance), and graphs of single measurement and running mean values will be used to ensure that the test is performing within expected limits and not showing 'drift' away from the central expected value.

Many countries also have *external quality assurance schemes* where reference samples are sent to all participating laboratories to ensure acceptable analytical performance. When a laboratory gives a quantitative result for a parameter that is under physiological control, a reference range is often given to facilitate interpretation of the result.

If a parameter shows normal (Gaussian) distribution in the local population, the 'normal' range is often given as two standard deviations below the mean to two standard deviations above the mean. If a value lies outside this range then it lies outside 95% of the results for that population and may be regarded as abnormal, but 2.5% of the healthy population will have values lying outside the range at either end. Thus,

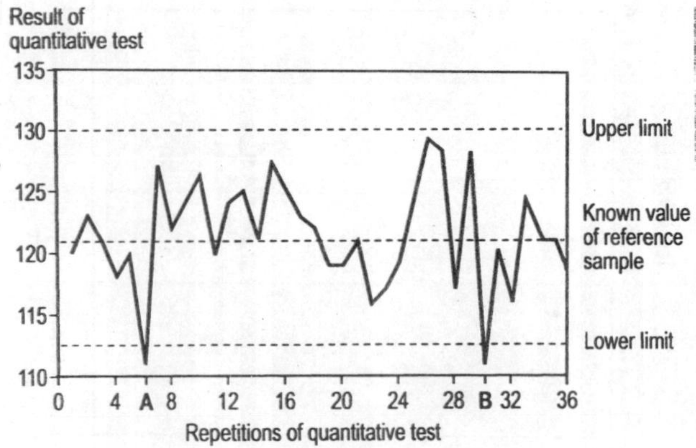

Figure 2.4: Internal quality assurance graph for a quantitative pathological test.

all the details of the individual case must be considered, including other measurements, as a number of results at the top end of the 'normal' range could be more significant than a single result just above the 'normal' range. If the distribution is not Gaussian it may require normalisation by transformation, or non-parametric methods must be used.

Prognostic Tests

In many tumours, assignment to a diagnostic category (e.g. adenoma or carcinoma) gives an indication of the prognosis for the individual patient, but within such groupings (e.g. colorectal carcinoma) there may be wide variation in the biological behaviour of the tumour.

In order to plan appropriate treatment and to be able to give useful information and counselling to individual patients many prognostic pathological tests have been developed. In tumour pathology one of the most predictive prognostic tests is *staging* of the tumour (extent of spread), which is always assessed in the histopathological examination of specimens.

One of the best examples of this is Dukes' staging of colorectal carcinoma. The *histological type* of tumour has important prognostic implications, particularly in some organs; subjects with papillary thyroid carcinoma have a life expectancy which is the same as the rest of the general population without the tumour, whereas subjects with anaplastic thyroid carcinoma have a median survival of a few months.

The *grade* of the tumour, an assessment of its degree of differentiation and proliferative activity, also has predictive value; well-differentiated tumours (closely resembling parent tissue) with few mitoses have a

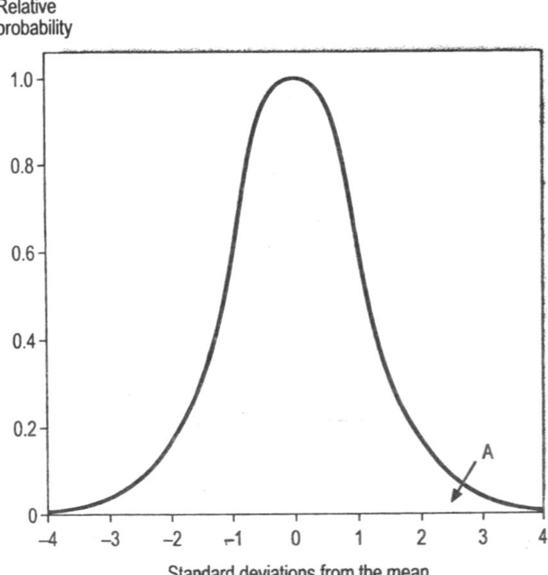

Figure 2.5 : Quantitative measurement with a normal (Gaussian) distribution in the population.

better prognosis. In tumours which produce substances that enter the blood or urine (e.g. α-fetoprotein produced by testicular teratomas), measurement of the levels of these at the time of diagnosis may be predictive of prognosis (and can be used in follow-up). As more becomes known of the molecular abnormalities of tumours, the possibilities for specific molecular tests that will have prognostic value increase, but the translation of an apparently significant research result into a routinely used prognostic test is not straightforward.

When evaluating any new prognostic test the significance for the individual patient has to be considered; a test which shows a statistically significant difference between two large groups of patients may not assign individual cases to a prognostic category with a sufficient degree of certainty to be useful in management decisions or patient information.

One recently developed test that has found usage is the detection of expression of the transmembrane receptor tyrosine kinase KIT, which is defined by the CD 117 antigen and is the product of the *c-kit* proto-oncogene in stromal tumours of the gastrointestinal tract. This can be detected by immunohistochemistry, which, if positive, predicts that the patient's tumour will respond to treatment with a specific tyrosine kinase inhibitor, imatinib mesylate.

SPECIALISED TESTS

- Clinical chemistry: measurement and interpretation of substances in blood, other body fluids and tissues
- Cytogenetics: analysis of chromosomal and genetic abnormalities
- Cytopathology: diagnostic interpretation of the morphology and other characteristics of cells; commonly used in cancer screening and diagnosis
- Haematology: diagnosis of diseases of the bone marrow and blood; blood transfusion
- Histopathology: diagnostic interpretation of tissue samples
- Immunology: investigation of immunological responses
- Microbiology: detection and identification of viruses, bacteria, fungi and parasites

Clinical Chemistry

Methods in clinical chemistry detect and measure subcellular substances-usually in the blood but also in other bodily fluids and tissue:

- blood
  - serum
  - plasma
  - red blood cells
- urine
- faeces
- gastric contents/aspirate
- effusions (e.g. pleural, pericardial).

The range of molecules measured is constantly expanding, ranging through electrolytes (such as sodium and potassium), larger inorganic molecules (urea), proteins (including many enzymes) and exogenous molecules (such as carbon monoxide and drugs):

- *blood gases:* e.g. oxygen, carbon dioxide
- *electrolytes:* e.g. sodium, potassium
- *smaller organic molecules:* e.g. urea, creatinine
- *hormones:* e.g. thyroid stimulating hormone, prolactin
- *non-enzymatic proteins:* e.g. albumin, lipoproteins
- *enzymes:* e.g. aspartate transaminase, amylase
- *drugs:* e.g. lithium, digoxin.

Since many of the tests in clinical chemistry are quantitative, the laboratories have extensive programmes of internal and external quality control, and laboratory reports quote reference ranges.

For many tests, ranges appropriate for the age and sex of the patient may be quoted. As with all pathological tests the clinician with direct responsibility for the patient must decide whether a particular test is an appropriate investigation and what sample is most appropriate for that test.

These considerations are especially important in clinical chemistry where large automated machines can measure a wide range of substances on a single sample and, if not used selectively, may generate non-essential data which may be difficult to interpret and require unnecessary further investigations. The type of sample and the circumstances in which it is taken are also important.

It is outside the scope of this chapter to give specific recommendations for individual tests but examples of inappropriate samples would be blood taken for glucose analysis shortly after a large carbohydraterich meal, blood taken for electrolyte analysis from a vein in an arm receiving an intravenous infusion, and blood taken for a digoxin level immediately after a dose of the drug.

The interpretation of results also requires knowledge about the substances being assayed, and the advice of a specialist clinical chemist is often useful. An example of this is the use of cardiac enzymes measured to determine whether a myocardial infarct has occurred.

The enzymes lactate dehydrogenase, aspartate transaminase and creatine phosphokinase normally reside intracellularly in muscle cells; if muscle is damaged, the enzymes gain entry to the blood and elevated levels may be detected. The interpretation of these assays requires knowledge about the time course of the enzyme release and the possible sites of enzyme release.

The enzymes are not released immediately when the myocytes become hypoxic because the cell membranes take some time to break down; Figure elsewhere in this chapter shows typical curves of the enzymes in blood after a myocardial infarct; it can also be seen from this graph that total creatine kinase and aspartate transaminase reach their peaks earlier than lactate dehydrogenase.

The interpretation of the enzyme results will thus require knowledge of these properties and an estimate of when the ischaemic myocardial event is likely to have occurred in the patient. Cardiac muscle is not the only tissue to contain these enzymes, they are also present in skeletal muscle, but different forms of the enzymes (isoenzymes) are

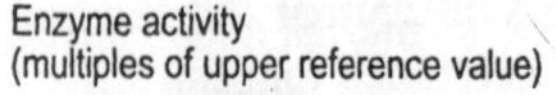

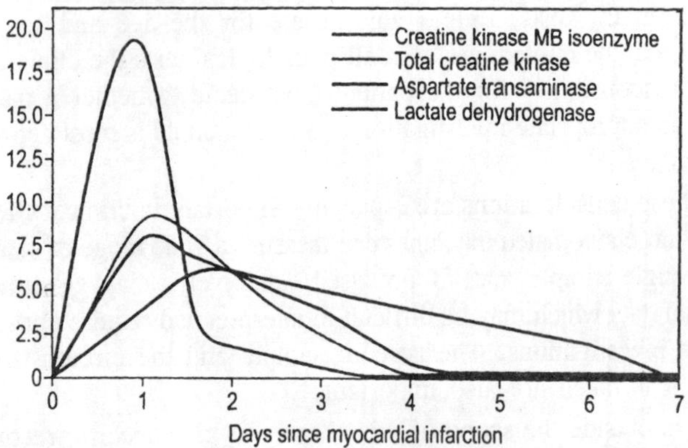

Figure 2.6: Enzyme assays.

present in the different sites. If an assay is used which measures the total amount of these enzymes, damage to skeletal muscle would produce elevations.

Thus, if a patient had been found collapsed at home and had been lying on the floor, measurement of the isoenzymes, such as creatine kinase MB, or muscle proteins would be required to ascertain whether an ischaemic myocardial event had precipitated the collapse. Similar interpretative considerations apply to all tests in clinical chemistry.

Cytogenetics and Molecular Pathology

Cytogenetics and molecular pathology are playing an increasingly important role in clinical pathology with more discrete genetic abnormalities being identified in specific tumours. Laboratory techniques may look at the number and form of chromosomes, the *karyotype,* or at more specific areas of DNA within chromosomes.

The techniques for investigating individual genetic abnormalities are described in other chapter of this book. The karyotype can be examined using a sample of peripheral blood. Phytohaemagglutinin is added to the blood, which stimulates the T-lymphocytes to divide; colchicine is then added to arrest the dividing cells in metaphase when the chromosomes will be most easily visible.

The chromosomes may be stained by several methods but the most common is the Giemsa method which produces alternate light and dark bands when the preparation is viewed by light microscopy (G-banding); the patterns of banding allow identification of each chromosome and visualisation of missing or additional material of about 4000 kilobases or more. Abnormalities may be divided into:

- numerical abnormalities
  - — aneuploidy
  - — polyploidy
- structural abnormalities
  - — translocation
  - — deletion and ring chromosome
  - — duplication
  - — inversion
  - — isochromosome
  - — centric fragment.

The number of chromosomal abnormalities associated with specific tumours is growing rapidly; currently there are over 30 human tumour types associated with non-random chromosomal abnormalities. One of the chromosomal abnormalities with the strongest association with a malignancy is the Philadelphia chromosome in chronic myeloid leukaemia.

This abnormality is a reciprocal translocation between chromosomes 9 and 22 resulting in the translocation of the *abl* oncogene to a breakpoint cluster region, which results in a hybrid gene producing a novel protein that may be responsible for the neoplastic transformation. Another chromosomal abnormality strongly associated with a specific tumour is the 13g14 microdeletion seen in retinoblastoma.

As more of these abnormalities are found it becomes increasingly important to send tumour samples for cytogenetic analysis as a diagnostic/ prognostic procedure. Cytogenetic analysis requires fresh tissue which has been placed in an appropriate transport medium and which must be transported rapidly to the cytogenetics laboratory.

It is important to send appropriate samples, which might include 'normal' background tissue as well as tumour; the most appropriate staff to do this might be the histopathologists if they receive the specimen fresh before immersion in a fixative solution.

Cytopathology

Cytopathology specimens consist of single cells or clumps of cells which are dissociated from their surrounding tissues. The technique is used mainly for the investigation and diagnosis of malignancy. The cells are distributed on glass slides, either by the person who takes the sample smearing them directly onto the slide at the time the sample is taken or by centrifugation methods in the laboratory.

The slides are stained by an appropriate method, which is most often the Papanicolaou technique, and examined by light microscopy. Since the cells are dissociated from their surrounding tissue, some features that are used in histopathological diagnosis, such as invasion and other architectural abnormalities, are not available for assessment. The main features used in cytopathological diagnosis are:

- variation in size of nuclei (nuclear pleomorphism)
- increased staining of DNA in the nucleus (nuclear hyperchromatism)
- ratio of nuclear area to cytoplasmic area (by subjective assessment).

Cells may be collected for cytological examination from epithelium shed or scraped from a body surface *(exfoliative cytology)* or by aspirating cells through a fine bore needle into a syringe *(aspiration cytology)*. Many cytopathological specimens are taken to assess dysplasia or malignancy in tissues but infective pathologies may also be diagnosed by this method (for example *Pneumocystis carinii* pneumonia in immunosuppressed patients may be detected by cytological examination of alveolar washings).

Cancer Screening

Cervix

One of the most frequent uses of cytopathological techniques is in the detection and assessment of dysplasia and neoplasia in the uterine cervix. The surface of the cervix is relatively accessible by speculum examination and cells are scraped from the surface at the junction between the squamous and glandular epithelium (the transformation zone) using a spatula.

The cells are spread directly onto a glass slide, fixed and sent to the cytopathology laboratory where they are stained using the Papanicolaou technique. Cells from areas of dysplasia or neoplasia are recognised by their abnormal nuclear (*dyskaryotic*) features and the degree of abnormality is graded in a range from mild to severe.

Mild abnormalities represent early dysplastic or reactive changes in the cervical epithelium, which may regress, so the usual management for those women is surveillance by further smears. More severe changes represent marked dysplasia or carcinoma; women whose smears show such changes are referred to gynaecologists for further assessment and probable surgical treatment.

In many countries cervical cytology is performed as a screening programme; the aim is to take samples at regular intervals from all women who are at risk of developing cervical cancer (which is most women with a uterus who have had sexual intercourse) and to detect early abnormalities which can be treated before invasive carcinoma has developed.

The method of cytopathological examination of cells from the uterine cervix is effective in detecting the abnormalities but most cervical screening programmes have not been totally effective because a significant proportion of women have failed to attend for screening.

Haematology

Haematology covers diseases of the blood; the pathology of these is described in other chapter of this book. The work of haematologists is usually divided into three areas:

- diagnosis of haematological disorders
- management of haematological disorders
- blood transfusion.

The diagnosis of haematological disorders is based on clinical history and examination, measurement of parameters in the blood, microscopic examination of blood films and often microscopic examination of bone marrow aspirates and trephine samples.

Automated machines measure many parameters in a sample of blood; the most common are:

- haemoglobin concentration
- red cell count
- packed cell volume (haematocrit)
- mean cell volume
- mean cell haemoglobin
- mean cell haemoglobin concentration
- white cell count and differential count
- platelet count
- coagulation times
  - — prothrombin time
  - — activated partial thromboplastin time
  - — thrombin time
- fibrinogen concentration.

Such machines can produce a plethora of data and the same problems of interpretation may occur as described in the section on clinical chemistry above, but in haematology many of the parameters (e.g.

haemoglobin, red cell count and mean cell volume) are linked and need to be examined together when making a diagnosis. Other measurements, such as of serum ferritin or cyanocobalamin (vitamin B_{12})· may need to be made to confirm the diagnosis.

Examination of the blood film can reveal abnormalities of red blood cell shape and size (e.g. anisocytosis, poikilocytosis, macrocytosis) and abnormal white blood cells such as blast cells in leukaemia. Some features, such as rouleaux formation by red blood cells, may suggest abnormalities in the non-cellular components of blood (in this case possible overproduction of antibodies or immunoglobulin).

Bone Marrow Examination

Samples of the bone marrow may be taken by insertion of a relatively large bore needle into a site, such as the iliac bone, and aspiration by a syringe. At the same time a tissue sample of marrow can be sampled with a trephine needle. A smear of aspirated cells, stained by the Giemsa method, allows identification of cells, and their relative proportions may be quantified.

This is an integral part of the diagnosis of leukaemia and assessment of its response to treatment. Trephine samples of bone marrow retain the architecture of the tissue and allow assessment of the overall cellularity, amount of reticulin and site of different cell types; such samples are essential in diseases that produce fibrosis of the bone marrow, such as myelofibrosis or metastatic prostatic carcinoma, as aspirates will usually produce a very low cellular yield.

Blood Transfusion

The primary purpose of blood transfusion is the supply of a product for the treatment of patients. The blood products that can be supplied include:

- red cell concentrates, for rapid correction of anaemia
- fresh frozen plasma, to replace coagulation factors
- platelets, for treatment of thrombocytopenia
- plasma fractions
  - — albumin, to correct hypoalbuminaemia
  - — immunoglobulin, for passive immunisation
  - — factors VIII and IX, to treat or prevent bleeding in haemophilia A or B.

Primary concerns in the operation of a blood transfusion laboratory will include an error-free system of crossmatching (as a mismatched transfusion may prove fatal), safeguards against transmission of microbiological agents (such as human immunodeficiency virus (HIV), hepatitis B and C) by transfusion, and balancing supply and demand of the products.

Histopathology

Histopathology involves the macroscopic examination of tissue with selection of tissue samples for light microscopic examination. Histopathology is usually the primary mode of diagnosis for tumours and also gives prognostic information by grading and staging of surgical resection specimens.

Diagnosis of infective and inflammatory conditions can also be made as, for instance, in the detection of *Helicobacter pylori* in gastric biopsies or the diagnosis of inflammatory conditions of the skin. Most diagnostic histopathology is performed on haematoxylin and eosin (H&E)-stained sections of paraffinwax-embedded tissue.

The tissue removed by surgical excision or biopsy is placed in a solution of fixative (most commonly formaldehyde) and transported to the histopathology laboratory. On receipt it is examined by the laboratory staff; a macroscopic description is given and tissue is selected for light microscopic examination.

Larger specimens, where most of the tissue will not be examined by light microscopy, are assessed and sampled by medicallytrained staff who are familiar with a wide range of macroscopic appearances and have a detailed knowledge of anatomy. The samples taken will vary but in a resection specimen would include samples of:

- tumour (for histogenetic pattern of differentiation and grading)
- resection margins
- lymph nodes
- background tissue.

The samples of tissue are processed by machine into paraffin wax, a process involving progressive dehydration through increasingly pure solutions of alcohol that is usually carried out overnight. The wax-embedded tissue samples are then mounted on a microtome and sections of 5-7 am thickness are cut, mounted on glass slides and stained. These slides are interpreted by expert pathologists and reports are issued to the clinicians who sent the specimens.

The reports are tailored to the type of specimen and the clinical details given on the request form. If a tumour is being examined the report will include the type of tumour, its grade (well, moderate or poorly differentiated), its stage (how far it has spread locally, whether any vascular invasion is detected and whether any sampled lymph nodes contain tumour) and comments on the surrounding tissue (e.g. whether there is dysplasia in background epithelium).

Table 2.2: Commonly used stains in histopathology Stain Use.

Haematoxylin and eosin (H&E)	Routine stain for histological sections
Masson's trichrome	Fibrous tissue
Perls'	Haemosiderin
Masson-Fontana	Melanin
Modified Giemsa	*Helicobacter*
Ziehl-Neelsen	Acid-fast bacilli
Gram	Bacteria
Periodic acid-Schiff (PAS)	Glycogen, fungi
Grocott's silver stain	Fungi
Alcian blue	Acidic mucin
Periodic acid-Schiff with diastase	Neutral mucin

Although H&E is the most commonly used stain, there are other stains that may be used to investigate specific features of the tissue. Many of these are standard tinctorial procedures.

Immunohistochemistry

An increasingly commonly used technique is *immunohistochemistry*. In this method antibodies are used which have been raised artificially to specific substances of interest (e.g. low molecular weight cytokeratins in a suspected epithelial tumour) and these bind to the specific substances if they are present in the tissue section.

The bound antibody is then visualised using one of a variety of methods, such as antibodies against the initial antibody and a dye complex such as diaminobenzidine. Immunohistochemistry is useful in:

- typing tumours that are poorly differentiated and so are difficult to categorise from appearances on H&E staining
- typing of lymphomas
- classification of glomerulonephritis.

In Situ Hybridisation (ISH)

DNA probes can be constructed which will bind to specific DNA or messenger RNA (mRNA) in tissue sections. The DNA probes are single-stranded sequences of DNA from tens to thousands of kilobases long and are labelled with radioisotopes, or now more commonly biotin or digoxigenin, to visualise the site of hybridisation using a colorimetric or fluorescent agent.

The DNA in the tissue section is made into a single-stranded form, by conditions such as strong alkalis, and the probe will bind to complementary sequences in the target DNA or mRNA. This technique is useful for detecting infectious agents in tissue sections, such as cytomegalovirus or Epstein-Barr virus.

It can also be used to detect production (rather than simply storage) of proteins in cells by detection of the mRNA for the specific protein. An excellent example of how all these histopathology techniques are integral to patient management is the current treatment of breast cancer.

Breast cancer may be detected by mammographic screening, or a woman may present with a self-discovered lump, but the diagnosis is made by histological examination of a sample of the lesion-most commonly by needle core biopsy. The most usual treatment of breast cancer is primary surgical excision, with sampling of the axillary lymph nodes to detect metastases.

These specimens are sent to the histopathology laboratory where examination produces a large amount of information that is vital for further management. Examination of H&E-stained sections will give the histological type of the breast cancer, its histological grade, the size of the cancer and whether the axillary lymph nodes contain metastases. This information makes a reasonably reliable prediction of the biological behaviour of the breast cancer.

A small, low grade tumour with no lymph nodes metastases is unlikely to have metastasised at the time of surgical resection and the sideeffects of adjuvant systemic chemotherapy will probably outweigh the possible benefits (i.e. the ablation of metastases that have not yet been detected). A large high grade tumour that has already metastasised to the axillary lymph nodes has a high risk of spread to other parts of the body, and the benefits of adjuvant systemic chemotherapy in eradicating or reducing the size and number of these is likely to be greater than the side-effects of this treatment.

Tamoxifen is a drug which is an antagonist for the oestrogen receptor. If a breast cancer expresses oestrogen receptors, i.e. has not become undifferentiated enough to lose this function, then tamoxifen has a strong beneficial effect in reducing the risk of tumour recurrence and distant metastases. Immunohistochemical staining of the excised breast cancer can assess the degree of expression of oestrogen receptor.

This test can be performed on the small samples obtained by needle core biopsy in elderly patients who can be treated with tamoxifen without surgical excision if the risk of surgery, or the desire to avoid it, is great. If breast cancer does recur with metastases there is a further therapy which can be used.

Trastuzumab (Herceptin) is a monoclonal antibody directed against the human epidermal growth factor receptor-2 (HER2). Immunohistochemical staining and fluorescent in situ hydrisation of the breast cancer can show whether this receptor is overexpressed in the original tumour and thus whether the patient will benefit from this therapy.

As more detailed molecular charateristics of tumours are defined, there are likely to be more histopathology tests that will predict response to specific therapies.

Electron Microscopy

Electron microscopy may be used to visualise subcellular detail in tissue samples. In the past this technique was used for detecting features of differentiation in tumours (such as melanosomes in malignant melanomas) but immunohistochemistry has largely replaced this function.

Electron microscopy is still used in the classification of glomerulonephritis, where the site and nature of immune complexes in the glomerular basement membrane may be visualised.

Immunology

Immunology is concerned with the immune response, both antibody and cell mediated, in health and disease. The range of antibodies and cellular features that can be detected and measured has increased so much in recent years that many centres have a separate immunology department to deal with these. The various tests may be divided into those measuring antibodies and those measuring cells.

Immunoglobulins and Antibodies

The overall levels of antibodies of certain classes can be measured but this is of little diagnostic use except in generalised immunodeficiencies such as hypogammaglobulinaemia. Detection or measurement of antibodies directed against specific antigens is important in the diagnosis and assessment of *autoimmune diseases*.

Samples of a patient's serum are placed on tissue sections and any bound antibody can be visualised by applying further antibodies against human immunoglobulin (or a specific subclass) to which is attached an immunofluorescent dye. Auto-antibodies detected in this way include antinuclear antibodies found in systemic lupus erythematosus.

To detect auto-antibodies bound to the patient's own tissues a sample of tissue is taken from the patient (this might be skin or a renal biopsy), antibodies against human immunoglobulins are applied to the biopsy and any bound antibody is visualised by immunofluorescent or other techniques. This technique is used in the assessment of glomerulonephritis and bullous skin disorders (pemphigus, pemphigoid, dermatitis herpetiformis, etc.).

Lymphocytes

There are now antibodies to the specific antigens of most subsets of lymphocytes, such as T-cells or B-cells, Tsuppressor cells, T-helper cells, etc., and in conjunction with other techniques (such as fluorescence-activated cell sorting-FAGS) the number of lymphocytes in each subclass can be measured. These measurements can give important information about a patient's immune status.

In acquired immune deficiency syndrome (AIDS) there is selective destruction of T-helper cells by HIV so that a reduction in the T-helper cell : T-suppressor cell ratio in HIVpositive subjects can indicate the onset of AIDS. In organ transplantation the detection of acute cellular rejection is important if appropriate immunosuppressive therapy is to be given in time to prevent loss of the graft.

Rejection is primarily detected by histological examination of a biopsy of the graft (e.g. kidney) but measurement of the T-cell helper : suppressor ratio provides useful additional information and, with more specific subtyping of lymphocytes, such tests may eventually replace graft biopsy.

Microbiology

Microbiology involves the detection and identification of micro-organisms, including viruses, bacteria, fungi, protozoa and helminths. These may be detected by direct examination of a sample from a patient or by culture of such a sample to increase the number of organisms before using a detection method.

Evidence of infection can also be inferred from serological tests for an antibody response to the organism. The susceptibility of cultured organisms to therapeutic agents, such as antibiotics, will also be assessed and microbiologists have wider responsibilities for general control of infection in hospitals and the community.

Direct detection methods in microbiology include:

- direct microscopy (by light or electron microscopy)
- specific antibody detection methods (visualised by enzyme-

linked immunosorbent assay (ELISA), radioimmunoassay or immunofluorescence)

- nucleic acid hybridisation technology with labelled probes or the polymerase chain reaction (PCR).

These methods give rapid results, which can be very useful to clinicians. Examples of direct detection include the identification of *Pneumocystis carinii* in bronchoalveolar washings from immunosuppressed patients (such as those with AIDS), immunofluorescent detection of *Cryptosporidia* in faeces, and immunofluorescent detection of respiratory syncytial virus in nasopharyngeal aspirates.

Viruses

Viruses are obligate intracellular parasites and so can be grown only in a cellular culture, such as 'immortal' cells derived from tumours or cultures with a finite life-span derived from embryonic tissues. The presence of a virus may be detected by the presence of a cytopathic effect, by haemadsorption/haemagglutination or by the direct methods described above.

The identity of the virus is confirmed by neutralisation of the cytopathic effect or haemadsorption/haemagglutination by antibodies raised against specific viruses. Serological tests are often used to diagnose viral infection: such tests involve the measurement of antibodies against specific viruses using a detection system such as ELISA, radioimmunoassay, immunofluorescence or complement fixation tests.

A detectable level of virus-specific IgM or a four-fold rise in the titre of other classes of virus-specific antibody is an indication of recent infection with that virus.

Bacteria

Bacteria may be cultivated in cell-free media. For most purposes the medium used is solid rather than liquid ('broth'). Most solid culture media are based on agar, to which blood or other nutrients are added. Where it is wished to identify a specific pathogen existing in the presence of other bacteria, substances may be incorporated which will inhibit the growth of these other bacteria while not affecting the specific pathogen being sought ('selective media').

For any given type of specimen a range of media is chosen which will support the growth of all pathogens relevant *to the clinical* condition. Cultures are then incubated at appropriate temperatures and atmospheric conditions (i.e. aerobic and anaerobic). Most bacteria will grow within a few days and can then be identified by:

- the specific conditions in which they have grown
- morphology of their colonies on the culture plate
- *Gram staining of* samples from the cultured colonies
- biochemical tests (such as the breakdown of carbohydrates)
- enzyme production (e.g. coagulase production by *Staphylococcus aureus)*
- serological tests of antigenic structure.

Some bacteria require specialised media and prolonged incubation in order to produce detectable colonies (for example *Mycobacterium tuberculosis* may need up to 8 weeks incubation on Lowenstein Jensen medium).

The *susceptibility* of bacteria to antibiotics may be determined by various methods, most commonly by observing inhibition of bacterial growth around antibiotic-impregnated filter-paper discs placed on culture plates prior to incubation. Microbiologists should provide advice on the empirical choice of antibiotics in cases where treatment may need to begin before the results of susceptibility tests are available.

Fungi

Fungi are grown on simple media (such as glucose peptone agar or blood agar with antibiotics to inhibit bacterial overgrowth) in aerobic conditions. Cultured fungi are identified by the method of spore production (asexual and sexual), *morphology* of the colony, morphology of vegetative and aerial hyphae, biochemical reactions and antigenic structure.

Parasites

Diseases caused by parasites are major problems in many countries, particularly those with tropical climates in which the vectors (e.g. insects) thrive. Parasites may be identified in, for example, tissue samples or faeces by their often distinctive morphology.

Precautions

When requesting microbiological tests it is especially important to send suitable specimens. Such samples should come from the likely site of infection, should not contain contaminants, should not contain substances likely to inhibit growth (such as antibiotics), should be put into a suitable container (which may contain a transport medium) and should be transported rapidly to the microbiology laboratory.

If septicaemia is suspected but no focus of infection has been identified, multiple samples, including blood and urine, should be sent before systemic antibiotic therapy is started. The risk to staff looking after patients with microbiological infections, or handling specimens from them, is roughly classified according to the degree of hazard. Most infective agents are included in category 2 (according to the scheme used in the UK).

If a patient potentially has a category 3 pathogen then all samples should be marked as such because laboratories receiving these samples will have to take special precautions in handling them (this includes samples sent for non-microbiological investigations).

Hospital-acquired Infections

Hospitals contain many patients with microbiological infections and there is considerable potential for spread to other patients. All hospitals should have agreed procedures for preventing the spread of infection, including adequate sterilisation and disinfection, and isolation or barrier nursing when required. Such policies will have been formulated in consultation with the microbiologists of the hospital.

The microbiological laboratory will be in a position to detect outbreaks of particular infections if there is suitable monitoring of laboratory results. An increasing problem in hospitals is the emergence *of* bacteria that are resistant to antibiotics, and this can be limited by the development of protocols for antibiotic usage.

AUTOPSIES

- May be performed for legal or medical purposes
- Information from autopsies is useful for clinical audit, education, medical research and allocation of resources
- Diagnostic discrepancies are revealed by autopsies in approximately 30% of cases

In most countries autopsies fall into two main categories:

1. those performed under the instruction of a legal authority
2. those performed with permission from the deceased's relatives for gathering further information about the nature and extent of the deceased's disease.

Medicolecal Autopsies

Medicolegal autopsies are performed to determine the cause of death and to collect evidence that may be used in the prosecution of those alleged to be responsible for the death. In many cases of murder the cause of death (e.g. bullet wounds or stab wounds) is obvious and most of the work of the pathologist is the collection of evidence, such as trace evidence confirming contact between the deceased and the

Table 2.3: Categories of risk (in the UK) for infectious organisms.

Category	*Risk*	*Examples*
1	An organism that is most unlikely to cause human disease	Algae
2	An organism that may cause human disease and may be a hazard to those handling it, but is unlikely to spread to the community and effective prophylaxis or treatment is usually available	Staphylococcus aureus, Escherichia coli
3	An organism that may cause severe human disease and present a serious hazard to those handling it. It may present a risk of spread to the community but there is usually effective prophylaxis available	Hepatitis B virus, Mycobacterium tuberculosis, Salmonella typhi
4	An organism that causes severe human disease and is a serious hazard to those handling it. It may present a high risk of spread to the community and there is usually no effective prophylaxis or treatment	Lassa fever virus, Marburg virus

person accused of the murder (e.g. blood stains, tissue beneath the deceased's fingernails, semen in body orifices) or evidence to link a specific weapon with the deceased's wounds (e.g. retrieval of bullets from wounds).

Clinical Autopsies

Non-medicolegal (clinical) autopsies performed on patients who die in hospital may appear to be diagnostic tests that have been performed too late, but much useful information can be gathered from these procedures.

Many studies have shown that the certified cause of death given by the clinicians with primary responsibility for the patient shows a discrepancy with the cause identified at autopsy, to the extent of being in a different organ system in about 30% of cases.

The hospital autopsy is therefore very useful in providing more accurate data about the cause of death; this is important for *clinical audit,* for *education* of clinicians, and for national *allocation* of health resources if the cause of death is used as an index of the prevalence of disease (which it is in many countries, including the UK). The hospital autopsy is also useful in defining the extent of disease and response to treatment.

If a patient has had a malignant tumour, such as malignant melanoma, which has spread to other sites in the body and that patient has then received systemic treatment, it is important to have the most accurate data available about the organs to which the tumour had spread and whether the therapy had had any apparent effect on the tumour.

Modern methods of in vivo imaging, such as computed axial tomography and nuclear magnetic resonance, may provide some of this data but, if the patient dies, an autopsy is a simple and cost-effective method of gathering accurate data. The rate of autopsies on patients dying in hospital has shown a decline in most countries over the past decade; this will inevitably lead to loss of much useful information about human disease.

Autopsy Techniques

Performing an autopsy is a relatively cheap, low technology procedure which has not changed much since the pioneering work of Virchow in the 19th century. A midline incision from the neck to the symphysis pubis is made and the thoracic and abdominal organs are removed. The scalp is reflected from the skull and the cranium is opened to remove the brain.

All the organs are dissected in detail by a medically-trained pathologist and the macroscopic appearances and weights are recorded; samples may be taken for microscopic examination, clinical chemistry analysis or microbiological culture.

Return of the organs to the body cavities and reconstruction of the body produces an acceptable cosmetic result so that relatives can view the body after autopsy. More limited examination of the body can still generate useful information and so the examination may be limited (by the deceased's relatives' wishes) to certain areas of the body.

This may allow an autopsy examination to be performed where permission would otherwise be refused (e.g. exclusion of examination of the cranial cavity in a patient who had received chemotherapy and had no hair, making any scalp incision clearly visible).

The ultimate limited autopsy is the *needle autopsy* where percutaneous samples of organs are taken for histological examination using a needle core biopsy needle or fine-needle aspiration techniques; such a technique is useful to assess liver disease in cases of hepatitis B or C where risk of infection may preclude a full autopsy.

3

Defeusive Pathology

DEFENSE AGAINST INFECTION

- Non-specific mechanisms include the skin barrier, lysozyme in some secretions, ciliary motion in the respiratory tract, and colonisation by harmless bacteria
- Innate *mechanisms* lack memory
- Specific immunity is characte-rised by specificity and memory

The immune system evolved as a defence against infectious diseases. Individuals with deficient immune responses, if untreated, succumb to infections in early life.

There is, therefore, a selective evolutionary pressure for an efficient immune system. *Specific immunity* is called into play only when micro-organisms bypass *non-specific* or *innate* mechanisms.

Non-specific Defences

Many non-specific mechanisms prevent invasion of the body by micro-organisms:

- *Mechanical barriers* are highly effective and their failure often results in infection: for instance, defects in the mucociliary lining of the respiratory tract, as in cystic fibrosis, are associated with recurrent lung infection.
- *Secretory factors* present formidable chemical barriers to many organisms. If the acid pH of the stomach is compromised, as in atrophic gastritis with achlorhydria, bacterial overgrowth may occur in the intestine.

Innate Immunity

The innate immune system can recognize a spectrum of pathogens using a repertoire of invariant receptors. Key components include:

- *Cellular* factors-include polymorphonuclear leukocytes and macrophages which phagocytose and kill microorganisms.
- *Complement-a* complex series of interacting plasma proteins which forms a major effector mechanism for antibody-mediated immune reactions but can also be activated directly by some bacteria.

Specific Immunity

The immune system has four essential features:

- specificity
- diversity
- memory
- recruitment of other defence mechanisms.

A specific or adaptive immune response consists of two parts: a *specific response* to the particular antigen and a *non-specific augmentation* of the effect of that response. For the specific response there is a quicker and larger response the second time that a particular antigen is encountered; memory of the initial specific immune response provides the efficiency.

The immune system has to recognize all pathogens, past and future and must have considerable diversity of response. This diversity is partly genetic (germ-line) and partly generated by somatic mutation during maturation of the immune system.

An immune response has two phases: first the *recognition phase,* involving antigen-presenting cells and T-lymphocytes, in which the antigen is recognised as foreign; and second the *effector phase,* in which antibodies and effector T-lymphocytes eliminate the antigen, often by recruiting innate mechanisms such as complement or macrophage activation.

KEY MOLECULES

- Antigens are substances able to provoke an immune response and react with the products of that response
- Antibodies are immunoglobulin molecules produced by plasma cells. Antigen-binding properties reside in the Fab fragments, while effector functions lie in the Fc fragment
- T-cells recognise antigens through their T-cell receptors associated with the CD3 molecule

- Major histocompatibility complex (MHC) antigens are of two main types-class I and class II. They play a fundamental role in the normal immune response by presenting antigenic peptides to T-cells
- Helper T-cells recognise antigen in association with major histocompatibility complex (MHC) class II molecules, while cytotoxic T-cells recognise antigen associated with MHC class I
- T-cell receptors will recognise antigen only as part of a complex of antigen peptide and the MHC molecule-a process termed MHC restriction
- Adhesion molecules play a key role in the migration of leukocytes into sites of inflammation and in the interactions between antigen-presenting cells and T-lymphocytes
- Cytokines are soluble mediators which act as stimulatory or inhibitory signals between cells. Cytokines which act between cells of the immune system are called interleukins

Antigens

Antigens are substances able to provoke an immune response and react with the immune products. They react both with the T-cell recognition receptor and with antibody. An antigenic molecule may have several antigenic determinants (epitopes); each *epitope* can bind with an individual antibody, and a single antigenic molecule can therefore provoke many antibody molecules with different binding sites.

Some low molecular weight molecules, called *haptens,* are unable to provoke an immune response themselves, although they can react with existing antibodies. Such substances need to be coupled to a carrier molecule in order to have sufficient epitopes to be antigenic.

For some chemicals, such as drugs, the carrier may be a host protein-called an auto-antigen. The tertiary structure, as well as the amino acid sequence, is important in determining antigenicity. Antigens are conventionally divided into thymus-dependent and thymus-independent antigens. *Thymus-dependent antigens* require T-cell participation to provoke the production of antibodies; most proteins are examples.

Thymus-independent antigens require no T-cell co-operation for antibody production; they directly stimulate specific B-lymphocytes by cross-linking antigen receptors on the B-cell surface but provoke poor immunological memory. Such antigens include bacterial cell wall polysaccharides.

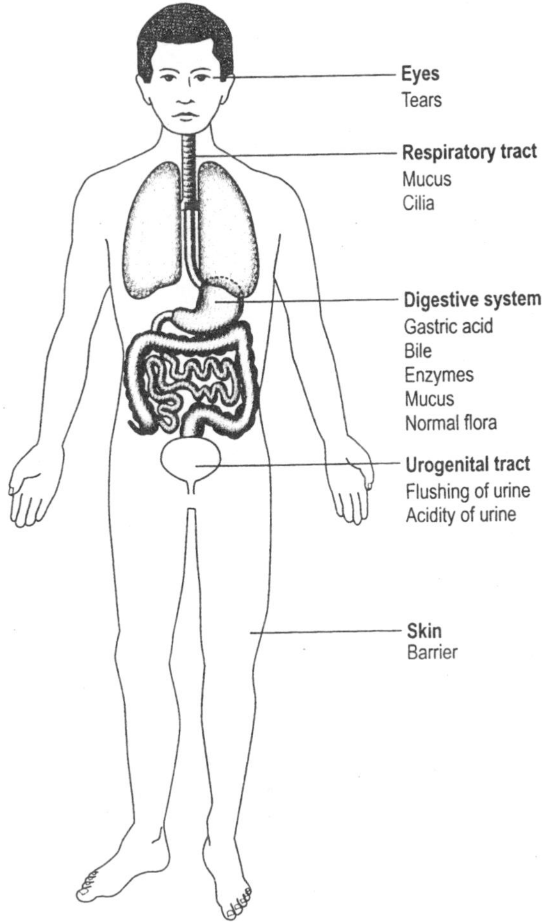

Figure 3.1: Mechanical and secretory barriers to infection.

Factors other than the intrinsic properties of the antigen also influence the quality of the immune response. These include:

- nature of molecule
- dose
- route of entry
- addition of substances with synergistic effects
- genetic background of recipient.

Substances which improve a host's immune response to a separate antigen are called *adjuvants;* these are routinely used in immunisation programmes in childhood.

Antibody

Humoral immunity is immunity that is dependent on the production of antibodies and their actions. All antibodies belong to the immunoglobulin class of proteins and are produced by plasma cells, themselves derived from Blymphocytes. The basic structure of an immunoglobulin molecule is shown in Figure elsewhere in this chapter.

It has a four-chain structure: two identical heavy (H) chains (molecular weight 50 kD) and two identical light (L) chains (mol wt 25 kD). There are two alternative types of light chain, known as kappa and lambda; an antibody molecule has either two kappa or two lambda light chains, never one of each.

There are no known differences in the functional properties between kappa and lambda light chains. In contrast, there are several different types of heavy chain, each with important functional differences. The heavy chains determine the class (isotype) of the antibody and the ultimate physiological function of the antibody molecule.

Once the antigen-binding site has reacted with its antigen, the molecule undergoes a change in the conformation of its heavy chains in order to take part in effector functions. The amino (N) terminal regions of the heavy and light chains include the *antigen-binding sites.*

The amino acid sequences of these N terminal domains vary between different antibody molecules of the same isotype and are known as

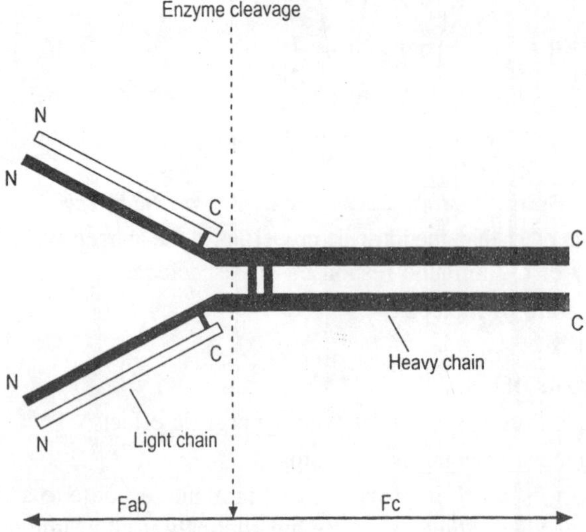

Figure 3.2: Basic structure of an immunoglobulin molecule.

variable (V) regions. Most of these differences reside in three hypervariable areas of the molecule, each only 6-10 amino acid residues long.

In the folded molecules, these *hypervariable regions* in each chain come together, with their counterparts on the other pair of heavy and light chains, to form the antigen-binding site. The structure of this part of the antibody molecule is unique to that molecule and is known as the *idiotypic determinant.*

In any individual, about 10^6 – 10^7 different antibody molecules could be made up by 10^3 different heavy chain variable regions associating with 10^3 different light chain variable regions. Somatic mutation during multiple divisions of B-lymphocytes generates further diversity of around 10^{14} antibody specificities.

IgM is the oldest class of immunoglobulin in evolutionary terms. It is a large molecule consisting of five basic units held together by a joining (J) chain; it penetrates poorly into tissues on account of its large size. The major physiological role of IgM is intravascular neutralisation of organisms (especially viruses) aided by its 10 antigen binding sites.

IgM also has multiple complement-binding sites; this results in excellent complement activation and lysis of the organism or removal of the antigen-antibodycomplement complexes by complement receptors on phagocytic cells. It is the first class of antibody to be formed in response to an initial encounter with an antigen *(primary immune response).*

IgG is a smaller immunoglobulin which penetrates tissues easily. It is the most abundant immunoglobulin in the plasma and extracellular fluid. It is the only immunoglobulin which crosses the placenta to provide immune protection to the neonate: this is an active process involving specific placental receptors for the Fc portion of the IgG molecule.

Polymorphs and macrophages also have surface receptors for the Fc fragment of IgG: thus binding of IgG to particulate antigen promotes adhesion of these cells and subsequent phagocytosis of the antigen.

There are four subclasses of IgG. IgG_1 and IgG_3 activate complement efficiently and are responsible for clearing most protein antigens. IgG_2 and IgG_4 react predominantly with carbohydrate antigens (in adults).

IgA is sometimes referred to as 'mucosal antiseptic paint'. It is secreted locally by plasma cells in the intestinal and respiratory mucosa and is an important constituent of breast milk. It consists of two basic units (a dimer) linked by a 'joining' or J chain. The addition of a 'secretory component' prevents digestion of the immunoglobulin molecule by enzymes present in intestinal or bronchial secretions.

Secretory component is a fragment of the polymeric immunoglobulin receptor synthesised by epithelial cells and which transports secretory IgA from the mucosa into the lumen of the gut or bronchi There is little free IgD or IgE in serum or normal body fluids. These two classes mainly act as cell receptors. *IgD* is synthesised by antigen-sensitive B-lymphocytes and is involved in the activation of these cells by antigen.

IgE is produced by plasma cells but taken up by specific IgE receptors on mast cells and basophils. IgE probably evolved as a way of expelling intestinal parasites via mast cell degranulation.

T-Cell Receptors

Like B-cells, each T-cell is committed to a given antigen, which it recognises by one of two types of T-cell receptors (TCRs), depending on the cell's lineage. T-cells have either TCR1, composed of gamma (γ) and delta (δ) chains (early in ontogeny), or TCR2, another heterodimer of alpha (α) and beta (β) chains. TCR2 cells predominate in adults, although 10% of T-cells in epithelial structures bear TCR1.

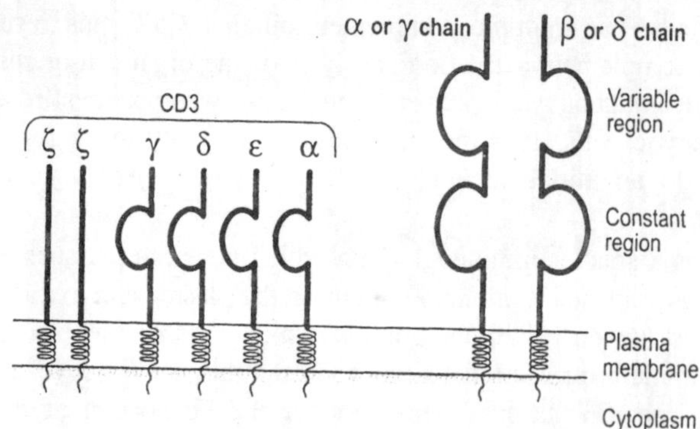

Figure 3.3: The structure of the T -cell receptor (TCR).

In either case the pair of TCRs are associated with several transmembrane proteins which make up the cluster differentiation 3 (CD3) molecule, responsible for taking the antigen recognition signal inside the cell (transduction). The CD3 antigen is widely used as a marker of mature T-cells in diagnostic and investigative pathology.

The T-cell receptor complex recognises small processed antigen peptides in the context of major histocompatibility complex (MHC) class I and II antigens (see below), depending on the type of T-cell. Helper T-cells recognise class II MHC in association with foreign antigen and use the CD4 molecule to enhance binding and intracellular signalling. Cytotoxic T-cells recognise antigen associated with MHC class I molecules and similarly use CD8 molecules for increased binding and signalling.

However, recognition of processed antigen alone is not enough to activate T-cells. Additional signals through soluble cytokines are needed: some of these are generated during 'antigen processing'.

Major Histocompatibility Complex Antigens

Histocompatibility antigens were so named because of the vigorous reactions they provoked during mismatched organ transplantation, but it soon became apparent that these antigens play a fundamental role in the normal immune response by presenting antigenic peptides to T-cells.

Human histocompatibility antigens are also known as *human leukocyte antigens* (HLAs), a term synonymous with the *major histocompatibility complex* (MHC). MHC antigens are cell surface glycoproteins of two basic types: class I and class II.

They exhibit extensive genetic polymorphism with multiple alleles at each locus. As a result, genetic variability between individuals is very great and most unrelated individuals possess different HLA molecules. This means that it is very difficult to obtain perfect HLA matches between unrelated persons for transplantation.

The antigen-specific receptor of an individual T-cell (TCR) will

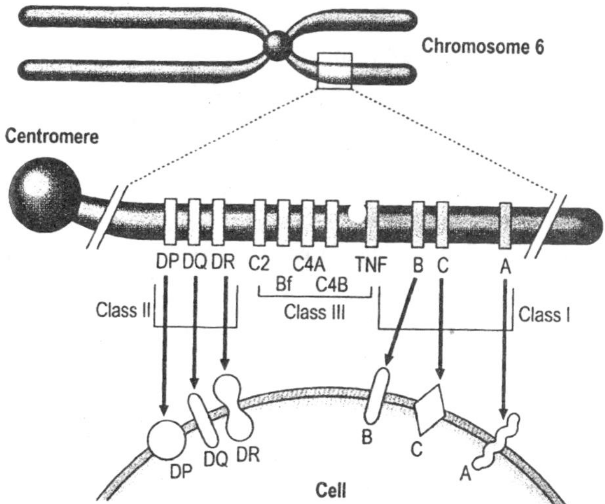

Figure 3.4: The major histocompatibility complex on chromosome 6 and MHC class I and II antigens.

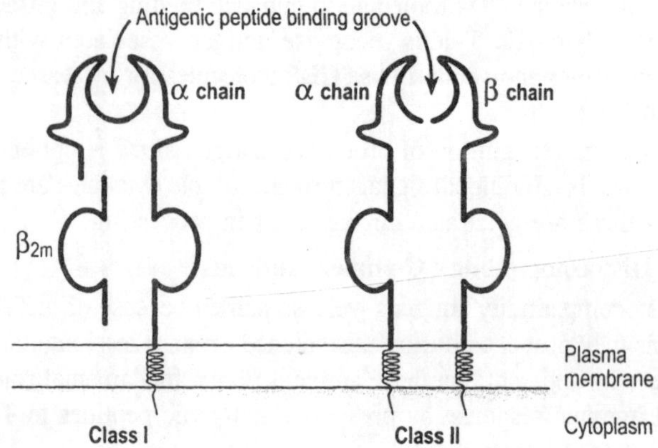

Figure 3.5: MHC class I and class II antigens.

only recognise antigen as part of a complex of antigenic peptide and that individual's MHC complex. This process of dual recognition of peptide and MHC molecule is known as *MHC restriction* because the MHC molecule restricts the ability of the T-cell to recognise antigen. T-cells from one person will not co-operate with antigen-presenting cells from a different person (i.e. of different HLA type).

MHC class I antigens are subdivided into three groups: A, B and C. Each group is controlled by a different gene locus within the major histocompatibility complex on chromosome 6. The products of the genes at all three loci are chemically similar.

MHC class I antigens are made up of a heavy chain (α) controlled by a gene in the relevant MHC locus, associated with a smaller chain called β_2-microglobulin, controlled by a gene on chromosome 12. The differences between individual MHC class I antigens are due to variations in the a chains; the β_2-microglobulin component is constant.

The detailed structure of class I antigens was determined by X-ray crystallography. This shows that small antigenic peptides are tightly bound to a groove in the surface a chains.

MHC class II antigens have a folded structure similar to class I antigens with the peptide binding groove found between the α and β chains. Whereas class I molecules are expressed by most nucleated cells, expression of class II molecules is restricted to a few cell types: B-lymphocytes, activated T-cells, macrophages, inflamed vascular endothelium and some epithelial cells.

However, other cells (e.g. thyroid, pancreas, gut epithelium) can be induced to express class II molecules under the influence of interferon-

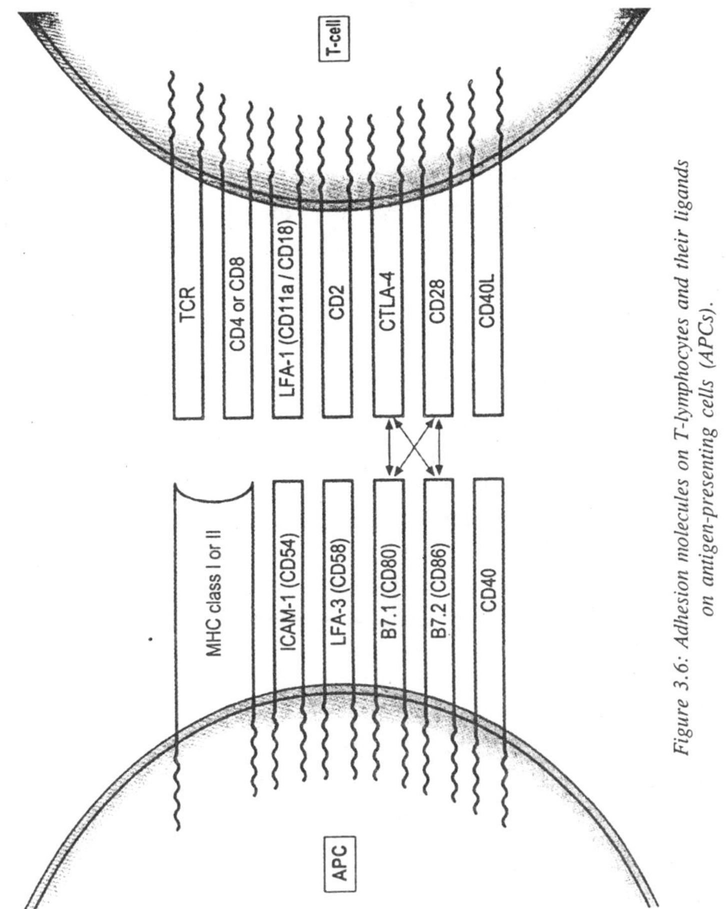

Figure 3.6: Adhesion molecules on T-lymphocytes and their ligands on antigen-presenting cells (APCs).

y released during inflammation. In humans, there are three groups of class II antigens: the loci are known as HLA-DP HLA-DQ and HLA-DR.

In practical terms, MHC restriction is a mechanism by which antigens in different intracellular compartments can be captured and presented to CD4+ or CD8+ T-cells. Endogenous antigens (including viral antigens) are presented by MHC class I bearing cells exclusively to CD8+ T-cells, while exogenous antigens are presented by MHC class II antigens to CD4+ T-cells.

MHC class III antigens constitute early complement proteins C4 and C2. Other inflammatory proteins, e.g. tumour necrosis factor (TNF), are encoded in adjacent areas.

Adhesion Molecules

T-cell activation needs more than just binding between the T-cell receptor and the MHC class II molecule and processed antigen on the antigen-presenting cell. Additional stimuli are provided by adhesion molecules on both cell surfaces.

Adhesion molecules comprise a diverse set of cell surface glycoproteins that play a pivotal role in the immune response by mediating cell to cell adhesion as well as adhesion between leukocytes and endothelial cells. Adhesion molecules are grouped into four main families:

1. integrins
2. selectins
3. immunoglobulin superfamily
4. cadherins.

Integrins mediate binding of lymphocytes and monocytes to the endothelial adhesion receptor called vascular cell adhesion molecule (VCAM-1). *Selectins* represent a family of three glycoproteins designated by the prefixes E-(endothelial), L-(leukocyte) or P-(platelet) to denote the cells on which they were first described. Selectins bind strongly to carbohydrate molecules on leukocytes and endothelial cells.

The *immunoglobulin superfamily* describes a group of adhesion molecules with a common immunoglobulin-like structure. These molecules strengthen the interaction between antigen-presenting cells and T-lymphocytes. They include CD2, lymphocyte function antigen 3 (LFA-3 or CD58) and intercellular adhesion molecules (ICAM-1, -2 and -3).

Cadherins are calcium-dependent adhesion molecules which establish molecular links between adjacent epithelial cells and play a key role during embryonic development.

The migration of leukocytes into sites of inflammation is dependent on three key sequential steps mediated by these adhesion molecules:

1. Rolling of leukocytes along activated endothelium is selectin-dependent.
2. Tight adhesion of leukocytes to endothelium is integrindependent.
3. Transendothelial migration is under the influence of chemotactic cytokines (chemokines).

Cytokines

Cytokines are soluble mediators secreted by lymphocytes *(lymphokines)* or by macrophages/monocytes *(monokines)*. They act as stimulatory or inhibitory signals between cells.

Cytokines which act between cells of the immune system are called *interleukins;* those which induce chemotaxis of leukocytes are called *chemokines.* All cytokines share common features:

- short half-lives
- rapid degradation
- local action within the microenvironment of cells
- may act on cytokine receptors on the surface of the cell of production to promote further activation and differentiation
- may affect multiple organs in the body
- exhibit overlapping functions.

Among the array of cytokines produced by macrophages and T-cells, interleukin-1 (IL-1) and interleukin-2 (IL-2) have a pivotal role in amplifying immune responses. IL-1 acts on a wide range of targets, including T- and B-cells. In contrast, the effects of IL-2 are restricted largely to lymphocytes: it has a trophic effect on T-cells, IL-2 receptor-bearing B-cells and natural killer (NK) cells. The considerable overlap between individual cytokines and interleukins is summarised in Table elsewhere in this chapter.

Table 3.2: Actions of interleukin-1.

Target cell	Effect
T -lymphocytes	Proliferation Differentiation Lymphokine production Induction of IL-2 receptors
B-lymphocytes	Proliferation Differentiation
Neutrophils	Release from bone marrow Chemoattraction
Macrophages **Fibroblasts** **Osteoblasts** **Epithelial cells**	Proliferation/activation
Osteoclasts	Reabsorption of bone
Hepatocytes	Acute-phase protein synthesis
Hypothalamus	Prostaglandin-induced fever
Muscle	Prostaglandin-induced proteolysis

Table 3.3: Cytokines and their actions.

Cytokine	*Source*	*Target cell*
IL-2	T-cells	Tcells, B-cells, NK cells
IL-3	T-cells	Mast cells, basophils, macrophages, eosinophils
IL-4	T-cells, basophils/mast cells	Tcells, B-cells, mast cells, monocytes
IL-5	T-cells, mast cells	Eosinophils, basophils, B-cells
IL-6	Macrophages, fibroblasts, T-cells, mast cells	Tcells, B-cells, hepatocytes, osteoclasts
IL-7	Stromal cells	Tcells, monocytes
IL-8	Monocytes/macrophages, Tcells, fibroblasts, keratinocytes, endothelial cells, NK cells	Neutrophils, Tcells, B-cells, monocytes, keratinocytes, endothelial cells
IL-9	Tcells	Tcells, macrophages
IL-10	Tcells, monocytes, keratinocytes	B-cells, Tcells, mast cells
IL-12	B-cells, monocytes/macrophages	Tcells, NK cells
IL-13	Tcells	Monocytes/macrophages, B-cells
GM-CSF	Tcells, macrophages, endothelial cells	Progenitors, Tcells
IFN-γ	Tcells, NK cells	Many cell types
TNF-α	Macrophages, Tcells, B-cells	Many cell types

STRUCTURAL ORGANISATION OF THE IMMUNE SYSTEM

- All lymphoid cells originate in the bone marrowly Lymphoid precursors destined to become T-lymphocytes mature in the thymus (hence T-cells)
- Development of B-lymphocytes occurs entirely in the bone marrow (hence B-cells)
- The thymus and bone marrow are primary lymphoid organs
- Lymph nodes, spleen and mucosa-associated lymphoid tissue are secondary lymphoid organs
- Peripheral blood T- and B-lymphocytes circulate in a defined pattern through secondary lymphoid organs. Circulation is strongly influenced by adhesion molecules
- Lymph node architecture is well adapted to its function

T- and B-Lymphocyte Development

All lymphoid cells originate in the bone marrow. An understanding of the developmental pathway is important, not only to clarify the physiology of the normal immune response but also because some leukaemias and immunodeficiency states reflect maturation arrest of cells in their early stages of development.

Lymphoid progenitors destined to become T-lymphocytes migrate from the bone marrow into the cortex of the thymus where further differentiation into mature T-cells occurs. Passage of T-cells from the thymic cortex to the medulla is associated with the acquisition of characteristic surface glycoprotein molecules so that medullary thymocytes resemble mature peripheral blood T-cells.

T-cell development in the thymus is characterised by a process of *positive selection* whereby T-cells which recognise and bind with low affinity to fragments of self-antigen in association with self-MHC molecules proceed to full maturation.

In contrast, T-cells which do not recognise self-MHC or which recognise and bind with high affinity to self-antigen are selected *out-negative selection*and do not develop further.

Negatively selected T-cells kill themselves by apoptosis, i.e. programmed cell death. This process is an important mechanism in preventing autoimmune disease. In summary, the thymus selects out the useful, neglects the useless and destroys the harmful, i.e. autoreactive T-cells.

In contrast, B-cell development occurs in the bone marrow and depends on the secretion of cytokines by stromal cells.

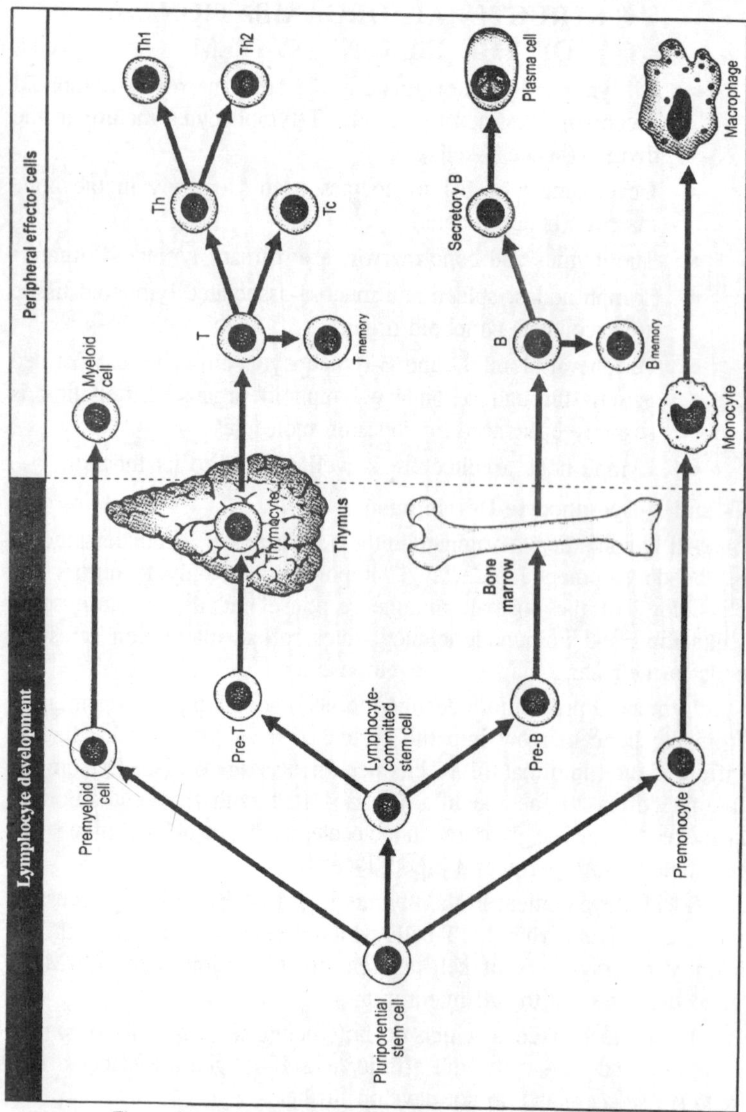

Figure 3.7: Development of lymphocytes from a pluripotential stem cell in the bone marrow.

Primary and Secondary Lymphoid Organs

The thymus and the bone marrow are *primary lymphoid organs.* They contain cells undergoing a process of maturation from stem cells to antigen-sensitive (and antigen-restricted) cells. This process of maturation is independent of antigenic stimulation within the animal. In contrast, *secondary lymphoid organs* are those which contain antigen-reactive cells in the process of recirculating through the body.

They include the lymph nodes, spleen and mucosa-associated lymphoid tissues. Antigenic stimulation changes the relative proportions of the mature cell types in secondary tissues.

Peripheral T- and B-cells circulate in a characteristic pattern through the secondary lymphoid organs. Most of the recirculating cells are T-cells and the complete cycle takes about 24 hours; some B-cells, including long-lived memory B-cells, also recirculate.

Lymphocyte circulation is strongly influenced by adhesion molecules on lymphocyte surfaces which act as homing agents directing cells to their respective ligands on endothelial cells.

Lymph node architecture is well adapted to its function. Lymphatic vessels draining the tissues penetrate the lymph node capsule and drain into the marginal sinus from which a branching network of sinuses passes through the cortex to the medulla and into the efferent lymphatic.

This network provides a filtration system for antigens entering the node from peripheral tissue. The cortex contains *primary follicles* of B-lymphocytes, surrounded by T-cells in the *'paracortex'*. There is a

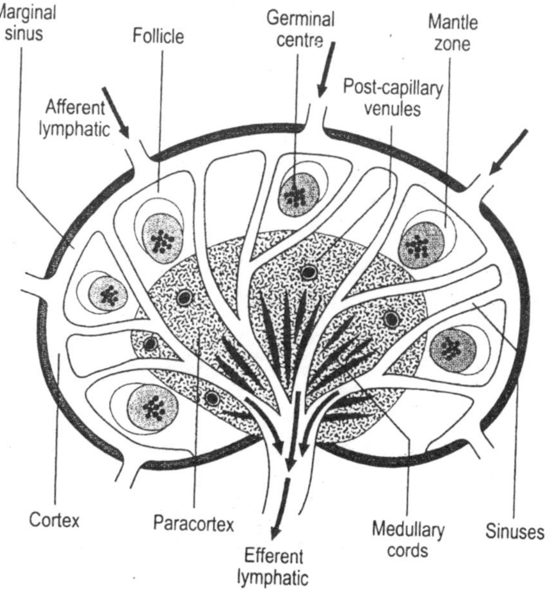

Figure 3.8: Structure of a normal lymph node.

meshwork of dendritic cells that express MHC class II antigen throughout the lymph node, and these cells filter and present antigen to lymphoid cells. On antigen challenge, the 'primary' follicles of the lymph node develop into 'secondary' follicles.

In contrast to primary follicles, secondary follicles contain *germinal centres*. These comprise mainly B-cells with a few helper T-cells and a mantle zone of the original primary follicle B-cells. B-cells in a secondary follicle are antigen-activated and more mature; most have IgG on their surfaces, whereas those in the primary follicle and mantle zone bear both IgD and IgM.

Activated B-cells migrate from the follicle to the medulla, where they develop into plasma cells in the medullary cords before releasing antibody into the efferent lymph. The majority of naive T-cells entering the lymph node will leave again immediately via efferent lymphatics. Naive T-cells which recognise specific antigen differentiate into effector T-cells before re-entering the circulation.

FUNCTIONAL ORGANISATION OF THE IMMUNE RESPONSE

- Processing and presentation of antigen to lymphocytes is performed by specialised antigen-presenting cells (APCs). The most efficient APCs are dendritic cells in lymph nodes
- Each B-lymphocyte is committed to the production of an antibody with a unique antigen-binding site-the idiotype
- The speed, vigour and efficiency of secondary antibody responses are the result of clonal expansion Antibody production usually requires a second signal provided by helper T-lymphocytes
- Helper T-lymphocytes (Th) fall into two subgroups which produce different cytokines-Thl and Th2 cells
- T-lymphocytes can directly kill virus-infected cells or release cytokines which contribute to inflammation

Antigen Presentation

The first stage of an immune response to any antigen is the processing and presentation of that antigen to lymphocytes by specialised *antigen-presenting cells* (APCs). T-cells cannot recognise antigen without it. The interaction between APCs and T-cells is strongly influenced by a group of cell surface molecules which act as *co-stimulators*.

Thus, CD80 and CD86 on the APC engage with their counterparts CD28 and CTLA-4 on the T-cell surface. Normal functioning of the co-

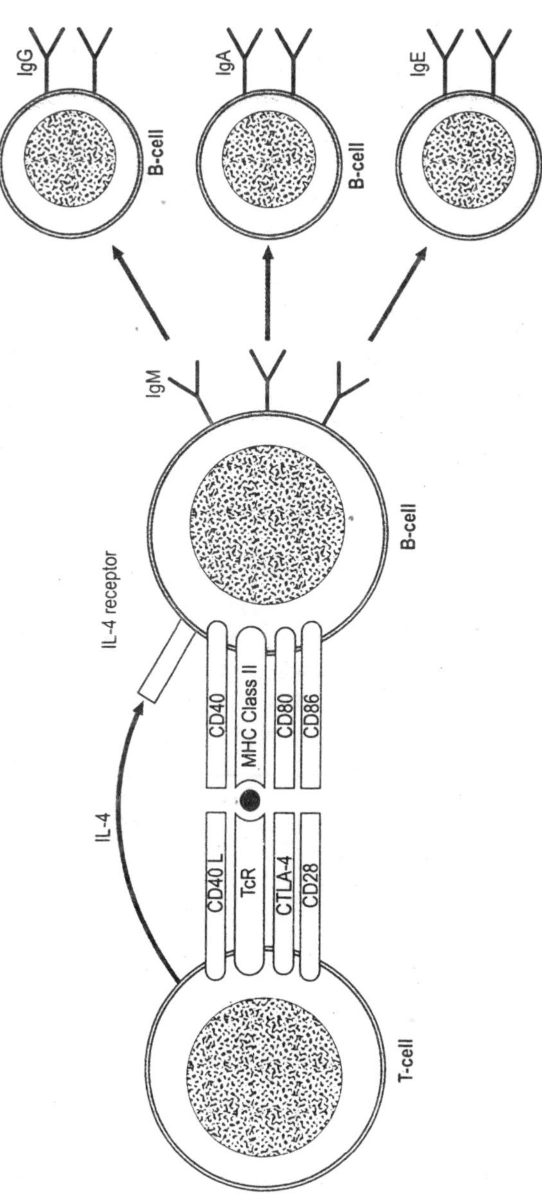

Figure 3.9: Interaction between CD40L on T-cells and CD40 on B-cells leads to isotype switching under the Influence of IL-4.

stimulatory pathway is vital for T-cell activation. Processed antigen is presented to T-cells alongside MHC class II antigens on the APC surface because T-cells do not recognise processed antigen alone.

The most efficient APCs are the interdigitating *dendritic cells* found in the T-cell regions of a lymph node. Such cells have high concentrations of MHC class I and II molecules, co-stimulatory molecules (CD80, CD86) and adhesion molecules on their surfaces but limited enzymatic powers, so enabling effective processing and presentation of antigen without complete digestion.

Antibody Production

Antibody production involves at least four types of cells: antigen-presenting cells, B-lymphocytes, and two types of regulatory T-cells which provide 'helper' or 'suppressor' signals. Antibodies are produced by B-cells, and their mature progeny are called *plasma cells*.

B-cells are readily recognised because they express immunoglobulin on their surfaces. During development, B-cells first show intracellular p chains and then surface IgM. These cells are able to switch from production of IgM to IgG, IgA or IgE as they mature, a process known as *isotype switching*.

This maturation sequence fits with the kinetics of an antibody response: the primary response is mainly IgM and the secondary response predominantly IgG. Isotype switching is mediated by the interaction of two important proteins: CD40 expressed on the B-cell surface engages with its ligand, CD40L, on activated T-cells (under the influence of IL-4) to induce B-cells to switch immunoglobulin production from IgM to

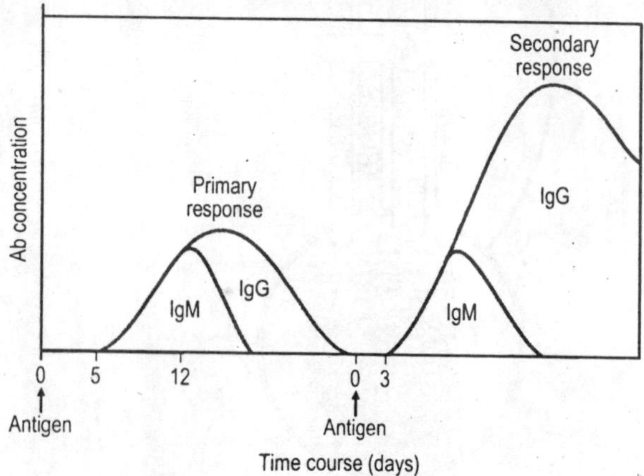

Figure 3.10: Primary and secondary antibody responses.

IgG, IgA or IgE. Each B-cell is committed to the production of an antibody which has a unique VH-VL combination, the idiotype, and the surface immunoglobulin and secreted immunoglobulin are identical. Contact with antigen and factors released by helper T -cells (IL-4, -5, -6) stimulate the B-cell to divide and differentiate, generating more antibody-producing cells, all of which make the same antibody with the same idiotype.

Simultaneously, a population of *memory cells* is produced which expresses the same surface immunoglobulin receptor. The result of these cell divisions is that a greater number of antigen-specific B-cells becomes available when the animal is exposed to the same antigen at a later date. This process, known as *clonal expansion,* helps to account for the amplified secondary response.

As well as being quicker and more vigorous, secondary responses are more efficient because the antibodies bind more effectively to the antigen, i.e. with higher affinity. A minority of B-cells will respond directly to antigens called T-independent antigens, which have repeating, identical, antigenic determinants and provoke predominantly IgM antibody responses. B-cells, however, will not usually respond directly to antigen, even when presented by appropriate accessory cells.

A second signal is needed to trigger the B-cell; this signal is

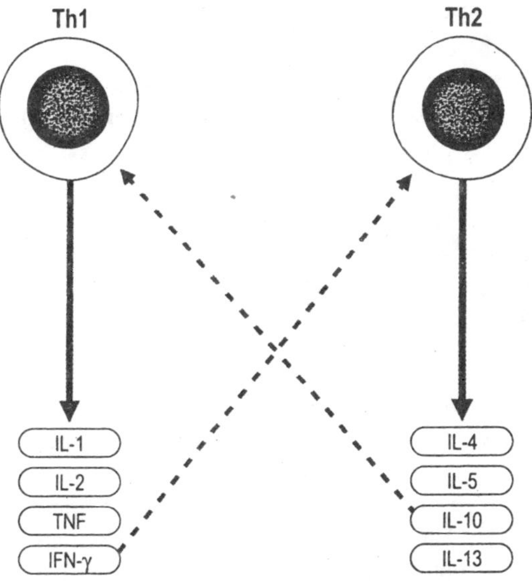

Figure 3.11: Thl and Th2 cells secrete different cytokines.

normally provided by helper T-cells (Th cells) which express CD4. T-cell help is antigen-specific. Only helper T-cells which have responded to antigen presented by macrophages can subsequently help B-cells already committed to that antigen.

Helper T-cells recognise both antigen and MHC class II antigens as a complex on the presenting cells. They then recognise the same combination of antigen and class II molecule on the corresponding B-cell.

When helper T-cells meet an antigen for the first time, the limited number reacting with that antigen are activated to provide help for B-cells. They undergo blast transformation and proliferation, i.e. *clonal* expansion, so the immune response on second and subsequent exposures is quicker and more vigorous.

Other mechanisms help to improve this efficiency. Memory cells (which bear the surface marker CD45RO) have increased numbers of adhesion molecules (LFA-1, CD2, LFA-3, ICAM-1) plus a higher proportion of high affinity receptors for the relevant antigen.

Memory cells are therefore easily activated and produce high concentrations of IL-2 to recruit more helper T-cells. Thus T-cell memory is a combination of an increase of T-cells and a qualitative change in the efficiency of those T-cells.

Helper T-cells are further grouped into two distinct subgroups depending on their cytokine profile. Thl cells secrete TNF and IFN-y and mediate cellular immunity. In contrast, Th2 cells predominantly secrete IL-4, IL-5, IL-10 and IL-13 and are responsible for stimulating vigorous antibody production by B-cells.

A Thl cytokine profile provides protection against intracellular pathogens, while a Th2 profile is found in those diseases associated with overproduction of antibodies, especially IgE.

The effects of helper T-cells are balanced by those of functional suppressor T-cells which express the characteristic surface glycoprotein CD8.

Cell-Mediated Responses

Antigen-specific cell-mediated responses are carried out by T-lymphocytes. T-cells can lyse cells expressing specific antigens *(cytotoxicity)* or release cytokines which trigger inflammation *(delayed hypersensitivity)*. These two types of T-cell response are mediated by the two distinct subpopulations: cytotoxicity is the role of cytotoxic T-cells and delayed hypersensitivity that of helper T-cells. These two types are responsible for fighting intracellular pathogens (all viruses, parasites and certain bacteria) which are inaccessible to antibodies.

Cytotoxic T-cells kill cells infected with virus. Such cytotoxicity is virus specific-only cells expressing the relevant viral proteins on their surfaces are killed. Since infected cells express surface viral proteins prior to the assembly of new virus particles and viral budding, cytotoxic T-cells are important in the recovery phase of an infection, destroying the infected cells before new virus particles are generated.

Cytotoxic T-cells recognise viral antigens together with MHC class I molecules. They show exquisite specificity for self-MHC antigens, in that they can only lyse cells expressing the same MHC class I molecules, i.e. express MHC restriction.

NON-SPECIFIC EFFECTOR MECHANISMS

- Complement is a complex series of proteins acting as an enzymatic cascade
- Complement can be activated by antibody (the classical pathway), by bacterial cell walls (the alternative pathway) or by mannose-binding lectin (the lectin pathway)
- Complement activation results in increased vascular permeability, chemoattraction of leukocytes, enhanced phagocytosis and cell lysis
- Monocytes and macrophages comprise the mononuclear phagocyte system
- Natural killer (NK) cells are important in the response to viral infection

Complement

Complement is a complex series of interacting plasma proteins which form a major effector system for antibodymediated immune reactions. Many complement components exist as inactive precursors; once activated, the component may behave as an enzyme which cleaves several molecules of the next component in the sequence.

Each precursor is cleaved into two or more fragments. The major fragment (usually designated 'b') has two biologically active sites: one for binding to cell membranes or the triggering complex, and the other for enzymatic cleavage of the next complement component.

Minor cleavage fragments (designated 'a') have important biological properties in the fluid phase. Control of complement activation involves spontaneous decay of any exposed attachment sites and inactivation by specific inhibitors. The major purpose of the complement pathway is to remove or destroy antigen, either by direct lysis or by opsonisation.

Complement Activation

Complement activation occurs in two sequential phases:

- activation of the C3 component
- activation of the 'attack' or lyric pathway.

The critical step is cleavage of C3 by complementderived enzymes called C3 convertases. The major fragment of activated C3-called C3b-mediates a number of vital biological activities, particularly opsonisation. The cleavage of C3 is achieved via three main routes, the classical, alternative and lectin pathways, all of which generate C3 convertases but in response to different stimuli.

Classical pathway activation

The classical pathway is activated when binding of IgM or IgG to antigen causes a conformational change in the Fc region of the antibody to reveal a binding site for the first component in the classical pathway, C1. C1 is a macromolecular complex of three subcomponents-C1q, Clr and Cls. Clq is a collagen-like protein composed of six subunits, resembling a 'bunch of tulips' when seen under the electron microscope.

Clq reacts with Fc regions via its globular heads but attachment by two critically spaced binding sites is needed for activation. IgM is more efficient than IgG in activating C1q. IgA, IgD and IgE do not activate the classical pathway. Once C1q is activated, C1r and C1s are sequentially bound to generate enzyme activity (C1 esterase) for C4 and C2, splitting both molecules into a and b fragments.

The complex C4b2b is the *classical pathway C3 convertase.* C4b2b cleaves C3 into two fragments, one (C3a) possessing anaphylotoxic and chemotactic activity and one which binds to the initiating complex and promotes many of the biological properties of complement. The C4b2b3b complex so generated is an enzyme, C5 convertase, which initiates the final lyric pathway (the 'attack' sequence).

Alternative pathway activation

The central reaction in this pathway, as in the classical one, is the activation of C3. The alternative pathway, however, generates a C3 convertase without the need for antibody, C1, C4 or C2. Instead, the most important activators are bacterial cell walls and endotoxin. Thus, the alternative pathway is responsible for innate defence against invading organisms, as it functions in the absence of preformed specific antibody.

The initial cleavage of C3 in the alternative pathway happens continuously and spontaneously, generating a low level of C3b. C3b is then able to use factors D and B of the alternative pathway to produce the active enzyme 'C3bBb' which can break down more C3, providing still more C3b. In the absence of any regulation, this positive feedback loop would continue to cleave C3 until the supply was exhausted.

Regulation is provided by the control proteins, factors H and I. H competes with factor B for binding to C3b, and I then cleaves and inactivates the displaced C3b. Microbial agents that activate the alternative pathway circumvent the effects of factor H and I and allow the pre-existing low grade turnover to be amplified. This self-destructive property seems to depend on the carbohydrate composition of the bacterial cell wall.

Lectin pathway activation

The lectin pathway is initiated by mannose-binding lectin (MBL), a circulating protein that binds avidly to carbohydrate on the surface of certain microorganisms. MBL is structurally related to Clq and activates complement through MASP (MBL-associated serine proteinase) which is similar to Clr and Cls of the classical pathway. The lectin pathway also contributes to innate immunity.

The Membrane Attack Complex

There are two ways of producing the C5 splitting enzymethe C5 convertase: in the classical pathway it is made up of C3b, C4b and C2b; in the alternative pathway it is composed of C3b, Bb and properdin. Thereafter, the final lyric pathway of complement is the same, involving the sequential attachment of the components C5, C6, C7, C8 and C9 and resulting in lysis of the target cell.

This target may be an invading organism or a virally infected cell. The lytic pathway complex binds to the cell membrane and a transmembrane channel is formed which leads to osmotic lysis of the cell.

Biological Effects of Complement

Complement-mediated *lysis* of antigen is dramatic but is not the most important role. Instead, complementdependent *phagocytosis* is crucial in defence. Microorganisms coated (i.e. opsonised) with C3b can be bound by cells that possess receptors-called complement receptors type 1 (CR1)-for this ligand.

CR1 receptors are present on phagocytic cells. Complement activation results in the release of the *pro-inflammatory mediators* C5a, C4a and C3a. These act as anaphylotoxins to increase vascular permeability, release vasoactive amines and induce smooth muscle spasm. C5a is a potent chemoattractant and stimulates neutrophils and macrophages to synthesise cytokines, undergo oxidative metabolism and release degradative enzymes.

Macrophages

Macrophages are the tissue equivalent of monocytes and together represent the *mononuclear phagocytic* system. Lymphocytes and macrophages are derived from closely related stem cells in the bone marrow but each cell lineage has different colony-stimulating factors.

Monocytes circulate for only a few hours before entering the tissues where they may differentiate and live for weeks or months as mature macrophages. Tissue macrophages are heterogeneous in appearance, in metabolism and probably also in function; they include freely mobile alveolar and peritoneal macrophages, fixed Kupffer cells in the liver and those lining the sinusoids of the spleen.

When found in other tissues, they are called *histiocytes*. A major function of the mononuclear phagocyte system is the phagocytosis of invading organisms and other antigens. Macrophages have prominent lysosomal granules containing acid hydrolases and other degradative enzymes with which to destroy phagocytosed material.

The material may be an engulfed viable organism, a dead cell, debris, an antigen or an immune complex. In order to carry out their functions effectively, macrophages must be 'activated'; in this state they show increased phagocytic and killing activity.

Stimuli include cytokines (see above), substances which bind to Fc receptors of IgG or soluble inflammatory mediators such as C5a. Toll-like receptors (TLR) are pattern recognition receptors on macrophages and other cells that contribute to innate immunity. They recognise combinations of sugars, proteins and lipids on pathogens such as gram-negative bacterial lipopolysaccharide-and trigger inflammatory responses by up-regulating cytokines such as TNF or IL-1, although cytokine release may cause further damage in inflamed tissues. Macrophages are also important for the presentation of antigen to other cells of the immune system, as described earlier.

Neutrophil Polymorphonuclear Leukocytes

Neutrophils play a major role in the body's defence against acute infection. They synthesise and express adhesion receptors so they can adhere to, and migrate out of, blood vessels into tissues. They do this in response to chemotactic agents produced at the site of inflammation;

such substances include IL-8, complement-derived factors (such as C3a and C5a), lymphokines released by Thl cells and chemokines produced by mast cells.

Neutrophils are phagocytic cells. Morphologically, the process *of* phagocytosis is similar in both neutrophils and mononuclear phagocytes. Neutrophils are also able to kill and degrade the substances they eat. This requires a considerable amount *of* energy and is associated with a 'respiratory burst' of oxygen consumption, increased hexose monophosphate shunt activity and superoxide production.

Antibody-Dependent Cell-mediated Cytotoxicity (ADCC)

ADCC is a mechanism by which antibody-coated target cells are destroyed by cells bearing Fc receptors natural killer cells, monocytes, neutrophils-with no involvement of the major histocompatibility complex. The mechanism of target cell destruction is not fully understood but includes the release of cytoplasmic components called perforin and granzymes.

Natural Killer Cells

Natural killer (NK) cells look like large granular lymphocytes. They can kill target cells even in the absence of any antibody or antigenic stimulation. They are activated non-specifically by mitogens, interferon and IL-12. NK cells are not immune cells in the strictest sense because, like macrophages, they are not clonally restricted, they show minimal specificity and have no memory.

The range of their potential targets is broad. Animals and rare patients with deficient NK cell function have an increased incidence of certain tumours and viral infections. NK cells are therefore thought to be important in the early host response to viral infection and in 'immune' surveillance against tumours.

OUTCOMES OF IMMUNE RESPONSES

- Antibody, especially IgM, can neutralise viruses and toxins
- Opsonisation of bacteria with IgG antibodies makes phagocytosis more efficient
- C3b generated by complement activation is also an efficient opsonin
- Target cells may be killed specifically by cytotoxic T-cells or non-specifically by macrophages or natural killer cells

- Many components of the immune response contribute to inflammation

Once the immune response is initiated, the end result depends on the nature and localisation of the antigen, on whether the predominant response has been humoral or cell mediated, on the type *of* antibody provoked and whether non-specific effector mechanisms have been involved.

Direct Effects of Antibody

Neutralisation is one direct effect of antibody, and IgM is particularly good at this. A number *of* antigens, including diphtheria toxin, tetanus toxin and many viruses, can be neutralised by antibody.

Once neutralised, these substances are no longer able to bind to receptors in the tissues; the resulting antigen-antibody complexes are usually removed from the circulation and destroyed by macrophages.

Indirect Effects of Antibody

Opsonisation is the process by which an antigen becomes coated with substances (such as antibodies or complement) that make it more easily engulfed by phagocytic cells. The coating of soluble or particulate antigens with IgG antibodies renders them more susceptible to cells which have surface receptors for the Fc portions of IgG (FcRIII).

Neutrophils and macrophages have Fc receptors and can phagocytose IgG-coated antigens; however, this process is relatively inefficient if only Fc receptors are involved. The activation of complement by antibody (via the classical pathway) or by bacterial cell walls (via the alternative or lectin pathways) generates C3b on the surface of microorganisms and makes them susceptible to binding by C3b receptors (CR1) on macrophages and neutrophils: C3 receptors are very efficient in triggering phagocytosis.

Killing of Target Cells

Target cells killed as a result of an immune response include organisms and cells bearing virally altered or tumourspecific antigens on their surfaces. They may be killed directly by antigen-specific mechanisms such as antibody and complement, antibody-dependent cell-mediated cytotoxicity or cytotoxic T-cells. Lymphokine production may result in non-specific killing, as does activation of NK cells and macrophages.

Inflammation

Inflammation is defined as increased vascular permeability accompanied by an infiltration of 'inflammatory' cells, initially neutrophil polymorphonuclear leukocytes and later macrophages, lymphocytes and plasma cells. Vascular permeability may be increased by complement fragments such as C3a or C5a. Some fragments (C3a, C5a and C567) also attract neutrophils and mobilise them from the bone marrow; lymphokines generated by activated T-cells have similar properties.

The triggering of mast cells via IgE also causes inflammation due to release of histamine and leukotrienes. Inflammation is covered in detail in other chapter of this book.

IMMUNODEFICIENCY

- Immunodeficiency presents as serious, persistent, unusual or recurrent infections-'SPUR'
- Secondary causes of immunodeficiency are much **more** common than primary disorders
- Patients with antibody deficiency present with recurrent bacterial infections of the respiratory tract
- Patients with defects in cellular immunity present with invasive and disseminated viral, fungal and opportunistic bacterial infections involving any organ
- Infants with severe combined immunodeficiency (5CID) will die before the age of 2 years unless bone marrow transplantation is performed
- Clinical presentations of defects in phagocytes and complement function show the dependence of humoral immunity on non-specific effector mechanisms
- In some primary immunodeficiencies, the gene responsible has been identified and somatic gene therapy is possible
- Secondary immunodeficiency occurs when synthesis of key immune components is suppressed (e.g. bone marrow infiltration or infection with an immunosuppressive virus) or their loss is accelerated (e.g. nephrotic syndrome or protein-losing enteropathy)
- Acquired immune deficiency syndrome (AIDS) is the result of infection with human immunodeficiency virus (HIV)
- The dominant clinical features of AIDS are opportunistic infections and tumours

Since the immune system evolved as a defence against infectious organisms, the most dramatic examples of its importance are provided by those disorders where one or more vital components of the immune system are missing or fail to function.

Defects in immunity can be classified as primary, due to an intrinsic defect in the immune system, or secondary to an underlying condition. These defects may involve specific or non-specific (innate) immune mechanisms. Underlying immunodeficiency should be suspected in every patient who has recurrent, persistent, severe or unusual infections, irrespective of age.

Primary Antibody Deficiencies

Defects in antibody synthesis can involve all immunoglobulin classes (panhypogammaglobulinaemia) or only one class or subclass of immunoglobulin (selective deficiency). Antibody deficiency can occur in children or adults although the underlying physiological defects may differ.

In congenital forms of antibody deficiency, recurrent infections usually begin between 4 months and 2 years of age, because maternally transferred IgG affords passive protection for the first 3-4 months of life. Some forms of primary antibody deficiency are inherited as Xlinked or autosomal recessive traits: a history of affected relatives, especially boys, is therefore of diagnostic value.

However, the average size of a family in developed countries is now so small that a negative family history does not exclude an inherited condition. Recurrent infections of the upper and lower respiratory tracts occur in almost all antibody-deficient patients.

Many patients also present with skin sepsis (boils, abscesses or cellulitis), gut infection, meningitis, arthritis, splenomegaly or purpura.

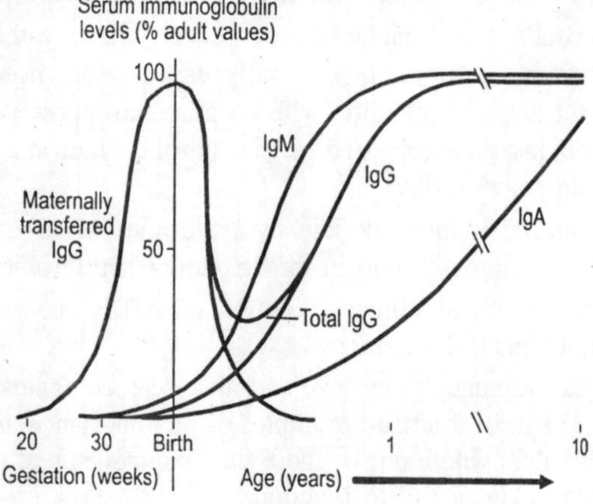

Figure 3.12: Serum immunoglobulin levels in relation to age.

The commonest infecting organisms in antibody deficiency states are pyogenic bacteria such as staphylococci, *Haemophilus influenzae* and *Streptococcus pneumoniae*.

In general, these patients are not unduly susceptible to viral or fungal infections because cellmediated immunity is preserved, but exceptions do occur. There are rarely any diagnostic physical signs of antibody deficiency, although examination often shows failure to thrive in children and the consequences of previous sepsis such as ruptured tympanic membranes or bronchiectasis.

Measurement of serum immunoglobulin levels will reveal any gross quantitative abnormality but the ability of a patient to make antibody is a better guide to susceptibility to infection than total immunoglobulin levels. Some individuals fail to make specific antibody after test immunisation despite normal serum immunoglobulins.

Transient Hypogammaglobulinaemia of Infancy

Maternal IgG is actively transported across the placenta to the fetal circulation from the fourth month of gestational life, although maximum transfer takes place during the final 2 months. At birth, the infant has a serum IgG at least equal to that of the mother; at first, catabolism of maternal IgG is only partly compensated by IgG synthesised by the newborn child.

The period between 3 and 6 months of age represents a phase of 'physiological hypogammaglobulinaemia'. The normal infant is not unduly susceptible to infection because functioning antibody is present despite the low IgG level, and T-cell function is intact. However, the trough in IgG is more severe and the risk of sepsis much greater if the gift of IgG acquired from the mother is severely reduced, as in extremely premature infants born around 28 weeks gestation.

X-linked Agammaglobulinaemia (XLA)-Bruton's Disease

Boys with this condition usually present with recurrent pyogenic infections between the ages of 4 months and 2 years. The sites of infection and the organisms involved are similar to other types of antibody deficiency, although these patients are susceptible to enteroviruses.

In almost all patients, circulating mature B-cells are absent but T-cells are normal and even increased. No plasma cells are found in the bone marrow, lymph nodes or gastrointestinal tract. The clinical diagnosis rests on the very low serum levels of all classes of immunoglobulin and the absence of circulating mature B-lymphocytes.

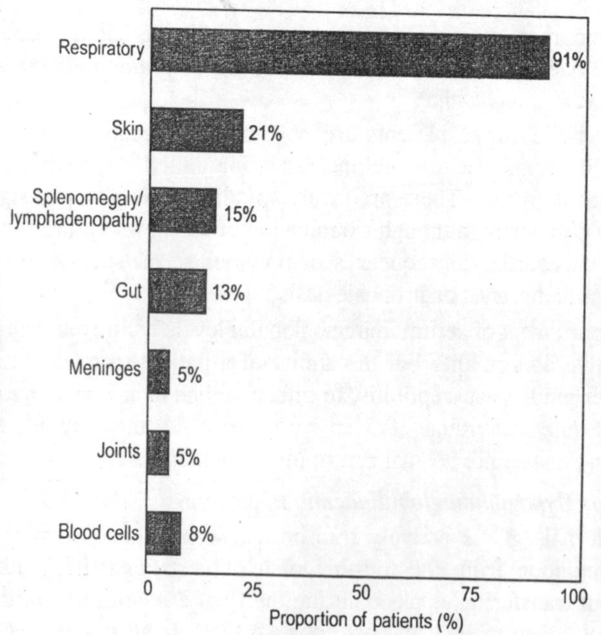

Figure 3.13: Clinical presentation in patients with primary antibody deficiency, irrespective of age.

The gene responsible for XLA is found on the short arm of the X chromosome. Its product is an intranuclear enzyme known as ***Bruton's*** *tyrosine kinase,* or Btk. In its absence pre-B-cells are unable to mature into B-cells. The identification of the gene confirms the diagnosis and enables asymptomatic female carriers to be identified and counselled. Management consists of replacement immunoglobulin for the affected boy.

Hyper-IgM Syndrome

Some boys with antibody deficiency have normal or high serum IgM levels. This X-linked disease is now known to be due to a failure of CD40 ligand expression on CD4+ T-lymphocytes. As a result, T-cells fail to trigger the switch from IgM to IgG or IgA production in antigenstimulated B-cells.

As well as bacterial infections, affected boys are susceptible to *Pneumocystis carinii* pneumonia because macrophage function is also impaired. Replacement immunoglobulin therapy and co-trimoxazole prophylaxis (to prevent Pneumocystis infection) are required in the long term, and bone marrow transplantation is indicated increasingly in many cases.

Selective IgA Deficiency

This is the commonest primary defect of specific immunity with a prevalence of 1:700 in the UK. It is characterised by undetectable serum IgA levels with normal concentrations of IgG and IgA. Most IgA deficient individuals are healthy but selective IgA deficiency is linked to a variety of disorders. About 20% of individuals make antibodies to IgA and may develop adverse reactions following transfusions of blood or plasma.

Common Variable Immunodeficiency (CVID)

CVID embraces a group of disorders presenting as antibody deficiency in late childhood or adult life. Patients experience the same range of bacterial infections as other patients with antibody deficiency. CVID is more common than XLA. CVID patients also have a 40-fold increase in incidence of lymphoma.

Primary Defects in Cell-Mediated Immunity

Impairment of T-cell function is usually accompanied by variable degrees of B-cell dysfunction, reflecting the T-B-cell co-operation needed for efficient antibody production. Most defects are therefore *combined* immunodeficiencies and this is reflected in the wide range of infections experienced by such patients. Some examples are illustrated below.

Severe Combined Immunodeficiency

Infants in whom there is major failure of both T- and Blymphocyte function have severe combined immunodeficiency (SCID). There are several genetic variants but all affected children present in the first few weeks or months of life with failure to thrive, chronic diarrhoea ('gastroenteritis') and respiratory infections.

Usually, there is lymphopenia, which is often overlooked. Immunisation with live vaccines and conventional blood transfusions must be avoided in patients with proven or suspected defects in cell-mediated immunity: live vaccines can lead to disseminated infection, and blood transfusion may result in *graft-versus-host disease.*

Infants with SCID die before they are 2 years old unless bone marrow transplantation is undertaken. In some forms of SCID due to a specific genetic defect, somatic gene therapy is an experimental alternative.

Di George Syndrome ('Catch 22' anomaly)

In this condition, severely affected neonates present with cardiovascular defects, hypocalcaemia and thymic dysfunction. Most deaths are due to the heart lesions and not to the immunodeficiency, which presents much later. The genetic defect (chromosome 22q11 deletion) results in impaired intrauterine development of the third and fourth pharyngeal pouches. The immune defect can be relatively mild.

Primary Defects in Phagocyte Function

Humoral immunity depends not only upon antibody synthesis but also upon effector mechanisms which eliminate antigen bound to antibody. Micro-organisms coated (i.e. opsonised) with IgG antibodies are readily bound and ingested by phagocytic cells.

Thus, specific immunity requires non-specific effector mechanisms for its efficient operation; this partly explains similarities between the infectious complications experienced by patients with defects of antibody synthesis and those with neutrophil dysfunction.

The major role of the neutrophil is to ingest, kill and digest invading micro-organisms, particularly bacteria and fungi. Failure to fulfil this role leads to infection. Defects in neutrophil function can be quantitative *(neutropenia)* or qualitative *(neutrophil dysfunction)*.

However, irrespective of the basic cause, the clinical features of infections are similar and certain generalisations are possible:

- Infections are recurrent and prolonged.
- Clinical features may be minimal despite severe infection.
- Infections are poorly responsive to antibiotics.
- They are commonly staphylococcal.
- They involve skin and mucous membranes.
- They are complicated by suppurative lymphadenopathy.

Chronic Granulomatous Disease

Chronic granulomatous disease (CGD) is a group of disorders resulting from a failure to produce bactericidal oxygen radicals during the 'respiratory burst' which accompanies activation of phagocytes.

The classic type is inherited as an X-linked recessive disorder, and typically presents in the first 3 months of life as severe skin sepsis caused by *Staphylococcus aureus* or fungal infections with *Candida albicans* or *Aspergillus fumigatus*.

The resulting complications include regional lymphadenopathy, hepatosplenomegaly, hepatic abscesses and osteomyelitis. Affected organs show multiple abscesses and non-caseating giant-cell granulomas.

Primary Complement Deficiency

Inherited deficiencies of complement components are associated with characteristic clinical syndromes. Many patients with Cl, C4 or

C2 deficiency present with a syndrome of malar flush, arthralgia, glomerulonephritis, fever or chronic vasculitis.

Patients with C3 deficiency occurring as a primary or secondary defect (due to deficiencies of factor H or factor 1) have an increased susceptibility to recurrent bacterial infections. Affected individuals present with lifethreatening infections such as pneumonia, septicaemia and meningitis, illustrating the important role of C3 in defence against infection.

There is a striking association between deficiencies of C5, C6, C7, C8 or properdin and recurrent neisserial infection. Most patients present with recurrent meningococcal meningitis, less commonly with gonococcal septicaemia and arthritis. However, many patients experience only one episode of meningitis, or many years may elapse between attacks.

Hereditary angioedema is caused by deficiency of the inhibitor of the first component of complement (C1 inhibitor). Patients experience recurrent attacks of cutaneous, intestinal or laryngeal oedema which can be fatal if the airway is occluded.

Secondary Immunodeficiency

Secondary causes of immunodeficiency are far more common than primary causes. Since levels of immune components represent the net balance of synthesis versus catabolism (or loss), low levels reflect either depressed production or accelerated catabolism or loss.

Protein loss severe enough to cause hypogammaglobulinaemia occurs mainly via the kidney *(nephrotic syndrome)* or through the gut *(protein-losing enteropathy)* in a variety of active inflammatory diseases such as Crohn's disease or ulcerative colitis. In intestinal lymphangiectasia, the dilated lymphatics leak lymphocytes as well as protein.

Impaired synthesis is exemplified *by protein energy malnutrition.* Malnourished individuals show impaired specific antibody production following immunisation, and even more striking defects in cell-mediated immunity, phagocyte function and complement activity. Many of these defects reverse after adequate protein and calorie supplementation of the diet.

Patients with *lymphoproliferative diseases* are very prone to infection. The infection risk in patients with multiple myeloma is 5-1.0 times higher than in age-matched controls, while untreated chronic lymphocytic leukaemia is commonly associated with hypogammaglobulinaemia and recurrent chest infections, which tend to become more severe as the disease progresses. Non-Hodgkin's lymphoma may be associated with defects of both humoral and cellmediated immunity.

Immunosuppressive drugs affect many aspects of cell function. Lymphocyte and polymorph activity are often impaired, although severe hypogammaglobulinaemia is unusual. Patients taking drugs to prevent organ transplant rejection can develop unusual opportunistic infections. An iatrogenic form of secondary immune deficiency is that associated with *splenectomy*. Death occurs from sudden, overwhelming infection due to *Streptococcus pneumoniae*. The risk of death from infection following splenectomy is 1-2% over 15 years.

All patients should receive immunisation with pneumococcal vaccine. In a number of *infections,* the micro-organism paradoxically suppresses rather than stimulates the immune system. Severe, though transient, impairment of cell-mediated immunity has been noted in many viral illnesses, particularly cytomegalovirus, measles, rubella, infectious mononucleosis and viral hepatitis; however, the most florid example is infection with the human immunodeficiency virus (HIV).

Acquired Immune Deficiency Syndrome (AIDS)

AIDS is a worldwide (pandemic) form of immuno-deficiency caused by the retroviruses human immuno-deficiency virus (HIV) types 1 and 2. Since its recognition in 1981, the number of people infected with HIV and cases of AIDS have risen progressively. At the end of 2001, the number of people living with HIV worldwide was estimated to be 40 million and growing at around 10% per year.

Sub-Saharan Africa is the most affected region and accounts for over two-thirds of all infected cases. Southern Africa is especially hard hit: in some countries, about 25% of all adults aged 15-49 years are living with HIV India has about 5 million infected people, more than any other country.

In 2001, women accounted for over 2.5 million new infections, and children under 15 years for nearly 700 000. Almost all new childhood infections are due to mother to child *(vertical)* transmission, before or during childbirth or through breastfeeding.

Transmission of HIV

HIV is transmitted through sexual intercourse, both heterosexual and homosexual, and through the sharing of contaminated needles and syringes by intravenous drug abusers or via therapeutic procedures in areas of the world where reuse of contaminated equipment occurs. Other methods of transmission are through the receipt of infected blood or blood products, donated organs or semen.

Cases of seroconversion and death among health care workers after

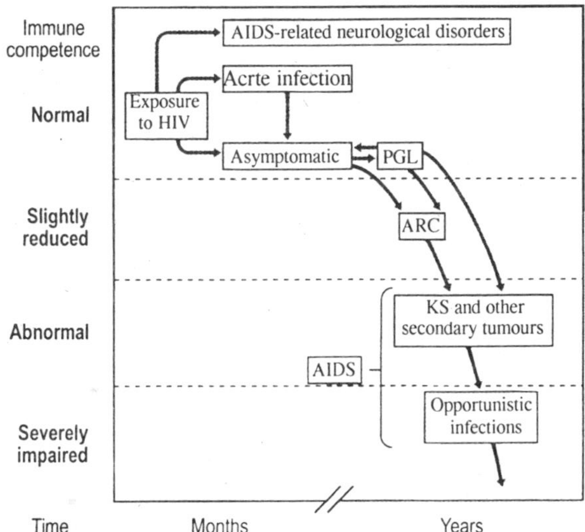

Figure 3.14: The spectrum of HIV infection and its progression towards AIDS.

needlestick injuries or blood splashes have also been reported (0.3% seroconvert).

Clinical spectrum of HIV infection

HIV produces a spectrum of disorders. A transient, acute *glandular fever-like illness* may occur in 10-20% of patients within a few weeks of initial HIV infection and precedes seroconversion (i.e. production of antibodies to HIV). Peripheral blood shows many atypical lymphocytes and an increased number of CD8+ T-cells at this time.

Most seropositive individuals then remain symptom-free for 2 to 10 or more years. Development of AIDS depends on the contribution of many co-factors, such as genetic background. After this latent period, some individuals develop asymptomatic *persistent generalised lymphadenopathy (PGL),* defined as enlarged nodes in two or more extra-inguinal sites persisting for at least 3 months in the absence of any illness associated with lymphadenopathy.

Some seropositive people show constitutional and clinical features such as unexplained lymphadenopathy, diarrhoea, night sweats, oral candidiasis and weight loss-the *AIDS-related complex*. HIV is *neurotropic:* acute aseptic meningitis, encephalopathy, myelopathy and neuropathy have been reported around the time of seroconversion while chronic meningitis, cerebral lymphoma, encephalopathy and dementia may occur later.

The dominant clinical manifestations of AIDS are *opportunistic infections* and *tumours*. Typical infections include *Pneumocystis carinii* pneumonia, cytomegalovirus or herpes simplex infections, cerebral toxoplasmosis, atypical mycobacterial infections, systemic fungal infection and parasitic infestations of the gastrointestinal tract.

Common tumours are the consequences of the activities of oncogenic viruses operating in an immunocompromised host: Kaposi's sarcoma is caused by human herpes virus type 8 (HHV8) and non-Hodgkin's lymphoma by Epstein-Barr virus.

Immunopathogenesis of HIV infection

HIV enters susceptible cells through binding of viral envelope glycoprotein (gp 120) to specific receptors on the cell surface, mainly the CD4 molecule itself, although another cell surface molecule-the chemokine receptors CXCR4 and CCR5-are also involved.

Any cell bearing the CD4 antigen can be infected by HIV: typically these are helper T-cells but some macrophages and glial cells of the central nervous system also express low amounts of CD4. The most striking effects of HIV are on T-lymphocyte mediated responses.

HIV replicates at a rate of 10^9-10^{70} new virions per day, resulting in up to 10^8 new mutants per day, so the immune system has an enormous task to limit HIV spread. The hallmark of disease progression is the inexorable fall in the absolute number of CD4+ T-cells, the result of the destructive, cytopathic effects of HIV While HIV infection may be latent clinically for many years, the destruction of CD4+ cells takes place continuously within lymph nodes and other lymphoid organs until the virus can no longer be contained and reappears in the blood stream—*HIV antigenaemia.*

Therapeutic options

Knowledge of the way in which HIV gains access into CD4+ cells and its method of replication has led to exploration of potential therapies. Binding of virus to the CD4 antigen in the cell membrane might be blocked by antibody to the viral envelope or to the CD4 or chemokine receptors.

Traditional vaccines, using killed or attenuated organisms, are unlikely to be of value. The fragile nature of the HIV envelope makes it a poor immunogen, while its high mutation rate poses a problem in selecting a stable common epitope able to provoke a protective immune response. Safety is a major concern because a mutation of an attenuated HIV back to its virulent state would be catastrophic. The search for a candidate AIDS vaccine' continues.

Inhibition of viral replication can be achieved by inhibiting activity of reverse transcriptase (RT) as this is a unique retroviral enzyme with no mammalian equivalent. Such inhibitors fall into two groups: nucleoside RT inhibitors and non-nucleoside RT inhibitors.

Protease inhibitors also prevent the assembly of new infectious virions. Current management uses combinations of 3-4 of these drugs from different therapeutic groups to control viral replication and limit progression of immune deficiency.

HYPERSENSITIVITY REACTIONS

- These are damaging immunological reactions to extrinsic antigens Immediate hypersensitivity (type I) reactions are due to the binding between antigen and IgE on mast cells or basophils
- Antibody to cell-bound antigen (type II) causes cell destruction by activating complement or promoting phagocytosis
- Type III reactions result from deposition of immune complexes

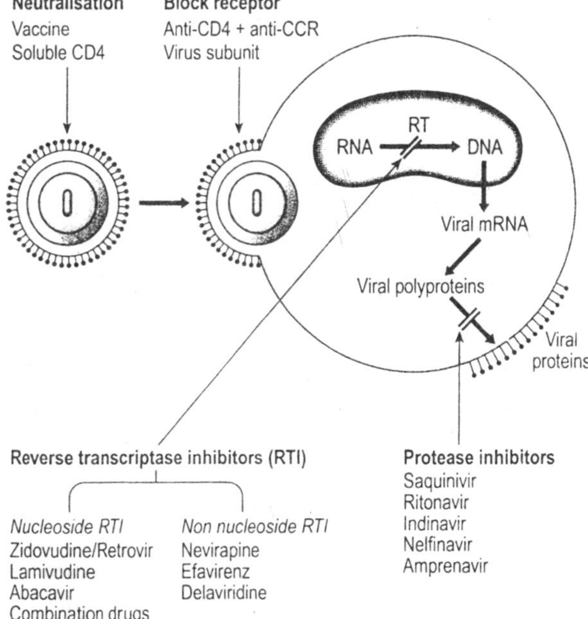

Figure 3.15: Potential therapeutic options for preventing or eliminating HIV infection.

in tissues, particularly the skin, joints and kidneys. Chronic immune complex nephritis accounts for most cases of glomerulonephritis in humans

- Type I, II and III reactions are caused by antibodies: type IV reactions are caused by T-lymphocytes
- Delayed-type hypersensitivity (type IV) reactions are mediated by interleukin-2, interferon yand other cytokines released by T-lymphocytes
- Complex hypersensitivity reactions cannot be explained solely on the basis of one type of reaction

Unfortunately, the recognition of foreign antigen by the immune system can cause incidental tissue damage as well as the intended destruction of the antigen. Such reactions are called 'hypersensitivity' reactions; Gell and Coombs defined four main types:

Type I: immediate hypersensitivity, or 'allergy,' due to overproduction of IgE antibody on mast cells or basophils

Type II: antibody to cell-bound antigen Type III: immune complex reactions

Type IV: delayed hypersensitivity mediated by T-cells.

Immediate Hypersensitivity (type I)

Immediate hypersensitivity (type I) reactions are those in which antigen interacts with IgE bound to tissue mast cells or basophils. IgE is embedded in the membranes of mast cells, exposing the antigen-binding sites of the molecule to the microenvironment of the cell.

Exposure to specific antigen bridges two adjacent IgE molecules and this bridging effect triggers the mast cell to release its mediators. There are two groups of mediators: those which are preformed and those which are newly synthesised.

The *preformed mediators* include histamine, lysosomal enzymes, chemokines and heparin. Because they are preformed, immediate (type I) hypersensitivity reactions are rapid: clinically the effects begin within 5-10 minutes and peak around 30 minutes.

This is well illustrated by skin prick tests: if the antigen is pricked or scratched into the skin of an allergic individual a 'wheal and flare' reaction rapidly appears. IgE responses are usually directed against antigens which enter at epithelial surfaces, i.e. inhaled or ingested antigens.

Allergic diseases are common: about 15-20% of the population has some form of allergy. Such patients are frequently *atopic:* atopy defines an inherited tendency for overproduction of IgE antibodies to common environmental antigens. Approximately 80% of atopic individuals have a family history of allergic disease.

Several genes predispose to this familial tendency but environmental factors must be involved because there is only 50% concordance in monozygotic twins. Typical atopic disorders include seasonal allergic rhinitis ('hay fever'), asthma and atopic eczema. However, life-threatening reactions can occur if the antigen enters the systemic circulation or if

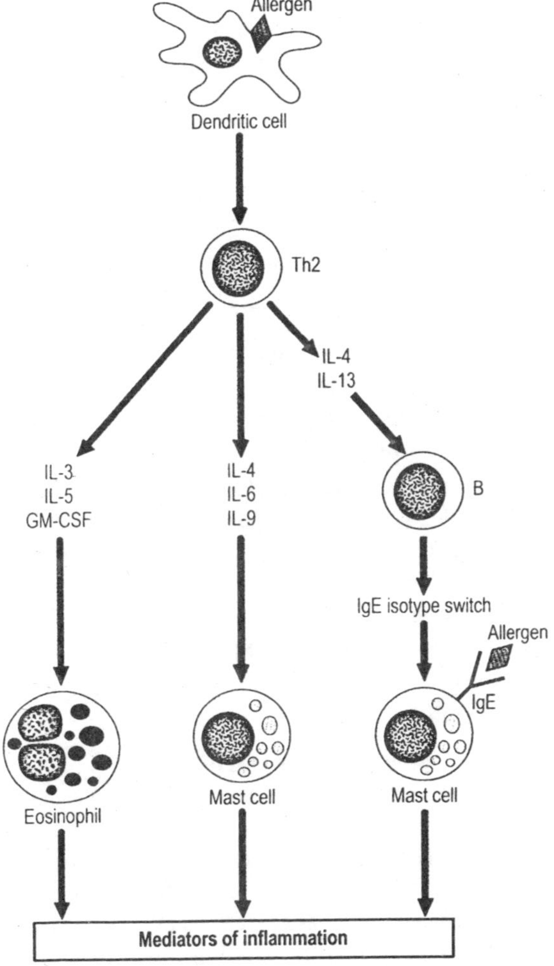

Figure 3.16: Cytokines produced by Th2 cells.

the patient has very high levels of circulating IgE antibodies. Generalised degranulation of IgE-sensitised mast cells and basophils leads to sudden hypotension, severe bronchoconstriction and collapse, a condition called *anaphylaxis*. Common causes are bee and wasp venom, antibiotics (e.g. penicillin), peanuts and latex.

Similar reactions which are not mediated by IgE antibodies are called *anaphylactoid:* the same mast cell mediators are responsible but the stimulus for their release differs. Substances inducing anaphylactoid reactions act directly on mast cells; they include anaesthetic induction agents and radiological contrast media.

Complex 'allergic' conditions such as asthma or eczema cannot be explained solely on the basis of IgE-mediated release of mediators. T-lymphocytes play a major role in the activation and/or recruitment of IgE antibody-producing B-cells, mast cells and eosinophils, the cellular triad involved in allergic inflammation.

Two major subsets of helper T-cells (Th) have been identified by their profile of cytokine secretion: Thl cells produce interleukin (IL)-2, interferon y and tumour necrosis factor; Th2 cells produce a range of cytokines including IL-4, IL-5, IL-10, IL-13 and GM-CSF. Sensitised T-cells found in bronchial biopsies and bronchoalveolar lavage fluid from allergic individuals are of the Th2 subset. When an atopic subject is exposed to the relevant antigen, immunological recognition can occur both via the T-cell receptor and via IgE bound to mast cells.

Once the lining of the airways becomes inflamed it is susceptible to any irritant, such as airways cooling, tobacco smoke, diesel particles or sulphur dioxide. Thus, *bronchial hyper-responsiveness is* the hallmark of asthma. Much of the inflammatory damage is induced by eosinophils which contain major basic protein (MBP) capable of damaging epithelial cells of the airways.

Damage to the epithelium by MBP, cytokines and mediators also exposes sensory nerve endings in the basement membrane and further increases irritability through neural triggering.

Antibody to Cell-Bound Antigen (type II)

Type II hypersensitivity reactions are triggered by antibodies reacting with antigenic determinants which form part of the cell membrane. The consequences of the reaction depend on whether or not complement or accessory cells are involved and whether the metabolism of the cell is affected. IgM or IgG antibodies are typically implicated.

Many examples of type II hypersensitivity involve drugs or their metabolites which have bound to the surface of red blood cells or platelets to form highly immunogenic epitopes. Antibodies formed against the drug or its metabolite inadvertently destroy the cell as well-'bystander lysis'-resulting in haemolytic anaemia or thrombocytopenic purpura.

The same mechanism is responsible for certain autoimmune disorders where the target antigen is intrinsic (i.e. self) antigen rather than extrinsic. Under these circumstances, auto-antibodies can also cause disease by binding to the functional sites of self-antigens, such as receptors for hormones or neurotransmitters, so mimicking or blocking the action of the hormone without causing inflammation or tissue damage.

Immune Complex Hypersensitivity (type III)

Type III reactions result from the deposition or formation of immune complexes in the tissues. Localisation of immune complexes depends on their size, their electrostatic charge, and the nature of the antigen. If they accumulate in the tissues in large quantities, they may activate complement and accessory cells and produce extensive tissue damage. A classic example is the *Arthus reaction,* an experimental model where an antigen is injected into the skin of an animal that has been previously sensitised.

The reaction of preformed antibody with this antigen results in high concentrations of local immune complexes; these cause complement

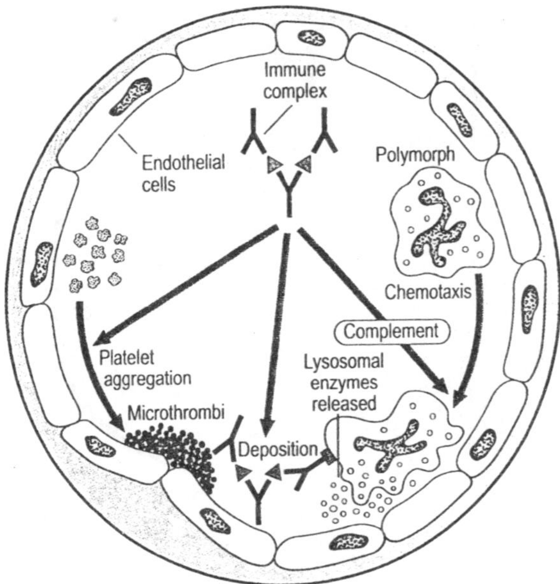

Figure 3.17: Vascular damage caused by immune complex deposition.

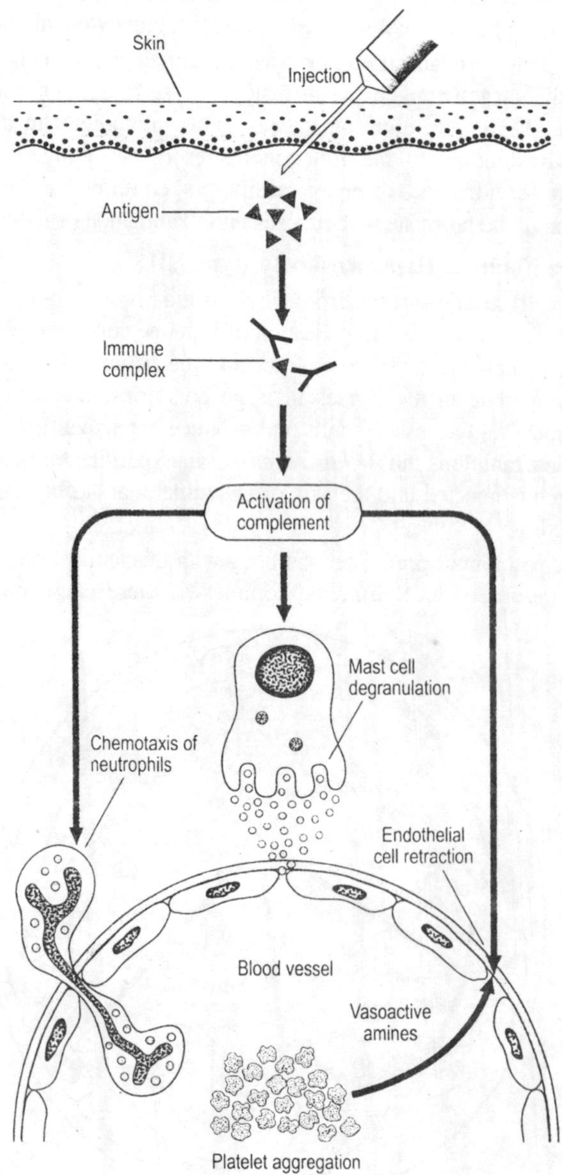

Figure 3.18: The Arthus reaction.

activation and neutrophil attraction and result in local inflammation 6-24 hours after the injection.

Acute 'one-shot' serum sickness is another example; in this condition, urticaria, arthralgia and glomerulonephritis occur about 10 days after initial exposure to the antigen. This is the time when IgG antibody, produced in response to antigen stimulation, reacts with remaining antigen to form circulating, soluble immune complexes.

As these damaging complexes are formed, the antigen concentration is rapidly lowered; the process continues only as long as circulating antigen persists and is usually self-limiting. Such reactions were common when antisera raised in animals were injected repeatedly into humans to neutralise bacterial toxins, e.g. tetanus anti-toxin. The animal serum immunoglobulins were highly immunogenic and resulted in an IgG antibody response to the foreign serum, hence *'serum sickness'*.

This reaction is now rare because animal serum is no longer used in this way. *Acute post-streptococcal glomerulonephritis* is caused by a similar mechanism. It occurs 10-12 days after a streptococcal infection of the throat or skin and results in deposition of immune complexes of IgG and C3 in the glomerular basement membrane.

Streptococcal antigens are rarely found in the complexes but antigenic fragments from certain 'nephritogenic' strains of streptococci bind to the glomerular basement membrane, so localising antibody to this site.

Chronic immune complex nephritis accounts for most cases of chronic glomerulonephritis in humans. When compared with the 'one-shot' model, chronic immune complex formation and deposition will occur if:

- antigen exposure is persistent
- the host makes an abnormal immune response
- local factors, such as defective complement function, promote deposition of complexes.

Persistent antigen exposure is most likely to occur if the antigen is a micro-organism capable of replication despite a host response, a medically prescribed drug, or an auto-antigen.

Delayed-type Hypersensitivity (type IV)

Type IV reactions are mediated by T-lymphocytes which react with antigen and release interleukin-2, interferon y and other cytokines. Once T-cells have been sensitised by primary exposure, secondary challenge is followed by a delayed-type hypersensitivity reaction (DTH), a local inflammatory response which takes 2-3 days to develop clinically. Histologically, these reactions consist of infiltrating T-lymphocytes,

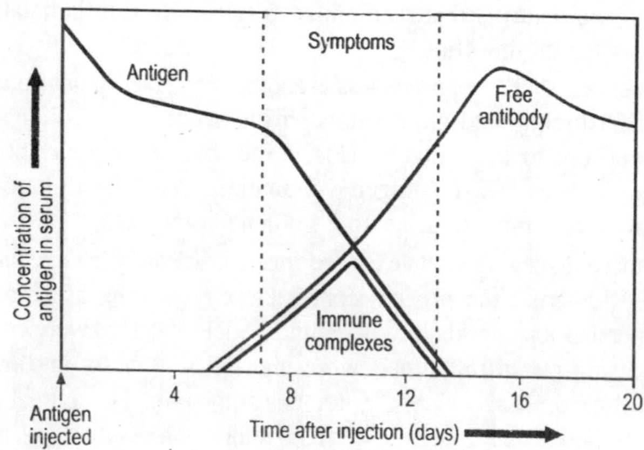

Figure 3.19: Acute 'one-shot' serum sickness and the time of deposition of immune complexes.

macrophages and occasional eosinophils. Experimentally, DTH can be transferred by T-lymphocytes but not by serum, i.e. antibodies are not involved.

A classic example of DTH is the *tuberculin reaction*. If a small amount of purified protein derivative (PPD) of tubercle bacilli is injected intradermally (Mantoux or Heaf test) into non-immune individuals, there is no effect. However, in individuals with cell-mediated immunity to tubercle bacilli, as a result either of previous tuberculous infection or immunisation with BCG (bacille Calmette-Guerin, a live but non-virulent strain of *Mycobacterium bovis*), an area of reddening and induration develops after 24-48 hours.

The dermis of the reaction site becomes infiltrated by lymphocytes and macrophages around small blood vessels, with oedema and vascular dilation. DTH may result from the normal cell-mediated immune response to infection with viruses, fungi and certain bacteria, notably *Mycobacterium tuberculosis* and *Mycobacterium leprae*.

If macrophages are unable to destroy ingested organisms, they may undergo differentiation into epithelioid cells or multinucleate giant cells. A collection of these cells forms *a granuloma*. Local tissue damage is an unwanted side-effect of this otherwise protective immune response. If the DTH response is absent or impaired, however, T-lymphocytes are unable to localise the invading micro-organism and patients develop invasive, aggressive disseminated disease, such as acute miliary tuberculosis.

Contact dermatitis to occupational and other antigens is also a type

IV reaction. Agents which do this are of relatively low molecular weight (< 1 kD) and not immunogenic in their own right: instead, they are highly reactive molecules that bind covalently to skin or tissue proteins. The sensitising chemical is known as a hapten and the host protein as the carrier.

The range of potential sensitising antigens is wide. Two phases of pathogenesis are recognised: the induction phase and the elicitation phase. In the *induction phase,* antigen-presenting cells in the skin-Langerhans' cells-bind the hapten-carrier protein complex and present it to T-lymphocytes in association with MHC class II antigen.

Induction of T-cells usually occurs after months of exposure to small amounts of antigen. Re-exposure to the relevant antigen triggers the *elicitation phase* where effector T-cells migrate to the skin to meet the protein complex presented by Langerhans' cells in the epidermis with consequent cytokine release and skin inflammation.

The diagnosis of the offending agent is made by *patch testing. A* suspected contact sensitiser is applied to normal skin on the patient's back and covered for 48 hours. The reaction site is inspected after 2 and 4 days. In a positive response, there is inflammation and induration at the test site. Delayed-type hypersensitivity is also a key mechanism underpinning the rejection of transplanted tissues and organs.

AUTOIMMUNITY AND AUTOIMMUNE DISEASE

- Autoimmunity is an immune response against a self-antigen
- Autoimmune disease is tissue damage or disturbed function resulting from an autoimmune response
- Disease may be restricted to a single organ (organ-specific), usually an endocrine gland, or involve auto-antigens widely distributed throughout the body (non-organ-specific)
- Most, but not all, autoimmune diseases are much commoner in females
- The immune system is normally specifically unreactive (tolerant) to self-antigens: autoimmune disease occurs when tolerance breaks down

Autoimmunity is an immune response against a self (auto) antigen or antigens. *Autoimmune disease* is tissue damage or disturbed physiological function resulting from an autoimmune response. This distinction is important as autoimmune responses can occur without resulting disease. Proof that autoimmunity causes a particular disease requires a number of criteria to be met, similar to Koch's postulates for micro-organisms in infectious diseases:

- Demonstrate immunological reactivity to a self-antigen.
- Characterise or isolate the inciting auto-antigen.
- Induce immunological reactivity against the same antigen by immunisation of experimental animals.
- Show pathological changes (similar or identical to those found in human disease) in the appropriate organs/tissues of an actively sensitised animal.

Patterns of Autoimmune Disease

Autoimmune diseases can affect any organ in the body although certain systems, such as endocrine glands, seem particularly susceptible. They are conventionally classified into organ-specific and non-organ-specific disorders.

Organ-specific Autoimmune Diseases

These affect a single organ; one or another endocrine gland is commonly involved. The antigen targets may be molecules expressed on the surface of living cells (particularly hormone receptors) or intracellular molecules, particularly intracellular enzymes.

Table 3.4: Some examples of self-antigens and associated autoimmune diseases.

Self-antigen	*Disease*
Hormone receptors	
TSH receptor	Hyper- or hypothyroidism
Insulin receptor	Hyper- or hypoglycaemia
Neurotransmitter receptor	
Acetylcholine receptor	Myasthenia gravis
Cell adhesion molecules	
Epidermal cell adhesion	Blistering skin diseases molecules
Plasma proteins	
Factor VIII	Acquired haemophilia
β_2 Glycoprotein I and other anticoagulant proteins	Antiphospholipid syndrome
Other cell surface antigens	
Red blood cells (multiple	Haemolytic anaemia antigens)
Platelets	Thrombocytopenic purpura

Intracellular enzymes	
Thyroid peroxidase	Thyroiditis, probable
hypothyroidism	
Steroid 21-hydroxylase (adrenal cortex)	Adrenocortical failure (Addison's disease)
Glutamate decarboxylase (β cells of pancreatic islets)	Autoimmune diabetes
Lysosomal enzymes (phagocytic cells)	Systemic vasculitis
Mitochondrial enzymes (particularly pyruvate dehydrogenase)	Primary biliary cirrhosis
Intracellular molecules involved in transcription and translation	
Double stranded DNA	Systemic lupus erythematosus
(SLE)	
Histones	SLE
Topoisomerase I	Diffuse scleroderma
Amino-acyl t-RNA synthases	Polymyositis
Centromere proteins	Limited scleroderma

Non-organ-specific Autoimmune Diseases

Non-organ-specific disorders affect multiple organs and are usually associated with autoimmune responses against self-molecules which are widely distributed through the body, particularly intracellular molecules involved in transcription and translation of the genetic code.

Many disorders are labelled as 'connective tissue diseases'; this is a misleading term as the 'connective tissues' are neither abnormal nor specifically damaged, but the term remains in widespread use.

Epidemiology of Autoimmune Disease

Around 3% of the population has an autoimmune disease. Many chronic disabling diseases are considered to have an autoimmune basis, including multiple sclerosis, rheumatoid arthritis and insulin-dependent diabetes mellitus.

Autoimmune diseases are rare in childhood; the peak years of onset are from 15 to 65 years, the major exception being the childhood onset form of diabetes mellitus. There are striking sex differences in the risk of developing an autoimmune disease.

Almost all are more common in women, and for some autoimmune diseases the risk may be eight times greater. A notable exception is ankylosing spondylitis, which is much commoner in young men.

Immunological Tolerance

Autoimmune responses are similar to immune responses to non-self-antigens. Both are driven by antigen, involve the same immune cell types and produce tissue damage by the same effector mechanisms. The key question, therefore, is 'What regulatory mechanisms prevent autoimmune responses occurring in everyone?'.

The immune system can generate a vast diversity of different T-cell antigen receptors and immunoglobulin molecules by differential genetic recombination. This process produces many antigen-specific receptors capable of binding to self-molecules.

To avoid autoimmune disease, the T- and B-cells bearing these self-reactive molecules must be either eliminated or down-regulated so that the immune system is made specifically unreactive-tolerant-to self-antigens.

Because T-cells (in particular CD4+ T-cells) have a central role in controlling nearly all immune responses, the process of T-cell tolerance is of greater importance in avoidance of autoimmunity than B-cell tolerance, since most self-reacting B-cells will not be able to produce auto-antibodies unless they receive appropriate T-cell help.

Those processes which induce specific tolerance arise inside the thymus (thymic tolerance) or outside (peripheral tolerance).

Thymic Tolerance

T-cell development in the thymus plays a major role in eliminating T-cells capable of recognising peptides from self-proteins. The principles of positive and negative selection are explained above.

This process of thymic education is only partially successful. Thymic tolerance can fail if self-peptides are not expressed at a sufficient level in the thymus to induce negative selection. Most peptides found bound to MHC molecules in the thymus are from either ubiquitous intracellular or membrane-bound proteins present in the extracellular fluid.

Thymic tolerance is not induced to many tissue-specific proteins (such as might be found in the brain, muscle, joints, islets of Langerhans, etc.) and it is not surprising that T-cells responsive to tissue-specific proteins can be detected in healthy people.

Peripheral Tolerance

A second level of control over potentially autoreactive cells is termed peripheral tolerance. Several mechanisms are involved.

Immunological ignorance

Some self-antigens are effectively invisible to the immune system-immunological ignorance. This occurs because the antigen is sequestered in an avascular organ such as the vitreous humour of the eye. Immunological ignorance also occurs because CD4+ T-cells will only recognise antigens presented in association with MHC class II molecules.

The very limited distribution of these molecules on professional antigen-presenting cells means that most organ-specific molecules will not be presented at levels high enough to induce T-cell activation. To prevent large amounts of self-antigen from gaining access to antigenpresenting cells, debris from self-tissue breakdown must be cleared rapidly and destroyed.

This is achieved by cell death through apoptosis, so preventing widespread spilling of cell contents, together with a variety of scavenger mechanisms which mop up cell debris.

Self-antigens and lymphocytes are also kept separate by the restricted routes of lymphocyte circulation which limit naive lymphocytes to secondary lymphoid tissue and the blood.

Anergy

Naive CD4+ T-cells need two signals to become activated and initiate an immune response: an antigen-specific signal through the T-cell antigen receptor and a second, non-specific costimulatory signal, usually signalled by CD28 (on the T-cell) binding to CD80 or CD86 on the stimulator.

If the T-cell receives both signals, then it will become activated and proliferate and produce cytokines. If no costimulatory molecules are engaged, then stimulation through the T-cell receptor alone leads to apoptosis or a state of longstanding unresponsiveness called *anergy*. Expression of these costimulatory molecules is tightly controlled and confined to specialised antigen-presenting cells such as dendritic cells.

Given their distributions, interaction between CD4+ cells and dendritic cells is only likely to occur in secondary lymphoid tissues such as lymph nodes. The restricted expression of costimulatory molecules means that even if a T-cell recognises a tissue-specific peptide MHC molecule complex (e.g. an antigen derived from a pancreatic islet cell), then anergy rather than activation is likely to follow, as no antigen-presenting cell will be available in healthy tissue to provide the co-stimulatory signal.

Suppression

Self-reactive T-cells may be actively suppressed by inhibitory populations of T-cells which recognise the same antigenso-called *suppressor T-cells.* The best defined mechanism involves cytokines produced by antigen stimulation which either inhibit or alter the activation of nearby T-cells.

B-cell tolerance

B-cell tolerance operates at a peripheral rather than a central level and is less complete than T-cell tolerance. The production of self-reactive antibodies is limited mainly by the lack of T-cell help for self-antigens, despite the fact that new B-cells are being produced continuously from bone marrow precursors and many of these are autoreactive.

Breakdown of Tolerance

For autoimmune responses to occur, the key mechanisms of immunological tolerance outlined above must be broken down.

Overcoming Peripheral Tolerance

This can result from inappropriate access of self-antigens to antigen-presenting cells, inappropriate local expression of costimulatory molecules, or alterations in the ways in which self-molecules are presented to the immune system.

All of these are more likely to happen when inflammation or tissue damage is present. The increased activity of proteolytic enzymes in inflammatory sites can cause both intra- and extracellular proteins to be broken down, leading to high concentrations of peptides being presented to responsive T-cells.

These novel peptides are known as *cryptic epitopes.* The structures of self-peptides may also be altered by viruses, free radicals or ionising radiation, thus bypassing previously established tolerance. For antigens which are sequestered from the immune system (e.g. in the eye), sufficient antigen may be released by tissue damage to initiate an immune response.

Molecular Mimicry

Structural similarity between self-proteins and microbial antigens may trigger an autoimmune response. In systemic infection, this cross-reactivity will cause expansion of the responsive T-cell population recognising the self-peptide if local conditions allow. The process is known as *molecular mimicry*.

Once tolerance has broken down, the resulting process of inflammation may allow presentation of further peptides. The immune response broadens and local tissue damage accelerates. This domino-like process is known as *epitope spreading*.

This is best demonstrated in experimental models, where immunis-

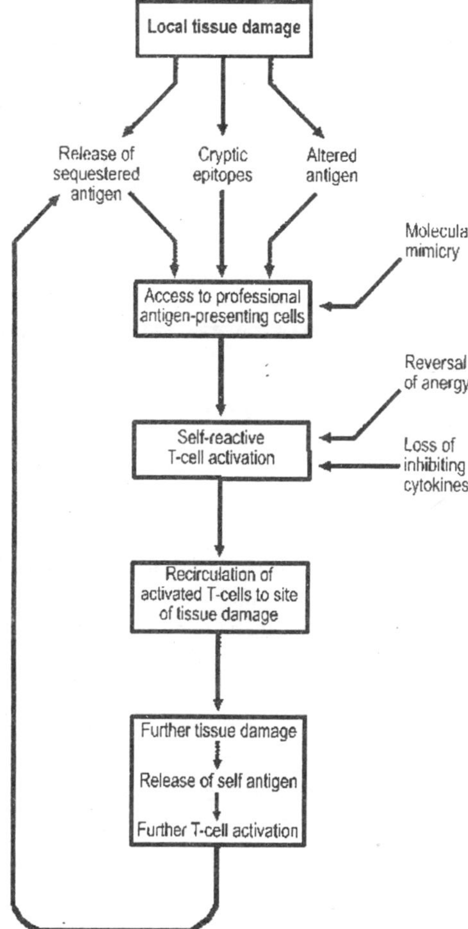

Figure 3.20: Ways in which peripheral tolerance might be overcome to produce autoimmune responses.

ation with a single peptide from a protein found in myelinated nerve sheaths (known as myelin basic protein or MBP) can lead to widespread inflammation in the central nervous system with an immune response against many peptides found in both MBP and other CNS proteins. This implies that, once the barrier of tolerance is broken down, autoimmune responses may be easier to sustain.

Aetiology of Autoimmune Disease

In autoimmune diseases, interactions between genetic and environmental factors are critically important.

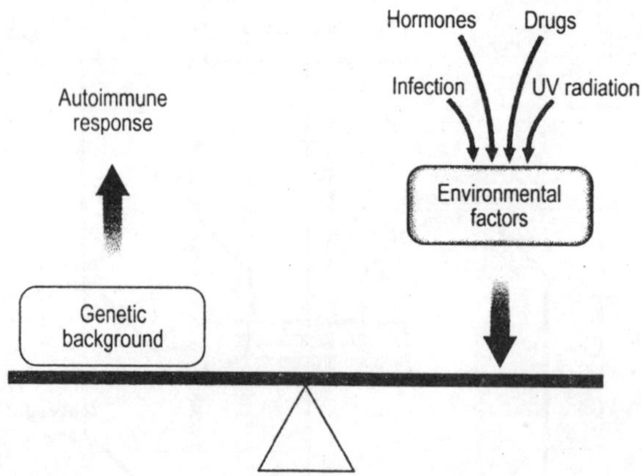

Figure 3.21: Interactions between genetic and environmental factors are important in the aetiology of autoimmune diseases.

Genetic Factors

Twin and family studies have confirmed a genetic contribution in all autoimmune diseases studied. Multiple autoimmune diseases may cluster within the same family, and subclinical autoimmunity is common among family members. The genetic contribution to autoimmune disease usually involves multiple genes but some single gene defects involve defects in apoptosis.

The strongest and best characterised associations involve alleles of the major histocompatibility complex (MHC), as might be expected from the central role of the products of many of these genes in T-cell function, and the involvement of other MHC genes in control of immunity and inflammation.

Environmental Factors

Environmental triggers in autoimmunity include:

- hormones
- infection
- drugs
- UV radiation.

Hormones

Females are far more likely than males to develop most autoimmune diseases. While this has an obvious genetic basis, hormonal factors must play a major role in this gender difference.

Most autoimmune diseases have their peak age of onset within the reproductive years and evidence implicates oestrogens as triggering

Table 3.5: Molecular mimicry

Microbial antigen	*Self-antigen with similar structure*	***Disease in which consequent molecular mimicry may play a role***
Group A streptococcal M protein	Antigen found in cardiac muscle	Rheumatic fever
Bacterial heat shock proteins	Self heat shock proteins	Links suggested with several autoimmune diseases but none proven
Coxsackie B4 nuclear protein	Pancreatic islet cell glutamate decarboxylase	Insulin-dependent diabetes mellitus
Campylobacter jejuni glycoproteins	Myelin-associated gangliosides and glycolipids	Guillain-Barre syndrome
DNA J heat shock protein from *Escherichia coli*	HLA-DR (3 chain subtypes containing the rheumatoid arthritis 'shared epitope'	Rheumatoid arthritis

factors. Removal of the ovaries inhibits the onset of spontaneous autoimmunity in animal models of SLE, while administration of oestrogen accelerates the onset of disease.

Infection

The relationship between infection and autoimmunity is clearest in the situation of molecular mimicry. Autoimmune diseases tend to be less common in parts of the world that carry a high burden of parasitic diseases and other infections.

Table 3.6 Common autoimmune diseases and their major HLA associations

HLA	*Disease association*	*Relative risk*
B27	Ankylosing spondylitis	85
	Reiter's disease	37
DR2	Goodpasture's syndrome	16
DR3	Sicca syndrome	10
	Addison's disease	9
	Hashimoto's thyroiditis	3
	Myasthenia gravis	3
DR4	Insulin-dependent diabetes mellitus	6

In some animal models of autoimmunity, the development of disease can be dramatically inhibited by keeping the animals in a laboratory environment with high prevalence of infection. Keeping the same animals in germfree conditions promotes the development of autoimmunity for reasons that are not clear.

Attempts to identify hidden infections in autoimmune diseases such as rheumatoid arthritis and multiple sclerosis have been unsuccessful.

Drugs

Drug-induced autoimmunity may involve mechanisms comparable to molecular mimicry, whereby the drug or a drug-self-molecule complex has a structural similarity to self and hence allows bypass of peripheral tolerance. Some drugs (e.g. penicillamine) have the ability to bind directly to the peptide-containing groove in MHC molecules and a direct capacity to induce abnormal T-cell responses.

Drug-mediated autoimmunity affects only a small proportion of those treated and is probably genetically determined. For example, HLA-DR2 is associated with penicillamineinduced myasthenia gravis, whereas DR3 is associated with nephritis. Genetic variation in drug metabolism is important.

The best example is the relationship between drug-induced systemic lupus erythematosus and the rate of acetylation of the triggering drug: slow acetylators are prone to SLE. It seems likely that this partial defect in metabolism may allow the formation of immunogenic conjugates between drug and self-molecules.

Ultraviolet radiation

Exposure to ultraviolet (UV) radiation (usually in the form of sunlight) is a well-defined trigger for skin inflammation and sometimes systemic involvement in systemic lupus erythematosus (SLE). UV radiation can modify self-antigens, so enhancing their immunogenicity, or lead to apoptotic death of cells within skin.

Apoptosis is associated with cell surface expression of auto-antigens usually found only within cells which are then able to bind related auto-antibodies and trigger tissue damage.

Mechanisms of Tissue Damage

Tissue damage in autoimmune disease is mediated by antibody, immune complexes, CD4+ T-cells, activation of macrophages or cytotoxic T-cells, or a combination of these mechanisms. In addition to their destructive effects, auto-antibodies can also cause disease by binding to the functional sites of self-antigens such as hormone receptors, neurotransmitter receptors and plasma proteins.

These auto-antibodies either mimic or block the action of the endogenous ligand for the self-protein, and thus cause abnormalities in function without necessarily causing inflammation or tissue damage. This phenomenon is best characterised in endocrine autoimmunity .

Treatment of Autoimmune Diseases

The treatment of autoimmune disease is based either on suppression of the damaging immune response or on replacement of the function of the damaged organ.

Replacement of Function

This is the usual treatment in autoimmune diseases with failure of the affected endocrine organ, such as hypothyroidism or insulin-dependent diabetes mellitus.

Suppression of the Autoimmune Response

Immunosuppression before irreversible tissue damage occurs is vital, but the early detection of preclinical autoimmunity presents a major challenge. In many autoimmune diseases, such as SLE, rheumatoid arthritis and autoimmune kidney disease, immunosuppression is the only means of preventing severe disability or death. However, all forms of immunosuppression are limited by their lack of specificity and toxic side-effects.

PRINCIPLES OF ORGAN TRANSPLANTATION

- Histocompatibility antigens have a crucial role in determining survival of transplanted organs
- The distinction between postoperative infection and graft rejection is vital
- Organ rejection can be hyperacute, acute or chronic T-lymphocytes play a central role in chronic rejection
- Immunosuppressive drugs, such as ciclosporin A, are vital in preventing graft rejection
- Immunosuppressed patients have an increased risk of infection and malignant disease
- Bone marrow transplantation is associated with the potentially fatal complication of graft-versus-host disease

Transplantation of living cells, tissues or organs is well established as a routine practice. Cells (e.g. red blood cells in transfusion), tissues (e.g. skin grafting in extensively burned patients), or whole organs (such as kidney, heart, pancreas or liver) may be successfully transferred between genetically dissimilar individuals *(allogeneic grafting)*.

The outcome depends on the degree of 'matching' of the relevant transplantation antigens between the two individuals and the success of therapeutic immunosuppressive measures to prevent rejection.

In contrast, grafting of a person's tissue from one part of their body to another *(autologous grafting)* is always successful, provided there are no surgical setbacks. Transplantation across a species barrier, for instance from pigs to humans *(xenogeneic grafting)* is currently the focus of interest because of the shortage of human organs.

Histocompatibility Genetics

The surfaces of all human cells express a series of molecules that are recognised by other individuals as foreign antigens. The most important antigens in organ transplantation are called 'histocompatibility antigens' as they have a crucial role in determining survival of transplanted organs. In humans, they are encoded by a segment of chromosome 6 known as the major histocompatibility complex (MHC).

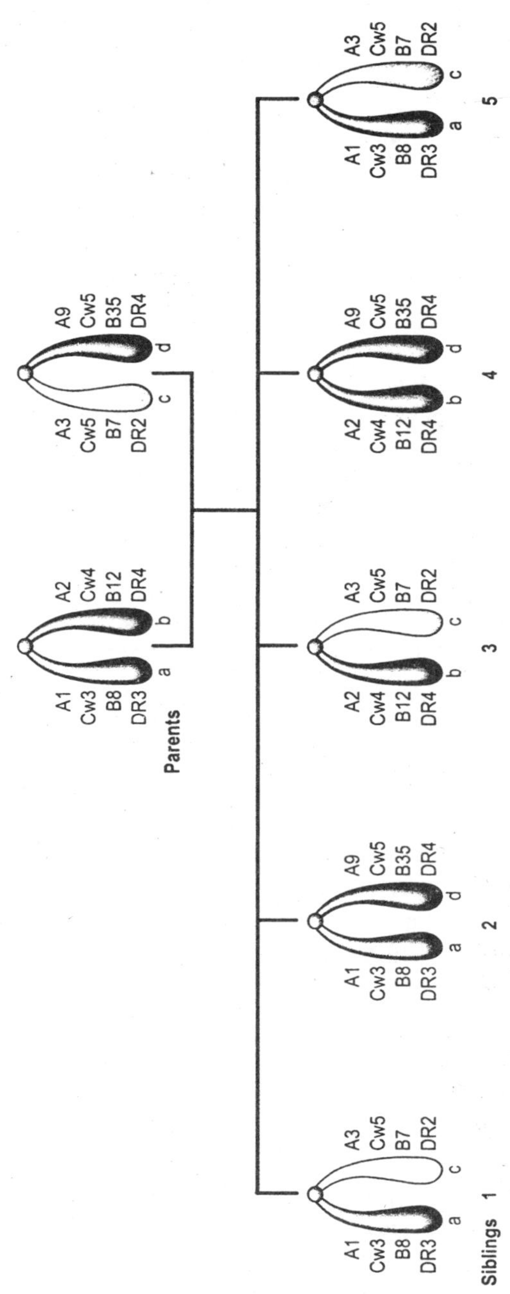

Figure 3.22: Inheritance of HLA haplotypes in a family.

Additional antigenic systems (minor histocompatibility antigens) play a more minor role in transplantation and are largely ignored. MHC antigens are described in detail above.

The HLA system is extremely polymorphic; that is, it has multiple alternative forms (alleles) of the gene at each known locus. The close proximity of the HLA loci means that their antigenic products tend to be inherited together as an *HLA haplotype.*

Because one haplotype is inherited from each parent, there is a one-in-four chance that siblings will possess identical pairs of haplotypes. These haplotypes are co-dominantly expressed.

Kidney Transplantation

Kidney transplantation is the treatment of choice for most patients with end-stage renal failure and illustrates the principles underpinning solid organ allografts.

Selection of Recipient and Donor

In kidney transplantation, organs can come from cadavers or living related donors. Because humans have two kidneys (unlike most other solid organs), a relative may choose to donate one to the recipient.

The selection of a donor kidney is rigorous. Knowing the ABO blood group and HLA type of a *cadaver kidney,* national and international registers of potential recipients can be searched by computer to find an ABOcompatible patient who matches the donor at as many loci as possible.

Once the recipient has been selected, the recipient's serum is then cross-matched against the donor's lymphocytes. If the patient has cytotoxic antibodies to donor MHC class I antigens (positive T-cell cross-match), then the kidney is unsuitable for that recipient.

Relatives who are anxious to donate *a live donor kidney* must be screened clinically and psychologically, and ABO and HLA typed so that the most suitable donor can be chosen.

The Post-transplantation Period

The transplanted kidney is usually sited in the iliac fossa. Great care is taken with the vascular anastomosis and implantation of the ureter. Once the vascular anastomoses are complete, the graft often starts to function immediately.

Renal function may deteriorate immediately after surgery for several reasons. Acute tubular necrosis can occur due to low blood pressure in either the recipient or the donor. If this happens, the recipient can be dialysed until renal function recovers. Alternatively, poor renal function

Table 3.7: Selection of donor and recipient in kidney transplantation.

Recipient selection

- ABO-compatible
- Negative serum cross-match with donor's T -lymphocytes
- HLA match-as near as possible, especially at D loci

Kidney selection *Cadaver donor:*

- Good renal function
- No infection (sepsis, HIV, etc.)
- No malignancy or systemic disease (diabetes, hypertension)
- Short warm ischaemia time

Living donor:

- *Two* functioning kidneys
- No transmissible disease
- No anomalous blood vessels
- Psychologically suitable
- Excellent health

may indicate hyperacute rejection or urinary obstruction, which must be relieved surgically.

It is crucial to distinguish rejection from infection, as the treatment differs. Rejection can be detected by percutaneous fine needle aspiration of the transplant. Immunosuppressive therapy is vital to prevent graft rejection.

Clinical Rejection

Rejection of the organ graft may be:

- hyperacute
- acute
- chronic.

Hyperacute rejection occurs minutes to hours following revascularisation of the graft. It is due to preformed circulating cytotoxic antibody which reacts with MHC class I antigens in the donor kidney. Activation of complement results in an influx of polymorphonuclear leukocytes, platelet aggregation, obstruction of the blood vessels, and ischaemia.

Histologically, the microvasculature becomes plugged with leukocytes and platelets, resulting in infarction. The kidney swells dramatically and is tender. Renal function declines; oliguria or anuria follows. There is no successful therapy and the kidney must be removed.

Acute rejection occurs a few weeks or months following transplantation. Early diagnosis is important because prompt treatment with immunosuppressive drugs reverses renal damage. Histologically, there is a mononuclear infiltrate in the renal cortex, and necrosis of arterial walls; after successful treatment, the inflammatory infiltrate clears.

Acute rejection is associated with increased expression of MHC class I and class II antigens in inflamed grafts, and with early infiltration of CD4+ T-lymphocytes. *Chronic rejection* is seen after months or years of good renal function. There is slowly progressive renal failure and hypertension.

Dominant histological findings are thickening of the glomerular basement membrane, hyalinisation of the glomeruli, interstitial fibrosis, and proliferation of endothelial cells. Chronic rejection must be distinguished from recurrence of the original glomerular disease, particularly when this is autoimmune.

Immunopathology of graft rejection

T-lymphocytes play a central role in rejection. Congenitally athymic ('nude') mice lack mature T-cells and cannot reject transplants. Injection of CD4+ T-cells into this mouse model leads to acute rejection, but CD8+ T-cells do not. Furthermore, ciclosporin A, which blocks interleukin-2 production by CD4+ T-cells, prevents rejection.

The rejection process has two parts:

- an afferent phase (initiation or sensitising component)
- an efferent phase (effector component).

In the *afferent phase,* donor MHC molecules found on 'passenger leukocytes' (dendritic cells) within the graft are recognised by the recipient's CD4+ T-cells, a process called *allorecognition,* which takes place either in the graft itself or in the lymphoid tissue of the recipient.

The *effector phase* of rejection is orchestrated by CD4+ T-cells which enter the graft parenchyma and recruit effector cells responsible for the tissue damage of rejection, namely macrophages, CD8+ T-cells, natural killer cells and B-lymphocytes. The most important cytokines in graft rejection are interleukin-2 and interferon γ (IFN-γ).

Not all parts of the graft need to be attacked for rejection to occur. The critical targets are the endothelium of the microvasculature and the specialised parenchymal cells of the organ, such as renal tubules, pancreatic islets of Langerhans or cardiac myocytes.

Immunosuppression

Immunosuppressive drugs are used to prevent graft rejection. Until relatively recently, azathioprine and corticosteroids were the mainstay of treatment. *Azathioprine* is inactive until metabolised by the liver but then affects all dividing cells, including lymphocytes, by inhibiting DNA synthesis.

Corticosteroids have their main immunosuppressive effects on macrophage activity but are ineffective alone in preventing the early phase of rejection. Graft rejection has been reduced dramatically by the discovery of *ciclosporin A, tacrolimus* and comparable agents. Ciclosporin is a powerful drug on its own or in combination with azathioprine and prednisolone.

Antibodies can also be used as immunosuppressive agents, such as those which destroy T-lymphocytes in the graft recipient. Antibodies to the IL-2 receptor have produced impressive reduction in rates of early rejection.

Graft Survival

Registry data show that survival rates for grafts from cadavers are around 60% at 10 years post-transplantation, while comparable rates for living donors exceed 70%.

Complications

Patients have an increased susceptibility to *infection* after transplant. Major causes of infection in the first month after transplantation are those related to surgical wounds, indwelling cannulae, or post-operative lung infections. The effects of such infections, however, are often considerable in the immunocompromised host.

After 1-4 months of immunosuppression, cytomegalovirus dominates a picture that includes various fungal, viral and protozoal infections. Infections occurring beyond 4 months fall into three main groups:

- chronic viral infections
- occasional opportunistic infections, such as cryptococcus
- infections normally present in the community.

A late complication of organ transplantation is *recurrence of the original disease.* This should always be considered in patients in whom there is functional deterioration following long periods of stable graft function.

The incidence of *malignancy,* particularly lymphoma, in transplant recipients is 40 times greater than in the general population. Both lymphoma and Kaposi's sarcoma are more common when profound immune suppression is used, and are related to persistent viral stimulation with Epstein-Barr virus (EBV) or human herpes virus 8 (HHV8).

Transplanted patients also have an increased risk of *acute myocardial infarction.* This may be linked to hypertension, hypertriglyceridaemia or insulin-resistant diabetes, as these conditions are often present before transplantation and are aggravated by steroids.

Transplantation of Other Solid Organs

Liver Transplantation

The results of human liver transplantation have improved dramatically in the last 10 years. Hepatic surgery poses unique problems; these include the bleeding tendency of a recipient with liver failure and the technically difficult surgery required to revascularise a grafted liver.

However, compared with transplants of other organs, rejection episodes are milder and require less immunosuppression. Recipients with life-threatening disease but residual liver function are best able to withstand major surgery.

Indications for liver transplantation include biliary atresia, hepatocellular carcinoma, primary biliary cirrhosis, posthepatic cirrhosis and alcoholic cirrhosis.

Heart Transplantation

Unlike renal transplantation, there is no satisfactory longterm support available. If the donated heart is rejected, early diagnosis is crucial. Electrocardiographic changes are closely monitored and serial endomyocardial biopsies show increased MHC class I expression by myocardial cells in early rejection.

A major postoperative problem is accelerated atherosclerosis in the graft coronary arteries. This is the major cause of death in patients who survive more than 1 year.

Pancreatic Transplantation

Improvements in surgical technique and better immunesuppression have resulted in 65-80% survival at 1 year of transplanted vascularised pancreatic grafts but longer-term results are disappointing.

Skin Grafting

Allogeneic skin grafting in humans is useful in providing skin cover in severely burned patients. HLA typing is not required because the endogenous immunosuppressive effect of severe burns allows prolonged survival of unmatched skin.

Although the graft is finally rejected, the short-term protective barrier afforded by covering burns during this time is vital to the patient in resisting infection.

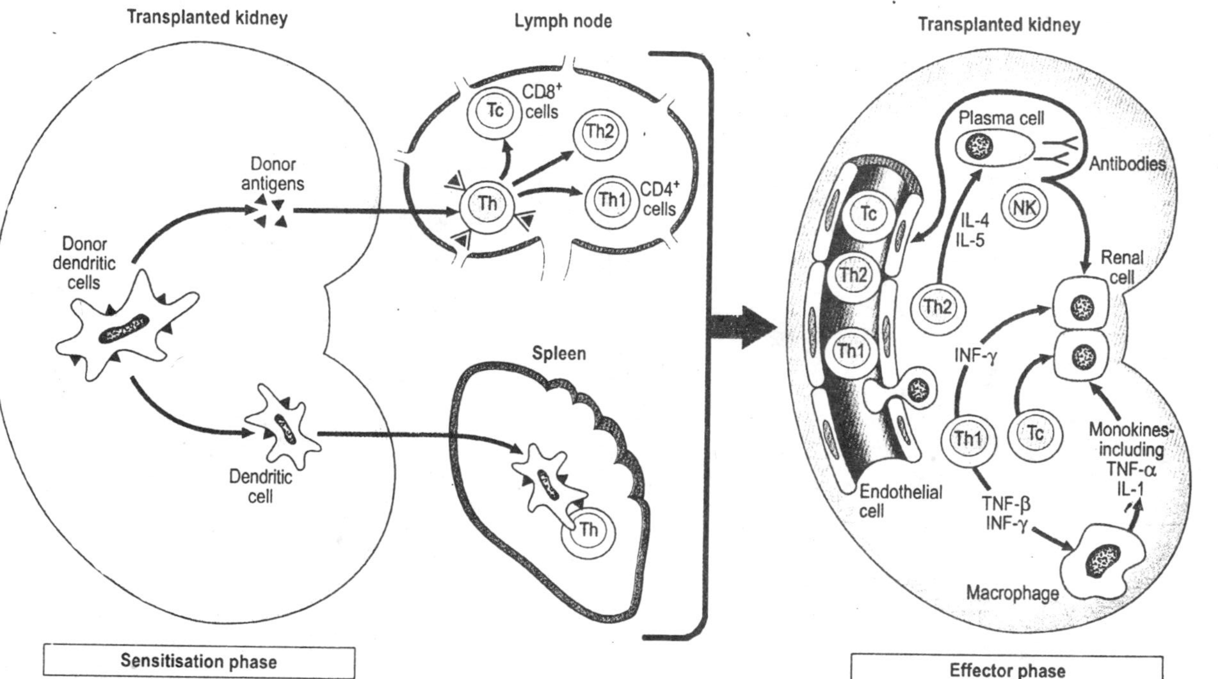

Figure 3.23: Immunopathology of graft rejection occurs in two phases.

Corneal Grafting

Corneas are obtained from cadaveric donors. There is no need to HLA type or systemically immunosuppress the recipient because corneal rejection does not occur unless the graft becomes vascularised. In grafts which do become vascularised following chemical burns or chronic viral infection, HLA matching significantly improves survival.

Bone Marrow Transplantation

Bone marrow transplantation offers the only chance of cure for many patients with a wide range of disorders:

- aplastic anaemia
- leukaemia
- immunodeficiency disorders
- inborn errors of metabolism.

Graft rejection is common, but bone marrow transplantation has the unique and often fatal complication of graft-versus-host disease (GVHD), in which the grafted immunocompetent cells recognise the host as foreign and mount an immunological attack.

Selection and preparation of patients

Theoretically, any abnormality of bone marrow stem cells is correctable by transplantation.

Preparation for transplantation begins 10 days before grafting. Measures to reduce infection risk include strict reverse-barrier nursing, decontamination of the skin and gut, the use of appropriate antibiotics and antimycotics, and immunoglobulin replacement if necessary.

The *grafting procedure* is straightforward; small amounts of marrow are taken from multiple sites under general anaesthetic. Bone spicules are removed by filtration through graded sieves. Cells can then be given either without fractionation or after removal of immunocompetent Tlymphocytes responsible for graft-versus-host disease (see below). Cells are then transplanted by intravenous infusion.

A successful graft is indicated by a rise in the peripheral white cell count and the appearance of haemopoietic precursors in the marrow 10-20 days after transplantation.

Complications

Three major problems dominate the post-transplant period:

- failure of engraftment
- infection
- graft-versus-host disease (GVHD).

Failure of engraftment can be due to using insufficient bone marrow cells or rejection of the grafted cells by the host. Patients with some residual immunity (e.g. as in leukaemia in remission or partial immune deficiencies) require immune suppression-conditioning-prior to grafting to ensure that rejection does not occur.

Patients with no immune function (e.g. severe combined immune deficiency) do not, in theory, require conditioning as they are unable to reject the graft.

Serious bacterial, fungal and viral *infections* occur despite the elaborate measures aimed at reducing their incidence and severity. Infection with CMV is a common cause of death; evidence of CMV reactivation is seen in 75% of patients who are CMV positive before transplant.

Graft-versus-host disease (GVHD) occurs in most patients who receive allogeneic bone marrow transplants. About 7-14 days later, a skin rash, fever, hepatosplenomegaly, bloody diarrhoea and breathlessness develop. In severe GVHD, the rash may progress from a maculopapular eruption to generalised erythroderma and exfoliative dermatitis.

Skin biopsy shows lymphocytic infiltration with vascular cuffing and basal cell degeneration. The mortality of GVHD is considerable; over *70%* of those with severe GVHD and about one-third with mild GVHD will die. Treatment requires an increase in immunosuppression but, once established, GVHD is very difficult to eradicate.

Commonly confused conditlons and entities relating to immunology and immunopathology

Commonly confused	*Distinction and explanation*
lnterleukins, cytokines, lymphokines and *chemokines*	*Cytokines* are soluble mediators of stimulatory or inhibitory signalling between cells; those produced by lymphocytes are called *lymphokines*. Cytokines acting between cells of the immune system (although some also have effects on other cells) are called *interleukins*. Cytokines inducing leukocyte chemotaxis are called chemokines.
Atopy *allergy* and *anaphylaxis*	All three terms apply to type I (immediate) hypersensitivity or allergy. *Atopy* is an inherited tendency to produce IgE antibodies to environmental allergens.

Exposure of the individual to an allergen may result in *allergy* as a result of mast cell degranulation. A severe, systemic, life-threatening allergic reaction is termed anaphylaxis.

Monocytes, macrophages and *histiocytes*

Monocytes are the newly-formed cells of the mononuclear phagocyte system. After a few hours in the blood, they enter tissues and undergo further differentiation into *macrophages*. Some macrophages in tissues have specific features and names (e.g. Kupffer cells); others are referred to as *histiocytes*.

Graft rejection and *graft-versus-host* disease

Graft rejection is an immunologically mediated reaction against a transplanted tissue or organ. *Graft-versus-host* disease occurs when immunologically active cells in the donor tissue (e.g. bone marrow transplant) damage the recipient's tissues.

Prevention of GVHD involves ways to eliminate or reduce the numbers of immunocompetent T-cells in the engrafted bone marrow. T-cell specific monoclonal antibodies can help deplete the T-cell load.

Peripheral Blood Stem Cell Transplantation

Because pluripotent stem cells can be mobilised from peripheral blood using colony-stimulating factors, stem cell transplants can theoretically be used as an alternative to bone marrow. There is interest in using umbilical cord blood as a source of stem cells in view of its ready availability.

Allogeneic or autologous stem cell transplantation is under investigation for the management of autoimmune disease such as rheumatoid arthritis or multiple sclerosis, solid tumours such as breast cancer and neuroblastoma, and for haematological malignancies.

4

Pathology of Digestive System

The alimentary system is constantly in contact with dietary contaminants, especially infective agents and environmental toxins, so it is not surprising that it is affected by many diseases. This chapter examines these diseases and, in those of major importance, attempts to relate them to the potentially pathogenic factors present in the human diet.

MOUTH, TEETH, PHARYNX AND SALIVARY GLANDS

The mouth and teeth masticate the food prior to swallowing and digestion. At the same time digestion is initiated by the addition of salivary amylases and lipases. The *mouth* is lined by stratified squamous epithelium overlying richly vascular connective tissue.

The epithelium is of variable thickness, being thickest over the tongue where there are also papillary projections which account for its rougher texture. The epithelium is mostly nonkeratinised, except over the lips, gums and hard palate where slight keratinisation occurs.

Elsewhere pathological keratinisation (keratosis) results in the formation of white plaques on the mucosa; this is termed leukoplakia. The *teeth* consist principally of *dentine,* which is similar to bone; it is composed of a collagen matrix mineralised by calcium phosphate (apatite) crystals.

It differs from bone, however, in that its cellular constituents (odontoblasts) form a layer over the surface of the dentine, from which long tubular processes ramify through the tissue. The dentine is covered over the exposed part of the tooth (crown) by *enamel,* which is composed almost entirely of inorganic material arranged in stacked crystalline rods.

The dentine of the root is covered by a thin layer of *cementum* which, as its name implies, attaches the tooth to the periodontal 'ligament' lining the socket. Centrally, the tooth has a connective tissue core, the *pulp,* which links with the narrow root canal. The *salivary glands* are usually categorised as either major or minor. The major glands are the parotid, submandibular and sublingual glands; minor glands are scattered throughout the oral cavity.

The parotids enclose branches of the facial nerve and a few lymph nodes. The glandular tissue comprises multiple small secretory acini lined by plump cells containing zymogen granules and surrounded by supporting myoepithelial cells. The secretion has a low protein content, hence these glandular units are referred to as *serous* acini. Small ducts lined by cuboidal epithelium drain the glandular lobules and unite to form the main secretory (Stensen's) duct.

The submandibular glands contain both serous and mucus-secreting cells in mixed acini; the sublingual and minor salivary glands are predominantly or entirely mucus-secreting. The main ducts of the submandibular glands (Wharton's ducts) are lined by partly ciliated epithelium to facilitate drainage of the more viscid mucous secretion.

CONGENITAL DISORDERS OF THE MOUTH

Hare-Lip and Cleft Palate

Hare-lip may appear as a sporadic defect of development but may also occur as an inherited condition exhibiting male sex linkage. The inherited form occurs both with and without a cleft palate. Where a cleft palate exists alone, a proportion of the cases are due to a dominant gene of low penetrance.

Other cases are not genetically determined, as for example in the rubella syndrome. Hare-lip may be unilateral or bilateral: it may involve the lip only, or extend upwards and backwards to include the floor of the nose and the alveolar ridge.

Cleft palate may vary considerably, from a small defect in the soft palate, which causes little disability, to a complete separation of the hard palate combined with hare-lip. With extensive lesions, there may be considerable difficulty with feeding as the child is unable to suck.

DISEASES OF THE TEETH AND GUMS

While of paramount importance to the dental student, diseases of the mouth, teeth and gums are soon evident to both patient and doctor, and frequently reflect generalised disorders. Their recognition and an understanding of the processes involved are therefore also of wider importance in clinical medicine.

Dental Caries

Caries is the result of acid destruction of the calcified components of the teeth. The acid is produced by bacteria, usually specific strains of *Streptococcus mutans,* acting mainly on refined sugar which is trapped in contact with the dentine by 'plaque', a mixture of adhesive sugar residues and bacteria. Penetration of the dentine is followed by bacterial invasion which can infect the pulp, causing *pulpitis.*

Gingivitis

Acute gingivitis (inflammation of the gums) is an uncommon infection caused by the anaerobic *Borrelia vincentii* and fusiform bacilli. It is a severe ulcerative disease, formerly referred to as Vincent's infection, which can spread widely along the gum margins and deeply to destroy bone.

Chronic gingivitis, by contrast, is a very common condition which represents the response of the gum to adjacent bacterial plaque. Proliferation of anaerobic bacteria, and possibly their production of proteolytic enzymes, leads to chronic periodontitis and gradual destruction of the supporting tissues of the teeth. This results in loosening and eventual loss of teeth.

DISEASES OF THE ORAL MUCOSA

Inflammatory Disorders

The oral mucous membrane is affected in a wide variety of mucocutaneous inflammatory disorders such as acute erythema multiforme, lichen planus, Behcet's syndrome and many others. However, some conditions (discussed below) are restricted to the oral mucosa.

Herpetic Stomatitis

Herpetic stomatitis is a very common manifestation of infection by herpes simplex virus. It is characterised by vesiculation and ulceration of the oral mucosa and is usually acquired during childhood. Many patients develop recurrences in later life which appear as similar lesions on the lips (herpes labialis).

Oral Candidiasis

Oral candidiasis (thrush), is caused by the yeast-like fungus *Candida albicans*. It appears as white plaques on the oral mucosa consisting of enmeshed fungal hyphae, which invade the epithelium, together with polymorphs and fibrin. The infection is seen in neonates, in patients receiving broad-spectrum antibiotics and in immunocompromised individuals.

Aphthous Stomatitis

Aphthous stomatitis is a very common disorder in which single or, more usually, multiple small ulcers appear in the oral mucosa. They are shallow, with a grey, necrotic base and a haemorrhagic rim. Many patients suffer from recurrent crops of ulcers which heal spontaneously after several days.

The aetiology is unknown but assumed to be immunological; some patients have an associated gastrointestinal disorder, such as coeliac disease or inflammatory bowel disease.

Reparative Lesions

The oral mucosa is frequently subjected to minor trauma. In some individuals the reparative processes that follow prove excessive, and the surplus fibrovascular tissue appears as a polyp. Such a reparative lesion in the mouth is termed an *epulis,* of which 'congenital' and giant cell forms are recognised.

There is also a similar angiomatous 'tumour' of pregnancy, and many of the so-called haemangiomas and fibromas of the mouth have the same histogenesis.

Leukoplakia

Leukoplakia is a clinical term used to describe patches of keratosis. Its importance is that it can be premalignant. Thus, in leukoplakia there is hyperkeratosis and hyperplasia of the squamous epithelium with, in some cases, dysplastic changes which herald the onset of malignant change.

In the UK and USA leukoplakia is associated with heavy cigarette smoking, excessive alcohol consumption and poor dental hygiene. The high incidence in India and Sri Lanka is attributed to the habit of chewing betel quids made up of tobacco dust, areca nut and lime wrapped up in a betel leaf.

Tumours

Cancer of the lip is more common than intra-oral cancers. It occurs mainly in elderly people and has a definite relationship to sunlight exposure. Thus it is much more common on the lower than the upper lip. Lip cancers are usually well-differentiated squamous carcinomas which spread directly into surrounding tissues, and through lymphatics to the regional nodes.

Intra-oral cancers most frequently affect the tongue and commonly develop in areas of leukoplakia. Like lip cancers, they are squamous carcinomas. Initially they are painless and can remain undetected, especially if situated on the posterior third of the tongue, until fixation and swelling interfere with swallowing and speech.

This tendency towards late presentation and towards spread to vital structures underlies the poorer prognosis of cancer of the tongue compared to that of cancer of the lip.

DISEASES OF THE PHARYNX

Pharyngitis

Viral Pharyngitis

The commonest cause of pharyngitis is viral infection, but the causative virus is rarely identified. Most cases are thought to be caused by adenoviruses, but other viral infections, notably those directed at the respiratory tract, can be responsible.

Patients with these infections either start with a pharyngitis or develop it during the illness. Thus pharyngitis is a common feature of the common cold, influenza, measles and infectious mononucleosis (glandular fever).

Streptococcal Pharyngitis

Although less common than viral infections, streptococcal pharyngitis is important for its complications. In nonimmune individuals a widespread skin rash (scarlet fever) develops and occasional patients will develop acute proliferative glomerulonephritis, rheumatic fever or Henoch-Schonlein purpura.

Ulcerative Pharyngitis

An ulcerative pharyngitis and tonsillitis is a common complication of agranulocytosis (deficiency of polymorphs) due to a leukaemia or marrow failure. Diphtheria was formerly an important cause of an ulcerative pharyngitis, but has now been largely eradicated in many countries by immunisation.

Tonsillitis

The faucial tonsils are collections of lymphoid tissue covered by non-keratinising squamous epithelium thrown into a series of clefts; these can harbour debris and act as a nidus for infection. The tonsils are thus a frequent site for bacterial infection, producing either an acute inflammation or, more frequently, recurring chronic inflammation leading to tonsillar enlargement and general debility.

Tumours

The pharynx can be the site of both squamous carcinoma and intermediate or 'transitional' cell carcinomas that exhibit features of epithelium transitional between squamous and columnar, respiratory-type epithelium. However, most carcinomas in this site are anaplastic (undifferentiated). In addition, the tonsils may be involved by lymphomas. *Nasopharyngeal carcinoma* is of interest because of the wide geographical variation in its incidence.

It is an uncommon carcinoma in Caucasians (less than 1%), but in some parts of China accounts for over *50%* of all malignant disease. A causative agent has not been identified, but patients with nasopharyngeal carcinomas have higher titres of antibody to Epstein-Barr (EB) virus than age-matched controls, and parts of the EB viral genome can be detected in the carcinoma tissue.

Genetic factors also appear to be involved; the susceptible Chinese show a higher frequency of the histocompatibility haplotypes HLA-A2 and -BW46 than other populations.

DISEASES OF THE SALIVARY GLANDS

Sialadenitis

Acute bacterial sialadenitis (inflammation of the salivary glands) is uncommon. It arises by ascending infection from the mouth and occurs in patients with abnormal dryness of the mouth (xerostomia), either as part of a generalised dehydration or as a result of an autoimmune-induced atrophy of the salivary glands *(Sjogren's syndrome)*.

Acute enlargement of the salivary glands is usually due to mumps virus infection. Recurrent sialadenitis is seen in patients who have some degree of duct obstruction, hyposecretion of saliva and ascending infection. Duct obstruction can be due to a stone (calculus) or to fibrosis.

Hyposecretion may be a direct consequence of duct obstruction but may also be due to the acinar atrophy resulting from sialadenitis itself. Bacterial infection leads to recurrent acute inflammation and also acts as a nidus for stone formation.

Tumours

- Pleomorphic adenoma: a benign mixed tumour

- Warthin's tumour (adenolymphoma): a benign tumour
- Muco-epidermoid tumour: both benign and malignant forms exist
- Adenoid cystic carcinoma: has a tendency for perineural invasion

Pleomorphic Adenoma

At least two-thirds of all salivary tumours are accounted for by the pleomorphic adenoma or 'mixed tumour'. As the name implies, this has a varied histological appearance and is composed of a mixture of stromal and epithelial elements.

The myxoid stroma, which is rich in proteoglycans, is thought to be produced by myoepithelial cells; thus, despite its biphasic appearance, it is a purely epithelial neoplasm. Occasionally the stroma has a cartilaginous appearance.

Pleomorphic adenomas are essentially benign tumours but are prone to local recurrence if surgical removal is incomplete. The facial nerve is vulnerable during attempts at surgical removal. A very small proportion undergo malignant change and are capable of metastasising; these are termed *malignant mixed tumours*.

Occasional tumours are composed entirely of ductular epithelial cells arranged in a tubular pattern and are referred to as *monomorphic adenomas*.

Warthin's Tumour

Warthin's tumour or adenolymphoma is a relatively common salivary gland tumour (5-10% of total). It has a very characteristic appearance: tall columnar epithelial cells line convoluted cystic spaces separated by a dense lymphoid stroma. The term adenolymphoma, with its connotations of lymphoid malignancy, is a misnomer; this is an entirely benign tumour.

Muco-epidermoid Tumour

True adenocarcinomas of the salivary gland do exist, but the malignant epithelial tumours are usually 'special' forms such as the muco-epidermoid tumour which consists of mucus-secreting cells, cells showing squamous differentiation and intermediate cells (small cells that are probable precuisors of the mucus-secreting and squamous cells). Malignancy is associated with an increasing proportion of intermediate and squamous cells with fewer mucous cells.

Adenoid Cystic Carcinoma

Adenoid cystic carcinoma is a distinctive malignancy composed of small epithelial cells arranged in islands showing microcystic change. This tumour has a propensity for perineural spread and is particularly difficult to eradicate surgically.

OESOPHAGUS

Normal Structure and Function

The oesophagus is a muscular tube lined mostly by squamous epithelium. It extends from the pharynx to the cardia of the stomach and is about 25 cm long in the adult. At the upper end there is the *cricopharyngeal sphincter;* close to the lower end there is a functional sphincter whose position can be determined only by manometry.

The upper sphincter contains striated muscle fibres enabling voluntary control over the initiation of swallowing, whereas the remainder of the muscular tube is composed of smooth muscle which propels the food bolus by peristalsis and is under autonomic control.

Entry of food into the stomach is facilitated by relaxation of the distal sphincter. Protection of the lower oesophagus against regurgitation of gastric contents is achieved by the distal sphincter assisted by constricting muscle bands in the diaphragm, and an acute valve-like angle of entry into the stomach. The distal 1.5-2 cm of the oesophagus is situated below the diaphragm and is lined by columnar mucosa of cardiac type.

The squamo-columnar junction is clearly visible on endoscopy and is usually found at about 40 cm (measured from the incisor teeth). Proximal extension of this junction is found in hiatus hernia or when there is columnar metaplasia. The squamous lining of the oesophagus consists of a layer of non-keratinising squamous epithelium overlying connective tissue papillae containing blood vessels and lymphatics.

A narrow layer 1-2 cells thick at the base of the epithelium forms the proliferative compartment from where cells migrate upwards, mature and desquamate at the surface. These cells acquire an increasing glycogen content as they mature. Scattered argyrophil cells and melanoblasts can also be found in the basal layer.

CONGENITAL AND MECHANICAL DISORDERS

Heterotopic Tissue

Patches of fundic-type gastric mucosa are occasionally found above the distal sphincter and separated from the columnar lining of the distal oesophagus. These are assumed to be congenitally misplaced (heterotopic) gastric tissue rather than an acquired change; they can lead to ulceration and stricturing due to local acid/pepsin secretion.

Atresia

Atresia is a failure of embryological canalisation. It is more frequent than agenesis of the oesophagus, which is extremely rare. Atresia is usually associated with an abnormal connection (fistula) between the patent part of the oesophagus and the trachea. The affected child cannot swallow and develops an aspiration bronchopneumonia.

Diverticula

Diverticula are outpouchings of the wall of a hollow viscus. Some represent a saccular dilatation of the full thickness of the wall; others are formed by herniation of mucosa through a defect in the muscle coat. Diverticula are more common in the pharynx but can develop in the oesophagus by either *traction* (external forces pulling on the wall) or *pulsion* (forcible distension).

These diverticula differ from congenital forms in lacking a muscle coat in their wall. They frequently become permanently distended with retained food and cause difficulties in swallowing (dysphagia).

Hiatus Hernia

The commonest mechanical disorder of the oesophagus is hiatus hernia, defined as the presence of part of the stomach above the diaphragmatic orifice. It was formerly believed that this could arise from congenital shortening of the oesophagus, but it is now thought that most, if not all, hiatus hernias are acquired.

The herniation of the stomach with subsequent retraction of the oesophagus is largely a consequence of increased intra-abdominal pressure and loss of diaphragmatic muscular tone with ageing. The consequent incompetence of the oesophageal sphincter leads to regurgitation and oesophagitis.

Achalasia

Achalasia is an uncommon condition in which the contractility of the lower oesophagus is lost and there is a failure of relaxation at the sphincter (cardiospasm).

Normal functioning of the oesophagus is dependent upon the integrity of its co-ordinated muscular activity, which in turn relies on normal neuronal transmission of peristaltic signals.

Thus dysphagia may arise from fibrosis and atrophy of the smooth muscle, as occurs in progressive systemic sclerosis, or by destruction or degeneration of the intrinsic nerves. The latter can occur in neurotropic

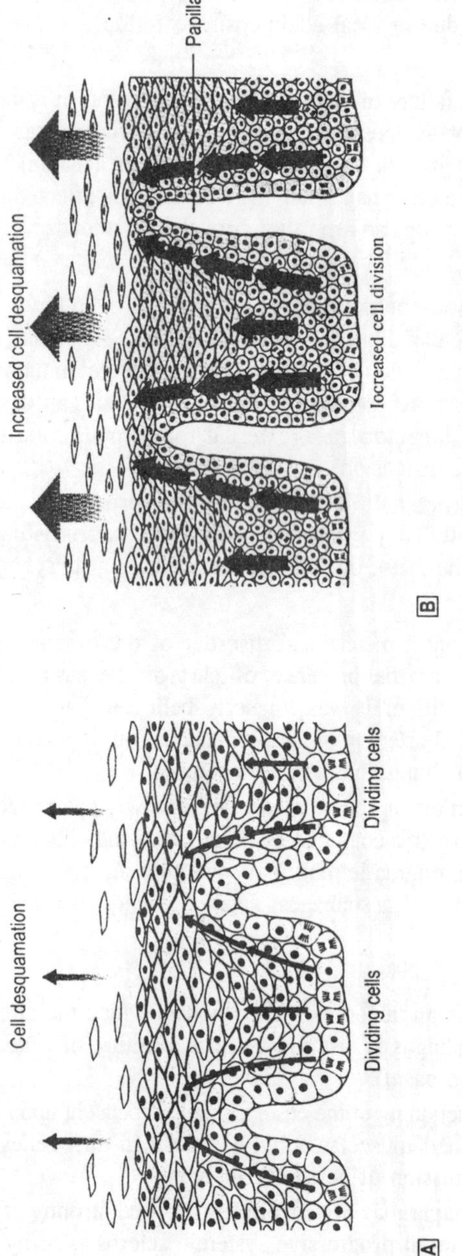

Figure 4.1: Basal cell hyperplasia in reflux oesophagitis.

infections such as Chagas' disease (South American trypanosomiasis), or by unknown mechanisms as in the condition of achalasia. Achalasia results in slowing or retention of the food bolus with increasing obstruction and dilatation of the oesophagus.

The cause of this condition is unknown, but there are reduced numbers of ganglion cells in the myenteric plexus, and both myelinated and unmyelinated axons of the extra-oesophageal vagus nerves show Wallerian degeneration.

Oesophageal Varices

Varices are localised dilatations of veins. The veins of the lower oesophagus are a potential site for porto-systemic shunting of blood when portal venous flow through the liver is impaired. Therefore, in portal hypertension (most commonly resulting from cirrhosis of the liver) the submucosal veins of the oesophagus become congested and dilate.

These enlarged veins elevate the mucosa and protrude into the oesophageal lumen where they are easily traumatised by the passage of food. Haemorrhage is thus a frequent complication and, because of the relatively high pressure within the vascular bed, can be torrential and fatal.

INFLAMMATORY DISORDERS

Oesophagitis

Acute Oesophagitis

Acute oesophagitis is clinically of only minor importance. Spread of bacterial infection from the nasopharynx to involve the oesophagus is a rare occurrence. More important are viral and fungal infections in immunocompromised individuals; for example, herpes simplex and cytomegalovirus infections are occasionally encountered in patients with leukaemias, lymphomas or AIDS.

Candidiasis is a more common infection which may give rise to difficulties in swallowing; it is endoscopically recognisable as white plaques with haemorrhagic margins. Candidiasis is also opportunistic in immunodeficiency states and in diabetes mellitus, but can sometimes be found in otherwise healthy individuals.

A further cause of acute inflammation and ulceration is the ingestion of *corrosive substances;* this may be either accidental (as when children swallow chemicals from unlabelled bottles) or taken with suicidal intent.

Chronic Oesophagitis

As with chronic inflammation in any site, chronic oesophagitis may be either specific or non-specific. Specific causes are rare, but involvement by tuberculosis and Crohn's disease are recognised. Non-specific oesophagitis is very common and usually results from regurgitation of gastric contents into the lower oesophagus; this is *reflux oesophagitis*.

Reflux Oesophagitis

The squamous lining of the oesophagus is easily damaged by regurgitated gastric contents and soon becomes chronically inflamed. A defective sphincter mechanism at the cardia predisposes to such gastro-oesophageal reflux, which is therefore an invariable accompaniment of hiatus hernia.

It may also be a consequence of increased intraabdominal pressure without herniation, or of gastric surgery. Other patients appear to have an underlying abnormality of upper gastro-intestinal motility which leads to gastrooesophageal reflux and/or duodeno-gastric reflux. The characteristic symptom is an awareness of acid regurgitation with central chest pain or discomfort ('heartburn').

Morphology

Exposure of the squamous mucosa to refluxed acid (together with bile in patients with entero-gastric reflux) leads to cell injury and accelerated desquamation. The increased cell loss is compensated for by increased proliferation of the germinative cells of the epithelium (basal cell hyperplasia); this results in less mature cells occupying most of the epithelial thickness and is accompanied by elongation of the connective tissue papillae.

Such elongation permits extension of the basal layer and possibly reflects an interaction between the proliferating epithelial cells and underlying mesenchyme. The epithelial injury is accompanied by a low-grade inflammatory cell response so that, in general, relatively small numbers of polymorphs (including eosinophils) and lymphocytes are seen within the epithelium and in the underlying connective tissue. Thus the response to reflux embraces both:

- an epithelial reaction-basal cell hyperplasia and elongation of papillae
- a conventional chronic inflammatory cell reaction.

Unfortunately, there is a poor correlation between the histological findings in biopsy specimens, the endoscopic appearances, symptomatology, and objective tests of reflux. However, the finding of typical histological changes in a patient who has no endoscopic evidence of reflux can be useful in management.

Where reflux is severe, cell proliferation cannot keep pace with cell desquamation and ulceration occurs. These areas of ulceration can be the source of haemorrhage, and may even perforate in the most severe cases. Healing is achieved by fibrosis and epithelial regeneration; subsequent shrinkage of fibrous tissue can produce a segmental narrowing *(stricture)* in the area of healed ulceration.

Restoration of epithelial continuity is usually achieved by proliferation of squamous cells, but in some patients the lost squamous epithelium is replaced by columnar epithelium, giving rise to a condition known as 'Barrett's oesophagus'.

BARRETT'S OESOPHAGUS

As a result of longstanding reflux, the lower oesophagus comes to be lined by columnar mucosa, an appearance referred to as Barrett's oesophagus. Opinions *vary* as to whether this is due to epithelial 'substitution'-migration of columnar epithelium from the distal two centimetres or from the ducts of submucosal mucous glands-or to an effect on the differentiation of progeny cells from a common stem cell (metaplasia).

The latter is held to be the main mechanism at work. In a patient with Barrett's oesophagus the endoscopist sees proximal extension of pink columnar mucosa replacing the pearly-white squamous epithelium. Such replacement is seen first as 'tongues' extending up from the cardia, and later as a complete 'cylinder' of columnar epithelium that can occupy much of the distal half of the oesophagus.

On microscopic examination the epithelium may resemble that of the gastric cardia but the characteristic 'specialised' Barrett's metaplasia consists of columnar epithelium, with goblet cells and tall intervening mucus-producing cells both secreting intestinal-type mucins-a form of intestinal metaplasia.

Metaplasias arise in response to an adverse micro-environment and can generally be considered a defence reaction in which the new cell lineage has a survival advantage over the 'native' epithelium it has replaced. Thus, an initial change from squamous epithelium to a columnar, gastric-type mucosa is readily understood as a response to acid reflux. However, the change to an epithelium with intestinal features cannot be explained solely as a reaction to acid.

It seems likely that other factors, such as bile reflux, are likely to play a part in the development of Barrett's metaplasia. Barrett's oesophagus has assumed increasing clinical importance in recent years following its recognition as a premalignant condition. Although cancer is not common in absolute terms, the risk of malignancy is about 100 times higher among patients with Barrett's oesophagus than in the general population.

Thus, once the condition has been diagnosed, it is advisable to put the patient on regular endoscopic surveillance and take multiple biopsies for the detection of dysplasia.

TUMOURS

Benign Tumours

Benign tumours are uncommon and comprise about 5% of all neoplasms of the oesophagus; the type most frequently encountered is a *leiomyoma.* The behaviour of smooth muscle tumours in the alimentary tract is generally difficult to predict (see below) but those arising in the oesophagus are almost invariably benign.

Other benign non-epithelial tumours-lipomas, haemangiomas and fibromas-are rare. The only benign epithelial tumour of note is squamous *papilloma.* Compared with squamous carcinoma (see below) these are rare lesions, certainly in terms of clinical presentation, but are of interest because they are likely to share a common pathogenesis with other squamous papillomas in that they result from human papillomavirus (HPV) infection.

Carcinoma

- Wide geographic variation in incidence
- Links with environmental factors
- Two main types: squamous carcinoma and adenocarcinoma
- Most adenocarcinomas arise from metaplastic columnar epithelium (Barrett's oesophagus)

There are two main types of oesophageal carcinomasquamous and *adenocarcinoma.* These differ markedly in their aetiology and epidemiology.

Squamous Carcinoma

Squamous carcinoma is much more common in males than females and shows marked geographical variation in incidence. In European countries, the age standardised annual incidence is around 5 per 100 000 population in males and 1 per 100 000 in females.

However, there are some well-defined high-risk areas, such as North-West France and Northern Italy, where the incidence rises to 30 per 100 000 in males and 2 per 100 000 in females. Globally there are more striking differences. Regions with very high incidence have been identified in Iran, South Africa, Brazil and Central China. In Henan Province in China the mortality rate from carcinoma of the oesophagus exceeds 100 per 100 000 in males and 50 per 100 000 in females.

Epidemiological studies in high-incidence areas have indicated that a high dietary intake of tannic acid, in the form of strong tea or sorghum wheat, or dietary deficiencies of riboflavin, vitamin A and possibly zinc may be important, but other factors such as fungal contamination of foodstuffs, opium usage and thermal injury may also be involved.

In Western countries, cigarette smoking and the drinking of alcoholic spirits are associated with a higher incidence. A factor of current interest is the possible involvement of HPV Some oesophageal cancers contain HPV in their cells, and viruses of similar subtype can be found in intact and apparently normal oesophageal mucosa. It is therefore possible that virus integrated into the host genome can bring about oncogene activation and carcinogenesis.

The involvement of papillomaviruses in the development of bovine oesophageal carcinoma is well established. Non-specific chronic oesophagitis is common among the general population in high-incidence areas, and biopsies will frequently reveal dysplasia. The squamous epithelium shows cellular pleomorphism: there is disordered maturation with immature cells and mitotic activity appearing close to the surface.

The degree of atypia can be categorised as low- or high-grade dysplasia; the latter condition will proceed to invasive carcinoma if surgical resection is not performed. As in the oropharynx, dysplasia is sometimes associated with abnormal keratosis of the squamous mucosa which appears to the endoscopist as an area of leukoplakia.

Adenocarcinoma

In the lower third of the oesophagus *adenocarcinomas* are the predominant type. They almost invariably develop on the basis of a Barrett's oesophagus and their incidence has risen dramatically in recent years among white, middle-aged men in European countries and the USA.

In the mid-1990s the incidence rate in Western countries of 1-4 per 100 000 males approaches, and in some areas exceeds, that of squamous carcinoma of the oesophagus. Carcinoma of the oesophagus, either *squamous* or *adeno*, usually commences as an ulcer, but spreads to become annular and constricting so that the patient develops dysphagia (difficulty in swallowing).

However, by the time most patients present, direct spread to adjacent organs has occurred and the surgical resection rate is only about 40%. Resectability and ultimate survival can be improved by pre-operative chemo-irradiation.

Those patients who cannot be surgically treated may undergo chemo- or radiotherapy alone, or receive palliative laser therapy. Unfortunately, a substantial proportion are simply intubated to facilitate adequate nutrition. The long-term outlook is therefore very poor, with only a 5% survival at 5 years.

Most patients die of local disease and bronchopneumonia exacerbated by malnutrition. Unlike many forms of cancer, metastases are rarely found at autopsy.

Other Tumours

Other rare malignant tumours arising in the oesophagus include malignant melanoma (from the melanocytes which are present in very small numbers in normal mucosa), small cell anaplastic (oat cell) carcinoma, mixed adeno-squamous carcinomas and sarcomas.

STOMACH

Normal Structure and Function

The stomach acts essentially as a 'mixing' reservoir for food during acid-pepsin digestion. Hydrochloric acid and pepsin are, however, only two of many products of the gastric mucosa. Histologically, the stomach can be divided into three regions-the *cardia, body* and *antrum.*

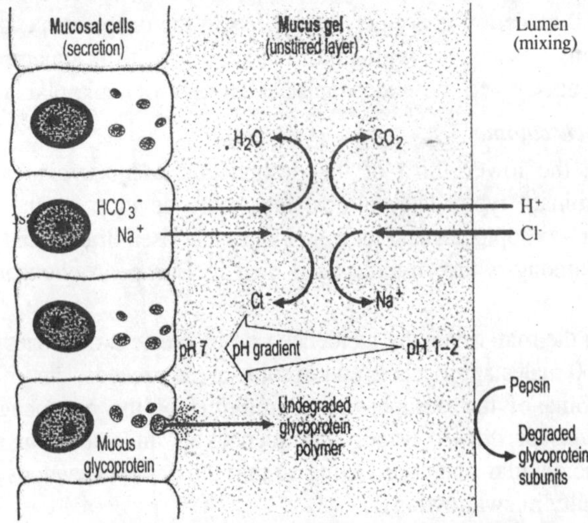

Figure 4.2: The gastric muscus barrier.

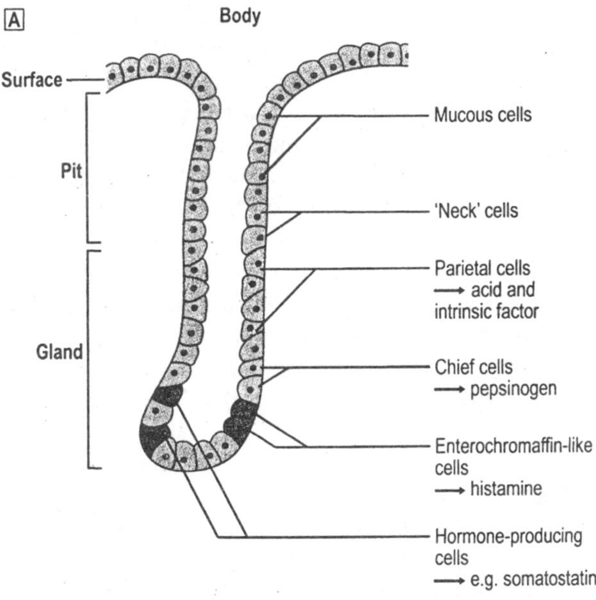

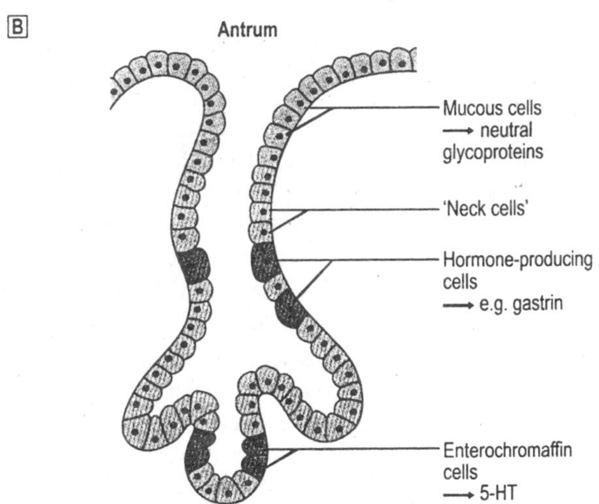

Figure 4.3: Structure of the gastric mucosa.

The surface of the gastric mucosa and its pits *(foveolae)* are lined throughout by columnar mucus-secreting epithelium. The mucus secreted by these cells, together with contributions from the antral mucous glands, forms a viscid gel covering the mucosa-the *gastric mucus barrier*.

Bicarbonate and sodium ions, also secreted by surface epithelial cells, diffuse into the unstirred gel and buffer the hydrogen ions entering from the luminal aspect. A pH gradient is thus established, ranging from 1 or 2 at the luminal surface of the barrier, to neutrality at the plasma membrane of the epithelium.

The glandular component varies from region to region. The *cardiac* (or *junctional) mucosa* is a narrow zone immediately below the termination of the squamous-lined oesophagus; it comprises simple tubular or cystic glands, lined by mucus-secreting cells, in which numerous endocrine cells and a few parietal (acid-producing) cells are scattered.

Body mucosa lines the proximal two-thirds of the stomach and consists of tightly-packed tubular glands, the upper parts of which are lined by parietal cells and the lower parts by chief cells.

In addition to acid, the parietal cells secrete intrinsic factor, essential for vitamin B_{12} absorption. Other cells present in body mucosa are mucous neck cells and endocrine cells. The neck cells are found at the bases of the gastric pits, i.e. at the junction between foveolar lining cells and glandular cells, and contain the stem cells of the mucosa together with some immature foveolar cells.

The majority of the endocrine cells are so-called enterochromaffin-like (ECL) cells which are readily identifiable by silver staining (argyrophil) techniques. These cells modulate parietal cell activity by releasing histamine in response to stimulatory hormones such as gastrin.

Antral (or *pyloric) mucosa* occupies a roughly triangular region proximal to the pylorus, with its base about onethird of the distance along the lesser curvature and its apex a few centimetres from the pylorus on the greater curve. The antral glands are more branched, tortuous and less tightly packed than those in the body.

The glands are lined by mucus-secreting cells with faintly granular cytoplasm and basal nuclei, together with endocrine cells. There may be occasional parietal cells. The endocrine cells of the antrum produce several hormones: G cells secreting gastrin are the most numerous, but others include D cells (which secrete somatostatin), EC cells (5-hydroxytryptamine, 5-HT), P cells (bombesin) and S cells (secretin).

CONGENITAL DISORDERS

Congenital abnormalities, apart from hypertrophic pyloric stenosis, are rare. They include accessory structures lined by gastric mucosa, which, are referred to as 'cysts' when saccular and not communicating with the gastric lumen, 'duplications' if tubular and non-communicating and 'diverticula' if they communicate.

Diaphragmatic Hernia

Maldevelopment of the diaphragm can lead to defects though which the stomach, together with parts of the intestine and the spleen, herniate into the left thoracic cavity.

Usually only part of the stomach is dislocated into the thorax, but after birth it may become expanded by swallowed air and can rapidly compress the lungs and, very rarely, cause death from respiratory failure.

Pyloric Stenosis

An abnormal hypertrophy of the circular muscle coat at the pylorus can lead to outflow obstruction from the stomach. The condition, found in approximately 4 per 1000 live births, usually presents with projectile vomiting. It is four to five times more common in males than females.

INFLAMMATORY DISORDERS

- Acute gastritis is commonly due to chemical injury (e.g. alcohol, drugs)
- Commonest form of chronic gastritis results from *Helicobacter pylori* infection
- Chronic gastritis can also result from an autoimmune process, often causing vitamin B_{12} deficiency
- Chemical (reactive) gastritis is caused by biliary regurgitation or drug-induced damage

Inflammation of the stomach, as with other organs, is usually considered as either acute (often described as 'haemorrhagic' or 'erosive') or chronic gastritis. Until recently chronic gastritis was a rather nebulous condition, ill-defined in pathogenetic terms and poorly correlated with endoscopic findings and symptomatology.

One form (type A) has long been recognised as an autoimmune disorder, but this type is uncommon; the generality of chronic gastritis (type B) was formerly attributed to non-specific irritants, whether exogenous (e.g. hot drinks and spices) or endogenous (e.g. bile reflux).

However, it is now recognised that type B gastritis is a response to bacterial infection, *Helicobacter pylori* and that reflux of bile into the stomach produces a distinctive histological picture.

Acute Gastritis

Acute gastritis is almost invariably an acute response to an irritant 'chemical' injury by drugs or alcohol. The principal drugs involved are non-steroidal anti-inflammatory drugs (NSAIDs), including aspirin, but many others have been implicated. These agents cause a prompt exfoliation of surface epithelial cells and diminished secretion of mucus such that the protective barrier against acid attack (see below) may be compromised.

Many of their effects are probably mediated by an inhibition of prostaglandin synthesis. Depending on the severity of the injury, the mucosal response varies from vasodilatation and oedema of the lamina propria, to erosion and haemorrhage. An erosion is an area of partial loss of the mucosa, as opposed to an ulcer where the full thickness, i.e. below the muscularis mucosae, is lost.

The erosions in acute gastritis are frequently multiple and the resultant haemorrhage can be severe and life-threatening. Fortunately the lesions are transient and heal rapidly by regeneration, so that erosions may well have disappeared 24-48 h after the bleeding episode.

An acute neutrophilic gastritis (i.e. one in which polymorph infiltration is a dominant feature) is characteristic of the initial response to *Helicobacter pylori* infection. Acute *Helicobacter* gastritis is a transient phase which in the majority of individuals is subclinical and over the course of 3-4 weeks gives way to chronic gastritis.

In a minority of individuals the infection is spontaneously eradicated and the inflammatory response resolves. The pathological features of acute bacterial gastritis are summarised in Table elsewhere in this chapter.

Chronic Gastritis

Autoimmune Chronic Gastritis

A few patients with chronic gastritis are found to have antibodies in their serum directed against gastric parietal cells and intrinsic factor binding sites. These patients exhibit varying degrees of hypochlorhydria (they are often achlorhydric), and have a macrocytic anaemia resulting from vitamin B_{12} deficiency; this association of autoimmune gastritis with macrocytic anaemia is called *pernicious anaemia.*

Histologically, the body of the stomach is maximally affected: there is marked loss of specialised cells (glandular atrophy) and replacement fibrosis of the lamina propria, together with an infiltrate of lymphocytes and plasma cells.

In addition, the surface and pit-lining epithelium may show *intestinal* metaplasia (IM), a change common to all forms of longstanding chronic gastritis. In this form of metaplasia, the neutral, mucin-secreting cells characteristic of the stomach are replaced by goblet cells containing acidic glycoproteins typical of the intestine.

In well-developed cases there may also be absorptive cells and Paneth cells. Intestinal metaplasia is generally regarded as a premalignant condition, because patients with gastric cancer frequently exhibit IM elsewhere in the stomach and because the cancers themselves frequently exhibit 'intestinal' features.

However, cancer develops in only a very small proportion of patients with IM, and the possession of intestinal features by a cancer does not necessarily imply origin from intestinalised epithelial cells. On the contrary, it is likely that IM is an essentially benign adaptive response.

Only when the change in differentiation is incomplete, giving rise to 'immature' or atypical phenotypes, is there an increased risk of cancer development. This is the situation in Barrett's oesophagus, and similar changes can arise in the stomach.

Thus, in the stomach only incomplete IM should be considered a pre-malignant condition.

Helicobacter-associated Chronic Gastritis

The cause of the most common form of chronic gastritis is bacterial infection *by Helicobacter pylori.* This is a Gramnegative organism that inhabits a peculiarly protected niche closely applied to the surface epithelium beneath the mucous barrier where the pH approaches neutrality.

The organism is not simply a commensal, as it attacks the surface cells, causes accelerated cell exfoliation and leads to a polymorph and chronic inflammatory cell response in the gastric mucosa. *H. pylori* is found in over 90% of biopsies showing active chronic (type B) gastritis but is uncommon in type A disease. The gastritis resolves after successful eradication of infection with antibiotics.

Interestingly, the organism is found only on gastric epithelium and does not colonise duodenal (or any other intestinal) epithelium. With this in mind, one explanation for intestinal metaplasia in the stomach is that it is a defence against bacterial colonisation.

The acute inflammatory response provoked *by H. pylori* is mediated by complement components which are liberated through activation of the alternative pathway and are chemotactic for polymorphs, together with low molecular weight chemotactic factors shed by the bacteria and interleukin-8 secreted by epithelial cells, macrophages and endothelial cells.

The polymorphs subsequently release proteases and reactive oxygen metabolites which may be responsible for the glandular destruction (resulting in atrophy) which characterises the established disease. In addition, anti-H. *pylori* IgA, IgG and IgM antibodies are produced locally by plasma cells in the lamina propria; these have a role in the prevention of bacterial adhesion and in opsonisation but fail to eliminate the infection.

Histologically, *Helicobacter-associated* gastritis affects the entire stomach but to a variable degree. The majority of patients exhibit diffuse involvement of the antrum and body with the gradual acquisition. over time of glandular atrophy, replacement fibrosis and intestinal metaplasia.

Patients with this distribution of gastritis are at an increased risk of gastric ulcer and carcinoma compared with uninfected individuals. A second main pattern is where the antrum is markedly inflamed but with little involvement of body mucosa. These individuals exhibit an increased acid output which renders the corpus mucosa more hostile to *H. pylori* colonisation.

Subjects with this antral-predominant gastritis are at greater risk of duodenal ulcer. The histological features of acute and chronic gastritis are summarised in Table elsewhere in this chapter.

Chemical (reflux) Gastritis

The presence of regurgitated bile and alkaline duodenal juice in the stomach provokes epithelial cell loss, compensatory hyperplasia of the proliferative compartment in the gastric foveolae, and vasodilatation and oedema of the lamina propria; this is reflux gastritis. In 'normal' people there is little or no regurgitation of duodenal contents into the stomach.

Reflux gastritis is seen in the post-operative stomach following operations which destroy or bypass the pylorus, as a result of secondary motility disturbances in patients with gallstones and after cholecystectomy, and in some patients who appear to have a disturbance of antroduodenal motility or co-ordination.

Unoperated patients with bile reflux appear to have a failure in pyloric competence resulting from a disturbance in pyloro-antral motor function; this may be either a primary disturbance, or a defective response to hormones, such as cholecystokinin and secretin, which normally increase pyloric tone during duodenal acidification. The ensuing reflux gastritis stimulates production of gastrin by the antral mucosa; this may also block the effects of cholecystokinin and secretin on the pyloric muscles.

Reflux gastritis may present with bilious vomiting or less severe dyspeptic symptoms; repeated damage to the mucosa may lead to the development of a gastric ulcer. A similar histological picture to that found with bile reflux can result from long-term usage of non-steroidal antiinflammatory drugs (NSAIDs); the common denominator is repeated chemical injury. The various types of chronic gastritis are compared in Table elsewhere in this chapter.

Other Forms of Gastritis

Less common forms of chronic gastritis have been distinguished from the three major types discussed above.

In *lymphocytic gastritis* the main histological feature is the presence of numerous mature lymphocytes within the surface epithelium. This form is occasionally seen in patients who have peculiarly heaped-up erosions running along prominent rugal folds.

Most patients are histologically H. pylori-negative at the time of diagnosis but most show serological evidence of infection. Some cases are related to villous atrophy and altered small intestinal function.

Table 4.1: Comparison of the epidemiology, incidence and aetiology of gastric and duodenal ulcers.

Feature	*Gastric ulcer*	*Duodenal ulcer*
Incidence (relative)	1	**3**
Age distribution	Increases with age	Increases up to 35 years of age
Social class	Higher in class V	Even distribution
Blood group	**A**	O
Acid levels	Normal or low	Elevated or normal
***Helicobacter* gastritis**	About 70%	95-100%

Eosinophilicgastritis is characterised by oedema and a large number of eosinophils in the inflammatory cell infiltrate. It is thought to be an allergic response to a dietary antigen to which the patient has become sensitised, or in some countries to parasitic infestation.

Granulomatous gastritis is a rare form of gastritis in which epithelioid cell granulomas are found. Such granulomas can be part of

Table 4.2: Types of chronic gastritis.

Aetiology	*Pathogenic mechanisms*	*Histological findings*	*Clinical consequences*
Autoimmune	Anti-parietal cell and anti-intrinsic factor antibodies	Glandular atrophy in body mucosa	Pernicious anaemia
		Intestinal metaplasia	
	Sensitised T -lymphocytes		
Bacterial infection	Cytotoxins	Active chronic inflammation	Peptic ulceration
(H. pylon)	Liberation of chemokines	gastric ulcer)	(duodenal/
	Mucolytic enzymes	Multifocal atrophy: antrum > body	?Gastric cancer
	?Ammonia production by bacterial urease	Intestinal metaplasia	
	Tissue damage by immune response		
Chemical injury	Direct injury	Foveolar hyperplasia	Gastric erosions
NSAIDs	Disruption of the mucus layer	Oedema	Gastric ulcer
Bile reflux	Degranulation of mast cells	Vasodilatation	
?Alcohol		Paucity of inflammatory cells	

Crohn's disease or sarcoidosis, but after exclusion of these causes there remains an isolated granulomatous gastritis of unknown aetiology.

PEPTIC ULCERATION

- Major sites: first part of duodenum, junction of antral and body mucosa in stomach, distal oesophagus, and gastro-enterostomy stoma
- Main aetiological factors: hyperacidity, *Helicobacter* gastritis, duodenal reflux, NSAIDs, smoking and genetic factors
- Ulcers may be acute or chronic

  Complications include haemorrhage, penetration of adjacent organs, perforation, anaemia, obstruction due to fibrous strictures, and malignancy

Peptic ulceration is a breach in the mucosa lining the alimentary tract as a result of acid and pepsin attack. Gastric and duodenal ulcers differ in their epidemiology, incidence and pathogenesis. They arise as either acute or chronic ulcers.

Acute ulcers

Acute peptic ulcers develop:

- as part of an acute gastritis
- as a complication of a severe *stress response*
- as a result of extreme *hyperacidity*.

Deeper extension of the erosions in acute gastritis resulting from NSAIDs or acute alcohol overdosage can produce frank ulcers. Acute ulcers occur also in a heterogeneous group of conditions where stress seems to be the common denominator.

For example, ulcers may be found following severe burns (Curling's ulcer), major trauma or cerebrovascular accidents. Such ulcers probably arise as a consequence of mucosal ischaemia, which lowers the mucosal resistance to acid. Extreme hyperacidity, as seen for example in patients with gastrin-secreting tumours (ZollingerEllison syndrome), can lead to multiple acute ulcers in the antrum, the duodenum and even the jejunum.

Chronic Ulcers

Chronic peptic ulcers seem to occur most frequently at mucosal junctions. Thus gastric ulcers are generally found in antral mucosa where it meets body-type mucosa; duodenal ulcers are found in the proximal duodenum close to the pylorus; oesophageal peptic ulcers are found in the squamous epithelium just above the cardiooesophageal junction; and stomal ulcers-those occurring following construction of a gastro-enterostomy linking stomach and jejunum-are found in the jejunal mucosa immediately adjacent to the gastric mucosa of the stomal margin. This suggests that ulceration is most likely to occur where acid and pepsin first come into contact with a susceptible mucosa.

Pathogenesis

For many years peptic ulceration has been attributed to excessive acid production. However, there are many problems with this hypothesis. People with gastric ulcers frequently have normal or even subnormal acid production, and over one-half of duodenal ulcer patients do not have hyperacidity.

Conversely, many people who are hypersecretors of acid do not get ulcers. Furthermore, while most ulcers respond initially to anti-acid treatment there are frequent relapses. It has therefore become increasingly apparent that mucosal defence against acid attack is of considerable importance. Failure of the mucosal defence mechanisms means that ulcers can result from normal or even decreased quantities of acid.

Gastric ulcers

The pH of the gastric juice under fasting conditions is extremely acidic (between 1 and 2) so that any unprotected gastric mucosa would rapidly undergo auto-digestion.

The mucosal defences against acid attack consist of

- a mucus-bicarbonate barrier
- the surface epithelium.

The *mucus barrier* is the more important of the two lines of defence. The pit-lining and surface epithelial cells of the stomach secrete viscid neutral glycoproteins which form a layer of unstirred mucus on the surface.

The mucus itself has acid-resistant properties, but its protective power is greatly enhanced by the establishment of a buffering gradient within the layer brought about by bicarbonate ions.

The *surface epithelium* constitutes a second line of defence; for its proper functioning it requires integrity of both the apical plasma membrane as a barrier to ion transfer, and cellular metabolic functions, including the production of bicarbonate. These functions are dependent upon an adequate mucosal blood supply. Ulceration can follow either destruction or removal of the mucus barrier, or a loss of integrity of the surface epithelium.

Dissolution of the mucus layer can occur as a primary event as a consequence of duodeno-gastric reflux. The regurgitated bile from the duodenum strips off the mucus barrier and paves the way for acid attack. Acid and bile in combination damage the surface epithelial cells, increasing the permeability of the mucosa.

This causes the congestion and oedema of the lamina propria seen in reflux gastritis. The epithelial barrier may be damaged by the effect of NSAIDs blocking the synthesis of the prostaglandins which normally protect the epithelium. Epithelial injury is also a consequence of *H. pylori* infection, either produced directly by cytotoxins and ammonia or indirectly as a result of the inflammatory reaction.

Thus in peptic ulcers in the stomach, breakdown of mucosal defence is much more important than excessive acid production.

Duodenal ulcers

Increased production of acid assumes more importance in the pathogenesis of duodenal ulceration; about one-half of such patients have an elevated maximal acid secretion, and even in those with a normal maximal acid output it may be that they have inappropriately sustained acid secretion without the normal sharp fall-off of acid production during sleep.

It has been shown that *H. pylori-infected* individuals secrete 2-6 times as much acid as non-infected controls when stimulated by gastrin-releasing peptide. Nevertheless, excess acidity is not the entire explanation and mucosal defence is also important.

The factors causing lowered resistance in the stomach do not usually apply in the duodenum: *Helicobacter* does not colonise normal duodenal epithelium; the duodenal mucosa is tolerant of bile and pancreatic alkaline secretions; and drugs are generally diluted or absorbed before reaching the duodenum.

Nevertheless, *Helicobacter is* involved in duodenal ulceration because there is gastric metaplasia in response to excess acid. Gastric metaplasia paves the way for colonisation *by Helicobacter,* which in turn sets up chronic inflammation in the duodenum and predisposes to ulceration.

Morphology

Grossly, chronic peptic ulcers are usually less than 20 mm in diameter but they may be larger and can exceed 100 mm in diameter. The edges are clear-cut and overhang the base. Microscopically, the base consists of necrotic tissue and polymorph exudate overlying inflamed granulation tissue which merges with mature fibrous (scar) tissue.

The latter frequently occupies the remainder of the wall, with the muscularis propria completely breached. Arteries within this fibrous base often show extreme narrowing of their lumina by intimal proliferation *(endarteritis obliterans)*.

Ulcers heal by epithelial regeneration, which reconstitutes the mucosa, and progressive fibrosis. Later, shrinkage of the fibrous tissue (cicatrisation) may lead to pyloric stenosis or a central narrowing of the stomach, the so-called *hourglass deformity*.

More immediate complications of peptic ulcers include:

- *perforation,* giving rise to spillage of gastric contents into the peritoneal cavity and peritonitis
- *penetration,* whereby the ulcer erodes into an adjacent organ such as the liver or pancreas
- *haemorrhage,* from eroded vessels in the ulcer base.

Although malignant change is claimed to occur in gastric peptic ulcers, this is a very uncommon event: as far as duodenal ulcers are concerned it can be assumed that they never become malignant.

BENIGN TUMOURS AND POLYPS

A polyp is simply a protuberant mass of tissue; it can either be neoplastic or form as a result of an excessive reparative or regenerative process. The commonest form of polyp involves simple elongation of the gastric pits separated by fibrous tissue or mildly inflamed lamina propria.

These are *hyperplastic* or *regenerative polyps* and are generally found against a background of *Helicobacter-associated* gastritis in the gastric antrum. A similar variety is seen in body-type mucosa, but in this instance the main feature is enlargement by cystic dilatation of the specialised fundic glands.

These were originally thought to be hamartomatous, but this is questionable and they are best termed *simple fundic polyps*. Much more rarely, true *hamartomas* occur, either as adenomyomas, which, as the term implies, are overgrowths of glandular and smooth muscle elements, or as part of the Peutz Jeghers syndrome, where the patient has multiple gastrointestinal hamartomatous polyps and circumoral skin pigmentation.

A further rare cause of a polypoid mass in the stomach is *heterotopic pancreas,* i.e. the presence of pancreatic tissue separate from the main gland.

A benign epithelial tumour of the stomach *(adenoma) is* uncommon in most Western countries but is a relatively frequent finding in Japan and other countries with a high incidence of gastric cancer. When polypoid, these tumours have a strong potential for malignant change and, if subjected to multiple sectioning, around 40% will be found to contain carcinoma on microscopic examination. However, *flat adenomas* with lower malignant potential are increasingly recognised and have to be distinguished from the higherrisk multifocal epithelial dysplasias.

There are two main benign mesenchymal tumours, the *leiomyoma* and the *Schwannoma* or nerve sheath tumour. Both are rare. However, the majority of connective tissue tumours are composed of interwoven spindle cells which can exhibit both neural and smooth muscle differentiation on immunostaining and are referred to as *gastric stromal tumours.*

Stromal tumours are of unpredictable behaviour and it is difficult to distinguish between benign and malignant tumours on histological criteria. Those features which indicate a benign course are small size, encapsulation, low mitotic activity and absence of necrosis.

MALIGNANT TUMOURS OF THE STOMACH

Carcinoma of the Stomach

- Majority are adenocarcinomas
- Many arise on a background of chronic gastritis and intestinal metaplasia
- Most cases present when clinically advanced
- Early cases (carcinoma confined to mucosa or submucosa) have a good prognosis
- All gastric ulcers must be regarded as potentially malignant

The incidence of gastric cancer, like that of carcinoma of the oesophagus, varies widely both between and within countries. There is a notably high incidence in Japan, China, Colombia and Finland, but even in these countries, as elsewhere in the world, the incidence of carcinoma of the stomach is declining.

Despite this fall, gastric cancer is still the second most common fatal malignancy (after lung cancer) in the world, with an estimated three-quarters of a million new cases diagnosed annually. In many countries gastric cancer remains the most common form of cancer.

Migrant studies indicate strong environmental influences; for example, when Japanese people move to Hawaii or California the incidence of gastric cancer in that group falls, and after only one generation approximates to that of the local population. While the causative environmental factors remain to be conclusively determined, it appears that *H. pylori* plays a major part.

Aetiology

For many years a sequence of events, starting with chronic gastritis and passing through atrophy and intestinal metaplasia to premalignant dysplasia, has been acknowledged as the precursor to cancer of the stomach. Given that *H. pylori* has now been accepted as the major cause of chronic gastritis, it is logical to implicate this infection in the causation of gastric cancer.

The prevalence of *H. pylori* infection frequently runs 'parallel with the incidence of gastric cancer in the same populations, and epidemiological studies have shown that patients with antibodies to *H. pylori* have a higher risk of gastric cancer.

The strength of the epidemiological links is such that the International Agency for Research into Cancer has declared that *H. pylori* is a gastric carcinogen, that is, the infection initiates the events leading to cancer. Given the high prevalence of infection and the comparative rarity of cancer it is unlikely that the organism or its products are direct-acting mutagens.

There are a number of possible indirect mechanisms linking *H. pylori* infection to gastric cancer. Long-term infection leads to glandular atrophy, which leads to a gradual decline in acid secretion. Hypochlorhydria allows other bacteria to proliferate in the gastric juice; these bacteria are capable of reducing nitrate ions to nitrite and can catalyse nitrosation of amines and amides present in the diet to give rise to potentially carcinogenic N-nitroso compounds.

H. pylori possesses an inducible alcohol dehydrogenase which is capable of producing acetaldehyde from alcohol substrates. Acetaldehyde is a highly reactive product which damages epithelial cells and can cause DNA damage, but its role in vivo is in dispute.

A more likely source of genomic DNA damage in *H. pylori* gastritis is reactive oxygen attack by superoxide and hydroxyl radicals, monochloramines and nitric oxide produced by activated polymorphs and macrophages. Interestingly, nitrosation and oxidative damage is minimised by anti-oxidant vitamins, among which ascorbic acid is the most important, and diets rich in fresh fruit and vegetables have long been recognised as protective against gastric cancer.

Ascorbic acid secretion into gastric juice is severely compromised in *H. pylori* gastritis. Perhaps the most important factor underlying the relationship between *H. pylori* and gastric cancer is a promotional effect through high cell turnover. The production of cytotoxins and ammonia by the organism, and indirect epithelial damage brought about by cytokines and polymorph products, induce increased cell turnover. DNA repair is compromised by increased cell proliferation, and the probability of a mutation escaping repair and being transmitted to daughter cells is increased.

Several molecular genetic changes have been demonstrated in gastric cancer. Loss of expression of cell adhesion molecules including E-cadherin and β-catenin, mutations and deletions of tumour suppressor genes, notably p53, K-ras and the APC gene, and over-expression of oncogenes like c-myc and *erbB-2,* have been demonstrated. However, while some of these mutations are consistent with exogenous chemical carcinogens or exposure to endogenous freeradical injury, one cannot infer the nature of the mutational agent from the genetic lesions with any certainty.

Nevertheless the overall evidence favours an aetiological link between *H. pylori* infection and gastric cancer. The implications for the prevention of this major cancer are clear. Eradication of this infection or, more practicably when a vaccine becomes available, vaccination in childhood will have a profound effect on the incidence of gastric cancer.

Premalignant Conditions

There are few clearly defined conditions in the stomach where an increased incidence of cancer is observed. In addition to atrophy and incomplete intestinal metaplasia in chronic *H. pylori* gastritis, a higher incidence of gastric cancer is seen in patients with pernicious anaemia and following partial gastrectomy for benign ulcer disease.

Patients with pernicious anaemia exhibit a threefold increase in the risk of gastric cancer over the general population, while post-gastrectomy patients develop an excess risk about 15-20 years after surgery. A common denominator in all such patients is the presence of hypochlorhydria or achlorhydria as a result of glandular atrophy and/or alkaline reflux; low gastric acidity allows the proliferation of large numbers of bacteria in the gastric juice.

Thus it may be that the development of most 'environmental' gastric cancers can be explained in terms of longstanding mucosal injury leading to gastric atrophy and low acid secretion, with a consequent rise in bacterial counts in the gastric juice. These bacteria, usually of enteric type, are capable of nitrate reduction and act as catalysts for the nitrosation of amines to carcinogenic nitrosamines.

There are a few patients with gastric cancer who have neither a recognised premalignant condition nor chronic gastritis and hypochlorhydria. Genetic factors are likely to be involved, but little is known of these beyond a link with blood group A and the appearance of frequent gastric cancers in certain families, often at a young age. It is possible that such individuals have inherited defects in DNA repair genes.

Dysplasia and Early Gastric Cancer

The dysplasia-carcinoma sequence is thought to characterise the development of most if not all gastric cancers, but the finding of dysplasia is relatively uncommon in lowincidence countries such as the UK and USA. Most cancers are advanced at the time of initial diagnosis and potentially curative operations are only possible in about 45% of cases.

This accounts for the poor prognosis of gastric cancer, which generally has only a 10-15% survival rate at 5 years after diagnosis. However, much better results are obtained when patients undergo radical operations with extensive lymph node clearance. Patients who have such 'potentially curative resections' with removal of all macroscopic cancer have about a 60% chance of survival to 5 years.

Gastric cancers are classified as either 'early' or 'advanced' on the basis of direct spread through the stomach wall. *Early* gastric cancer is confined to either the mucosa (intramucosal carcinoma) or submucosa; *advanced* tumours extend into or beyond the main muscle coats. Cancers can thus still be 'early' even if spread has occurred to regional lymph nodes.

The importance of this categorisation lies in their differing prognosis, cases of early gastric cancer having a 5-year survival in excess of 90%. The prognosis of advanced cases rests largely on whether or not surgery has been truly 'curative' in removing the entire tumour.

Thus involvement of the resection margins by carcinoma carries a dire prognosis, as does the presence of covert hepatic or distant lymph node metastases. The best guide to prognosis in potentially curative cases appears to be the number of involved lymph nodes and, to some extent, the histological type of carcinoma.

Morphology

Foci of high-grade dysplasia and intra-mucosal carcinoma may be endoscopically visible as slightly elevated plaques or shallow depressions. If either of these lesions is diagnosed in a gastric biopsy, resection is essential. Histologically, they may be distinguished according to whether invasion of the lamina propria has occurred, but this can only be excluded in high-grade dysplasia by examination of multiple sections from the entire area of involvement.

With increasing size, the elevated lesions develop into *polypoid* and later into fungating carcinomas, while the depressed areas present an excavated *ulcerated* appearance mimicking that seen in chronic peptic ulcer. The distinction between carcinoma and chronic peptic ulcer cannot be made with certainty on clinical, endoscopic or radiological grounds, so that all gastric ulcers should be subjected to cytology or multiple biopsy both before and after therapy.

Carcinomas of the stomach are almost exclusively adenocarcinomas derived from mucus-secreting epithelial cells. Like other carcinomas, they can be graded according to their degree of differentiation; poorly differentiated carcinomas behave more aggressively than well-differentiated types.

However, a better guide to prognosis results from division into either 'intestinal' or 'diffuse' types according to the scheme devised by Lauren.

- Intestinal-type carcinomas show glandular formations lined by mucus-secreting cells with plentiful cytoplasm; they tend to have an expansile growth pattern with a well-demarcated 'pushing' border.
- *Diffuse* carcinomas, on the other hand, consist of chains of non-cohesive, single cells infiltrating the wall with a poorly demarcated invasive margin. Mucus secretion is generally less apparent, and usually takes the form of intra-cytoplasmic vacuoles which may compress the nucleus to form so-called 'signet ring' cells.

Intestinal-type gastric carcinomas carry a better prognosis than the diffuse type. Interestingly, the intestinal form predominates in high-incidence countries and has a strong correlation with pre-existing H. pylori-associated chronic gastritis. Diffuse carcinomas form a higher proportion of the total in low-incidence countries; this may reflect the increased contribution of genetic factors to cancer development among these populations.

Carcinomas spread directly to involve the serosa, which can lead to peritoneal dissemination. This can result in the formation of a malignant effusion (ascites) or involvement of other organs by transcoelomic spread, of which metastases in the ovaries (Krukenberg tumours) are a classical example.

Depending upon the site of the tumour, direct spread can also occur into the pancreas, transverse colon (when fistulation can occur), liver and spleen. Lymphatic spread is initially to local nodes along the right and left gastric arteries, extending to coeliac nodes, then to more distant sites like the classical (but rare) involvement of the left supraclavicular nodes (Troisier's sign). Blood-stream spread occurs via the portal vein; liver metastases are frequently evident at the time of presentation.

Other Malignant Tumours

Other malignant tumours include carcinoid tumours (p. 396), malignant stromal tumours and lymphomas.

Stromal Tumours

The stomach is the commonest site for gastrointestinal stromal tumours; approximately 45% of these are maligrfant and can give rise to metastases. They frequently present with symptoms referable to secondary ulceration, namely haemorrhage, anaemia, anorexia and weight loss.

Endoscopically they protrude into the lumen and often have a central deep ulcer crater. Malignancy is recognised by the presence of metastases at the time of surgery and can be predicted, to some extent, by the finding of increased mitotic activity in tumour tissue.

Lymphomas

The stomach is the commonest site for primary lymphomas to arise in the gastrointestinal tract, accounting for around 40% of all cases, and the incidence is steadily increasing. Lymphomas of the stomach represent about 5% of all gastric malignancies and are most frequently of the non-Hodgkin B-cell type; they are closely related to preceding *H. pylori* infection.

The normal gastric mucosa is virtually devoid of lymphocytes. *H. pylori* infection provokes a mucosal immune response characterised by an influx of lymphocytes and plasma cells and an active chronic inflammatory reaction.

The appearance of lymphoid follicles with germinal centres in the gastric mucosa together with an increase in intraepithelial lymphocytes in the immediately overlying epithelium recapitulate the features of mucosa-associated lymphoid tissue (MALT) and it is this acquired MALT which provides the tissue of origin for gastric B-cell lymphomas.

As with gastric carcinoma, epidemiological studies reveal a much increased risk for the subsequent development of gastric lymphoma when *H.* pylori-infected individuals are compared with uninfected controls. Indeed patients with these B-cell lymphomas (MALTomas) are almost always *H.* pylori-positive.

The emergence of a monoclonal proliferation of B-lymphocytes associated with aggressive features evidenced by invasion and destruction of epithelium *(lympho-epithelial* lesions) and replacement of germinal centres by atypical centrocyte-like B-cells are the characteristic features of a low-grade malignant MALT lymphoma. High-grade (large-cell) lymphomas consist of dense sheets of large 'blast' cells and are almost invariably of B-cell lineage.

The transition from chronic gastritis to lymphoma is associated with genetic changes but the cause of these DNA changes remains unknown.

Interestingly, the low-grade B-cell lymphomas *(marginal zone lymphomas)* appear to require continuing antigenic stimulation of helper T-cells to maintain B-cell proliferation. As a consequence, these lymphomas can show complete regression following successful elimination of *H. pylori* infection.

Deeply infiltrating low-grade tumours and all high-grade lymphomas require treatment with chemoand/or radiotherapy. Even so, high-grade lymphomas have a relatively good prognosis (compared to adenocarcinoma) when confined to the stomach (50% survival at 5 years), but the outlook worsens considerably when penetration of the serosa or involvement of regional lymph nodes has occurred.

The stomach may also be involved by lymphomas which have arisen elsewhere; the outlook in these systematised cases depends upon the overall extent, histological type and grade.

INTESTINE

Normal Structure and Function

Small intestine

The main functions of the small intestine are:

- enzymatic digestion
- absorption of nutrients.

By providing a vast surface area of specialised epithelium, the villous structure of the mucosa optimises absorption; this can be either passive or under active control. The *villi* are covered by tightly packed absorptive cells *(enterocytes),* which themselves have *microvilli* on the luminal surface along their plasma membranes.

This microvillous or 'brush' border further increases surface area and, together with the adherent glycoproteins of the glycocalyx, is also the site of hydrolytic enzyme activity, for example, disaccharidases and peptidases.

Endocrine Cells

Scattered among the absorptive cells are mucus-secreting goblet cells and endocrine cells; the latter produce a wide variety of gut 'hormones', such as enteroglucagon, cholecystokinin, gastrin, motilin, secretin and vasoactive intestinal polypeptide (VIP). Endocrine cells are also found among the proliferating cells *(enteroblasts)* of the intestinal crypts.

Here, many of the endocrine cells are of the *enterochromaffin* type and produce serotonin (5-HT), which has an important role in the control of gut motility and blood supply. Endocrine cells of the gut are often considered as part of a diffuse system of APUD (amine precursor uptake and decarboxylation) cells, which are found in many organs and from which distinctive neoplasms may originate.

Paneth cells

These are distinctive granulated cells also found at the bases of the small intestinal crypts. Paneth cells secrete an a-defensin, human α-defensin 5, which is an important antibacterial peptide within the bowel lumen. It is secreted as a propeptide which is cleaved by a trypsin isoenzyme, also produced by the Paneth cell, to form the bactericidal active peptide.

Brunner's glands

The duodenal submucosa contains Brunner's glands, collections of mucus-secreting acini most plentiful proximally. They are much less frequent in the jejunum. Brunner's glands produce an alkaline mucous secretion that is also rich in epidermal growth factor (EGF). The secretion not only neutralises acidic gastric juice entering the duodenum but, through its high content of luminally-active EGF, promotes mucosal regeneration after injury.

Mucosa-associated lymphoid tissue

The connective tissue of the mucosa (lamina propria) contains prominent lymphatics (lacteals), blood capillaries, and a cellular infiltrate comprising lymphocytes, plasma cells, eosinophils and mast cells. The lymphoid cells form an important arm of mucosal immunity, and most of those in the lamina propria are T-helper cells, whereas the intraepithelial lymphocytes are predominantly T-suppressor cells thought to be important in maintaining tolerance to food antigens.

Lymphoid aggregates or follicles with germinal centres are found throughout the intestinal mucosa; they frequently straddle the muscularis mucosae and extend into the superficial submucosa. Dense aggregates are found in the terminal ileum where they form *Peyer's patches*. The flattened epithelium over these aggregates contains *M-cells,* specialised cells capable of antigen binding and processing; they pass antigenic material to underlying helper T-lymphocytes.

Large Intestine

The large intestine has several functions:

- the storage and elimination of food residues
- the maintenance of fluid and electrolyte balance
- the degradation of complex carbohydrates and other nutrients by luminal bacteria.

The large intestine can be divided into six parts-caecum, ascending colon, transverse colon, descending colon, sigmoid and rectum. These divisions are imprecise, but are useful for describing the sites and extent of disease.

Mucosa

The mucosa of the large bowel is devoid of villi. Instead, it comprises perpendicular crypts extending from the flat surface down to the muscularis mucosae, separated by a little lamina propria. Numerically, the predominant cell is of columnar absorptive type, but in tissue sections such cells often appear less numerous than the intervening goblet cells.

As in the small intestine, several types of endocrine (or APUD) cell are present, but in health Paneth cells are confined to the right side of the colon and then only sparsely. Also, in contrast to the small intestine, large bowel mucosa has only scanty lymphatics which are concentrated towards the muscularis mucosae. This restricts the metastatic potential of intra-mucosal malignant cells.

Vascular supply

The vascular supply to the colon derives from the superior and inferior mesenteric arteries:

- The caecum, ascending and proximal transverse colon are supplied by branches of the superior mesenteric artery.
- The distal transverse, descending, sigmoid colon and upper rectum are supplied by branches of the inferior mesenteric artery.
- The remainder of the rectum is supplied by the middle and inferior rectal arteries which are branches of the internal iliac and internal pudendal arteries respectively.

These patterns of blood supply are important in determining the sites and consequences of ischaemia (for example, the 'watershed' territory around the splenic flexure is especially vulnerable) and, because lymphatic drainage follows similar patterns, in predicting the likely distribution of lymph node metastases from the site of the tumour.

Nerve supply

The intestine has a complex nerve network comprising autonomic motor and sensory neurones and a separate enteric nervous system. The sympathetic supply originates from ganglia outside the gut in the coeliac and mesenteric plexuses.

The parasympathetic ganglia are found within the gut wall, and these, together with the associated neurones, form two nerve networks, the submucosal (Meissner's) plexus and the myenteric (Auerbach's) plexus. The nerve plexuses create and conduct the basic electrical rhythm of the gut.

Stimulation of parasympathetic nerves increases muscular contraction (particularly in the inner circular layer), blood supply and secretory activity; stimulation of the sympathetic supply has the opposite effects. The enteric nervous system has sensory receptors in the mucosa and bowel wall which respond to changes in volume and composition of the bowel contents, and through neuronal connections elicits the appropriate response in the effector system.

These activities are mediated by a wide variety of neurotransmitters, such as VIP, cholecystokinin and somatostatin, some of which were formerly thought to be gut hormones.

Appendix

The appendix arises from the caecum. It is a blind-ended structure lined internally by colonic-type mucosa, surrounded by submucosa and muscle coats. In children and young adults the mucosa contains numerous prominent lymphoid follicles. In the elderly, the lumen often shows fibrous obliteration.

CONGENITAL DISORDERS

The duodenum derives from the distal end of the primitive foregut; the jejunum, ileum and proximal colon from the midgut; and the distal colon and rectum from the hindgut. Proper development involves canalisation (development of a lumen), temporary herniation into the extra-embryonic coelom, rotation, and eventual retraction back into the abdominal cavity. Defects arising in the course of this complex process are relatively common.

Atresia and Stenosis

Atresia represents either a failure of the gut to canalise or a failure of a segment to develop during fetal growth. A congenital stenosis is a constriction of the bowel arising during fetal development. These lesions are most commonly found in the duodenum or small intestine, and are rare in the colon.

Duodenal atresia seems to be a failure of organ development, and around 30% of affected children also have Down's syndrome; jejuno-ileal atresia commonly appears to be the result of an intra-uterine accident, such as incarceration of the midgut in the physiological umbilical hernia or some other form of vascular occlusion.

Malrotation

The commonest type of malrotation occurs when the large bowel fails to descend into the right iliac fossa after emerging from the physiological umbilical hernia. This means that the caecum remains high in the abdomen and the bands that should fix it in the right iliac fossa (Ladd's bands) cross the duodenum and compress it, causing extrinsic obstruction.

Duplication and Diverticula

Duplication of the bowel may either present as a tubular double-barrelled appearance, or form a cyst in the mesentery. These anomalies can produce an abdominal mass, cause intestinal obstruction, or initiate a volvulus. Congenital diverticula are out-pouchings of the full thickness of the bowel wall and are found mainly in the duodenum and jejunum.

These rarely have clinical consequences, but some patients develop bacterial overgrowth, steatorrhoea and vitamin B_{L2} malabsorption. The diverticula can also undergo perforation and haemorrhage.

Meckel's Diverticulum

Meckel's diverticulum arises as a result of incomplete regression of the vitello-intestinal duct, such that a tubular diverticulum is present in the ileum. The diverticulum is usually lined by normal small-intestinal mucosa, but occasionally it may contain heterotopic gastric or pancreatic elements.

If gastric elements are present, acid and peptic secretion may lead to ulceration at the mouth of the diverticulum and give rise to haemorrhage and perforation. The diverticulum may also become inflamed and present as an acute abdomen which can mimic appendicitis.

Meconiurn ileus

The term meconium ileus refers to small-intestinal obstruction resulting from thickening and desiccation (inspissation) of the viscid meconium produced by children with cystic fibrosis. It is seen in about *15%* of affected babies and may be complicated by perforation, secondary atresia or volvulus.

Hirschsprung's Disease

Hirschsprung's disease, or aganglionosis of the intestine, results from a failure of migration of neuroblasts from the vagus into the developing gut, such that the intramural parasympathetic nerve plexuses fail to develop.

The distal colon and rectum have an additional parasympathetic supply from extramural nerves derived from the sacral plexus. Under normal circumstances the parasympathetic tone, which controls the contraction of the circular muscle coat, is modulated at the ganglia by the sympathetic innervation.

However, in the absence of the myenteric ganglia, the intact extramural parasympathetic supply is unchecked by sympathetic modulation and results in spasm of the circular muscle and intestinal obstruction.

There is a proliferation of cholinergic nerves derived from this extramural supply throughout the affected segment, and their high content of acetylcholinesterase can be utilised to diagnose Hirschsprung's disease in frozen sections of rectal mucosa.

Hirschsprung's disease affects the distal large intestine extending proximally from the ano-rectal junction for a variable distance. The rectum and distal colon are usually involved, but the extent varies from 1-2 cm to total colonic aganglionosis, or even extension into the small intestine.

The effects of the aganglionosis vary from life-threatening total obstruction to mild cases causing chronic constipation. The main cause of death in Hirschsprung's disease is the development of an acute enterocolitis with endotoxaemia.

Anorectal Anomalies

A large variety of malformations have been described which affect the termination of the large bowel. These include:

- a *primitive cloaca,* where the alimentary, urinary and genital tracts open into a single orifice
- *anorectal agenesis* and *rectal atresia,* where there is a failure of development or canalisation from above the level of the levators

- an *ectopic* or *imperforate anus*.

Anorectal anomalies occur in approximately 1:5000 live births. Most are amenable to surgical correction.

MALABSORPTION

Malabsorption can result from pancreatic disease or various biochemical disorders such as lactase and sucrase-isomaltase deficiency, as well as from small-intestinal diseases. Smallintestinal causes include:

- *coeliac disease,* the major small-intestinal cause of malabsorption in Western countries
- *extensive surgical resection,* for example in patients with Crohn's disease
- *lymphatic obstruction,* which gives rise to a protein-losing state
- *'blind loop syndrome',* where bacterial overgrowth in partly obstructed or bypassed loops robs the patient of vital nutrients.

Coeliac Disease

- Results from sensitivity to gluten in cereals
- Diagnosis by finding villous atrophy and crypt hyperplasia on duodenal or jejunal biopsy
- Clinically, results in malabsorption
- Complicated by splenic atrophy and, less commonly, lymphoma and small-intestinal ulceration

Coeliac disease is due to an abnormal reaction to a constituent of wheat flour, gluten, which damages the surface enterocytes of the small intestine and severely reduces their absorptive capacity.

Incidence

Coeliac disease affects about 1 in 2000 individuals in the United Kingdom but in the west of Ireland this rises to 1 in 300. However, these incidence rates are set to increase as the range of disturbances resulting from gluten intolerance becomes more widely appreciated. In family studies the incidence of coeliac disease in siblings is between 10 and 20% and there is a raised incidence in their parents.

Aetiology and pathogenesis

The toxic component of gluten is probably gliadin, but the mechanism by which gliadin induces tissue damage remains unknown. It seems increasingly likely that tissue injury is more a consequence of the immune response than a direct toxic effect. There is an apparent increase in intraepithelial lymphocytes (IELs) in this condition and an increased proportion of a specialised subpopulation of T-lymphocytes among the

IELs, but the significance of these findings remains obscure. Genetic factors are also involved and there is a strong association with HLA-B8.

Approximately 80% of patients have this phenotype; furthermore, coeliac disease is associated with the skin disease dermatitis herpetiformis, which seems to be associated independently with the HLA-B8 antigen. These genetic associations are likely to be linked to mucosal immune responsiveness and thus determine susceptibility to the disease.

Sensitivity to gliadin and the development of coeliac disease might be 'triggered' in susceptible individuals by some other factor such as viral infection. This would explain the variable age of onset of the disease and its occasional appearance in middle-aged or even elderly people.

Morphology

Under normal circumstances, enterocytes are constantly shed from the tips of the villi and replenished by migration of cells up the villi from the proliferative compartment in the crypts. The entire cycle from cell birth through functional maturation to extrusion takes about 72 hours.

Moderately accelerated cell loss can be compensated for by increased cell proliferation. With higher rates of cell loss, a stage is soon reached when the increased proliferative compartment cannot maintain a normal number of maturing and functioning 'end cells', the size of this compartment diminishes, and villous atrophy results. Shrinkage of villi and reduction in epithelial surface area are thus inevitable consequences of any injury causing a high rate of cell loss in the small intestine.

In coeliac disease the ultimate stage of this process is seen; despite a marked increase in size of the proliferative compartment, evidenced by elongation, hypercellularity and high mitotic activity of the crypts (crypt hyperplasia), there is a flat surface (total villous atrophy) and even this is populated by immature cells incapable of proper absorptive activity.

The disease is therefore characterised by a total malabsorption, affecting sugars, fatty acids, monoglycerides, amino acids, water and electrolytes; the failure to absorb fat is the dominant abnormality in most cases. The loss of mature surface epithelial cells also gives rise to a secondary disaccharidase deficiency, so that patients become intolerant of lactose and other sugars.

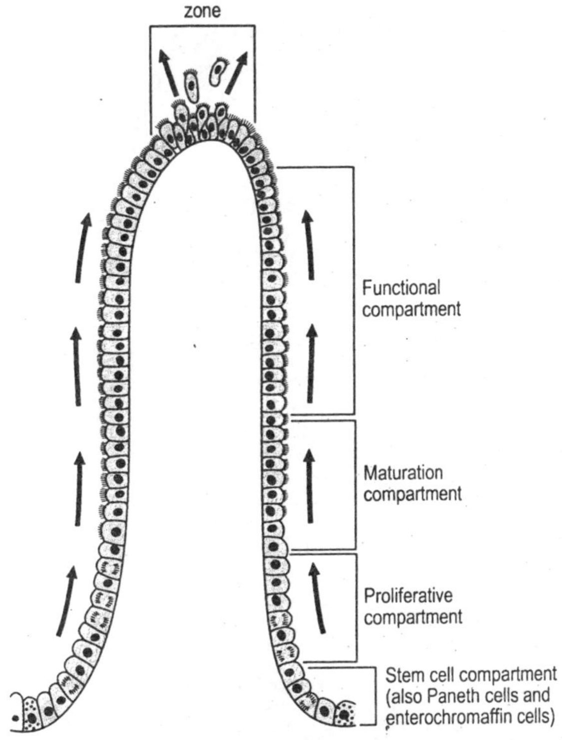

Figure 4.4: Cell proliferation and maturation in the small intestine.

The degenerate surface epithelium is infiltrated by large numbers of T-lymphocytes (IELs). Damaged epithelial cells may produce tumour necrosis factor a (TNF-a) which enhances the proliferation and migration of IELs.

The lesion is more severe in the proximal small intestine-the duodenum and proximal jejunum-and may spare the ileum, although the latter is susceptible to injury if exposed to gluten. In addition to malabsorption, intestinal hormone production from the proximal small bowel is impaired; there may be secondary reduction in pancreatic secretion and bile flow as a result of reduced production or release of pancreozymin, secretin and cholecystokinin.

Thus, gallstones are commonly present in older patients. Lesser degrees of gluten-intolerance short of classical coeliac disease are increasingly recognised. Investigation of older patients with unexplained weight loss or anaemia sometimes brings to light an increase in IELs

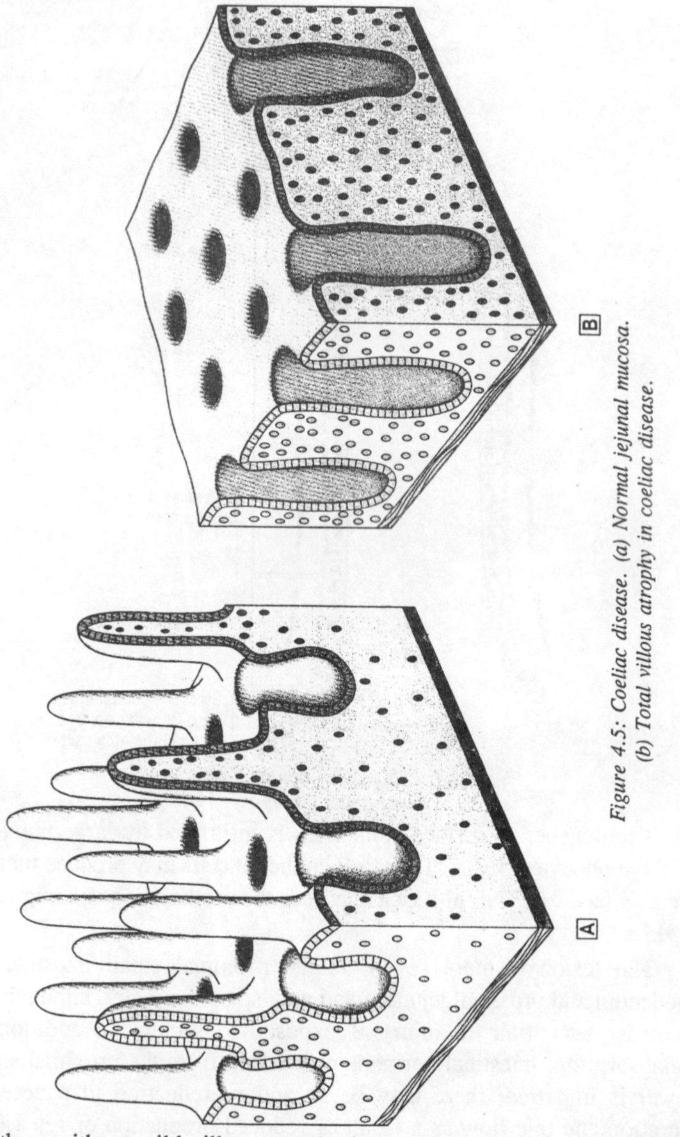

Figure 4.5: Coeliac disease. (a) Normal jejunal mucosa. (b) Total villous atrophy in coeliac disease.

with or without mild villous atrophy in duodenal biopsies. Such patients also respond to gluten withdrawal.

Complications

Now that the primary lesion and clinical consequences of coeliac disease can be managed by gluten-free diets, the later effects of the disease are becoming of greater concern. The main long-term problem is the development of malignant lymphomas in the small intestine, but there is also a higher incidence of other gastrointestinal cancers.

In general, small bowel lymphomas are of B-cell lineage, but in coeliac disease they are frequently of a large cell type derived from T-cells (enteropathy-associated T-cell lymphoma).

The patient presents with either haemorrhage, perforation, small-bowel obstruction or systemic symptoms. A few patients with coeliac disease develop ulceration of the small intestine which is non-lymphomatous; microscopic examination simply reveals non-specific chronic inflammation (chronic ulcerative enteritis).

Tropical Sprue

Pathological changes identical to those found in coeliac disease (but usually less severe) are evident in tropical sprue, a form of malabsorption found, as the name indicates, in the tropics and sub-tropics but not apparently in Africa. It is characterised by chronic diarrhoea, weight loss and a macrocytic anaemia due to folate or vitamin B_{12} deficiency.

A gluten-free diet has little or no beneficial effect, but the condition may be relieved by broad-spectrum antibiotics. The cause of the disease remains uncertain, but abnormal bacterial colonisation of the upper small bowel is probably involved.

Repeated bacterial and viral infections are virtually the norm in tropical countries and these may lead to mucosal changes which fall short of those seen in tropical sprue. In tropical Africa for instance, jejunal biopsies from apparently healthy subjects will reveal reduced villous height and an increase in inflammatory cells when compared to normal Europeans.

These minor morphological abnormalities found in asymptomatic residents of tropical countries have been called 'tropical enteropathy' but from a local perspective could be considered 'normal'.

Giardiasis

Mild malabsorption sometimes occurs in giardiasis.

BACTERIAL INFECTIONS

Bacterial infections of the intestinal tract are a major cause of morbidity and mortality throughout the world. Bacterial contamination of water supplies and the consequent diarrhoeal diseases are the major cause of infant mortality in developing countries.

Salmonella

Food poisoning by *Salmonella* organisms is a common and increasing problem in the United Kingdom. Whereas the organisms *S. typhi* and *S. paratyphi* cause bacteraemic illnesses, *Salmonella* infection of food poisoning type (salmonellosis) is generally confined to the gastrointestinal tract.

In some patients this results in vomiting and profuse watery diarrhoea, usually with colicky, peri-umbilical pain suggesting predominantly gastric and small-intestinal involvement. However, in others the features relate to the large intestine, with frequent, small-volume bloody motions, tenesmus and tenderness over the sigmoid colon.

In the latter cases, sigmoidoscopic examination discloses a range of abnormalities varying from mucosal oedema and hyperaemia, to mucosal friability with slough formation and contact or spontaneous haemorrhage.

The histological appearances are similarly varied. Some biopsies show oedema, focal interstitial haemorrhage and a mild increase in neutrophil polymorphs; more severe cases show a marked increase in polymorphs, with occasional crypts distended by polymorphs and mucus in the lumen ('mucoid crypt abscesses'). The crypt pattern, however, remains normal.

Bacillary Dysentery

Bacillary dysentery is an acute infection of the large intestine characterised by painful diarrhoea, often with blood and mucus in the stools. *Shigella sonnei* is the commonest cause; it produces relatively minor lesions and seldom causes ulceration.

However, *Sh. flexneri* and *Sh. dysenteriae* can produce necrosis, sloughing and haemorrhage, giving rise to a picture closely resembling ulcerative colitis.

Cholera

Cholera is a form of enterotoxigenic diarrhoea resulting from infection with *Vibrio cholerae*. The cholera toxin binds to a specific receptor on epithelial cells which leads to increased adenylate cyclase activity; this in turn results in high cyclic-AMP levels in the intestinal mucosa.

The affected enterocytes secrete fluid and sodium ions, and the ensuing watery diarrhoea can be extreme, with overwhelming fluid loss and a rapidly fatal outcome. Because the effects are mediated by an exotoxin and there is no bacterial invasion of host tissues, the histological changes are remarkably slight; the mucosa shows mild oedema and goblet cell depletion.

Campylobacter colitis

It has been known since the early 1900s that *Campylobacter* organisms cause dysentery and abortion in cattle and domestic animals, but recognition of their role in human disease is relatively recent.

Contamination of milk and water supplies with *C. jejuni* and C. coli is now recognised as a frequent cause of severe gastroenteritis and colitis, particularly in debilitated and malnourished individuals. The histological changes seen in rectal biopsies are nonspecific, and are similar to those seen in other forms of infective colitis.

Neonatal Diarrhoea

In some of the diarrhoeas of neonates and infants, various strains of *Escherichia* coli can be isolated. Such infections are more common in bottle-fed infants, and epidemics may occur in children's wards. Certain defined enteropathogenic serotypes are involved, and these differ from non-pathogenic types in their powers of adhesion to colonocytes and their ability to invade the mucosa.

Diarrhoea may be severe and lead to dehydration and death. At autopsy, the smalland large-intestinal mucosa shows mucosal congestion and oedema with focal ulceration.

Staphylococcal Enterocolitis

The form of enterocolitis due to staphylococcal infection is rare, but potentially fatal. The injudicious use of broad spectrum antibiotics can so alter the normal ecology of the intestinal bacterial flora that the way is open for invasion by organisms that are either completely foreign to the bowel or normally present only in small numbers.

The most dangerous of these is *Staphylococcus aureus*, which, when present in large numbers, can liberate sufficient endotoxin to produce a severe enterocolitis. Staphylococcal enterocolitis is usually the result of cross-infection, and typically affects the hospital inpatient who has had contact with an antibiotic-resistant staphylococcus.

Patients present with sudden onset of severe diarrhoea, accompanied by shock and dehydration. A smear of the stools stained by Gram's method will reveal numerous staphylococci and often no other organisms. The course can be relatively mild and respond to treatment, but is often severe with a high mortality.

There is widespread superficial ulceration predominantly affecting the small intestine. Microscopically there is acute inflammation of the mucosa with intense congestion and widespread necrosis. The surface of the mucosa is covered in an exudate containing numerous staphylococci.

Gonococcal Proctitis

Gonococcal proctitis (inflammation of the rectum) is an acute exudative inflammatory condition which develops by genito-anal spread in females, and results from anal intercourse in males. The histological changes are non-specific, but the demonstration of numerous Gram-negative diplococci in the exudate leads to a presumptive diagnosis. As with other forms of infective colitis, definitive diagnosis depends on culture of the organisms.

Tuberculosis

Tuberculosis is almost entirely confined to the small intestine. In primary infection, an inconspicuous intestinal lesion is accompanied by gross enlargement of mesenteric nodes. This was the form of infection characteristic of bovine tuberculosis, a variety now virtually eliminated from the UK through the introduction of tubercle-free herds of cattle and the pasteurisation of milk.

Secondary tuberculous enteritis is a complication of extensive pulmonary tuberculosis which results from the swallowing of infected sputum. The typical alimentary lesion is ulceration of the ileum, the ulcer having formed by coalescence of caseous foci in the mucosa and submucosa.

As the ulcers enlarge they follow the path of the lymphatics around the circumference of the intestine and eventually encircle the bowel. Healing is by fibrosis, and strictures may result from subsequent cicatrisation. The inflammatory exudate on the serosal aspect of the bowel may organise and form fibrous adhesions.

Ileo-caecal tuberculosis is a distinctive form of infection consisting of an ulcerative, granulomatous and fibrotic process occurring around the ileo-caecal valve, with variable extension into both ileum and caecum. The thickening and stenosis present a picture which is frequently indistinguishable from Crohn's disease, although, in tuberculosis, distinct pale tubercles can be seen in the serosa.

Patients recognised as having active intra-abdominal tuberculosis are treated by chemotherapy, but surgery may be required for the treatment of complications or for diagnosis. The major complications are intestinal obstruction by strictures and adhesions, perforation of ulcers (although this is uncommon because of the marked fibrous reaction), and malabsorption resulting from widespread mucosal involvement or blockage to lymphatic drainage.

Actinomycosis

Actinomycosis usually presents as a localised chronic inflammatory process most commonly related to the appendix or caecal area. The organism, *Actinomyces israelii*, is a normal commensal of the mouth, and when swallowed may resist acid digestion and infect the bowel.

The infection is protracted and characterised by chronic suppuration and the formation of sinuses (openings on to the skin) and fistulae (abnormal connections with other hollow viscera). Histology reveals inflamed granulation tissue, and foci of suppuration containing the characteristic colonies of organisms visible to the naked eye as 'sulphur granules' in the watery pus.

Whipple's Disease

Whipple's disease is a rare bacterial infection usually involving the small intestine. The causative organism has been identified as *Tropheryma whippelii,* and this infection, in combination with alterations in immune responsiveness, produces multisystem involvement with joint pains, weight loss, pigmentation, lymphadenopathy and malabsorption.

The mucosa from affected individuals shows infiltration of the lamina propria by numerous granular macrophages containing abundant glycoprotein. On electron microscopy, the Whipple bacillus and granular material derived from the bacterial cell wall can be found in these macrophages. Patients usually respond to prolonged treatment with tetracyclines.

Antibiotic-associated Colitis

Many patients taking a broad-spectrum antibiotic develop diarrhoea. In most cases this is not severe and responds to withdrawal of the antibiotic. However, a small proportion develop a fulminant colitis with profuse diarrhoea and dehydration, leading in the more debilitated patients to death.

On biopsy, there is superficial loss of epithelial cells and a 'volcano-like' eruption of mucin, polymorphs and fibrin forming a pseudomembrane on the surface; this is *pseudomembranous colitis.* It has been established that this form of colitis results from the suppression of the normal bowel flora and the overgrowth of *Clostridium difficile,* which causes a widespread toxic mucosal injury.

VIRAL INFECTIONS

In many cases of presumed infective gastroenteritis or colitis no bacteria are isolated, and viral infection is probably responsible. Acute viral gastroenteritis is a major public health problem and as a cause of illness is second only to the common cold.

However, the positive identification of viruses in contaminated food is difficult. The minute infecting dose required and the insensitivity of the available tests mean that laboratory identification is not always possible.

The principal agents are parvoviruses and 'small round structured' viruses including calicivirus. The most prevalent examples of the latter are the co-called 'Norwalk-like' viruses, a common cause of non-bacterial acute gastroenteritis resulting from contamination of food.

In the small intestine these viruses produce degenerative changes in absorptive cells, minor shortening of villi and crypt hyperplasia, and inflammatory cell infiltration of the lamina propria. Rare viral infections of the large bowel include *cytomegalovirus* and *lymphogranuloma venereum.* Cytomegalovirus colitis has been described both as a primary infection and as a complication of ulcerative colitis.

Infection is readily recognised by the presence of large intranuclear inclusions in cells within the mucosa. Proctitis due to lymphogranuloma venereum is principally a disease of females. The infection begins in the genital tract and is thought to spread to the rectum via lymphatics. The deeper tissues are most heavily involved, and rectal stricture is the likely clinical problem.

While non-specific chronic inflammation is usually pronounced, granulomas are a characteristic histological finding and these may show central necrosis when the disease is active.

FUNGAL INFECTIONS

Fungal infections of the alimentary tract are rare. Histoplasmosis may produce a striking picture of multiple inflammatory polyps in the small and large intestines, and on microscopy the intracellular *Histoplasma capsulatum* can be identified.

Mucor and *Rhizopus* are phycomycetes with non-septate hyphae which are widely distributed in nature. Although these organisms are usually non-pathogenic, gastrointestinal involvement in debilitated or immunosuppressed patients is becoming increasingly common.

The oesophagus, stomach and colon are most frequently involved, and in addition to ulceration there is thrombosis of submucosal vessels with intravascular growth of the fungi. Despite this propensity for vascular infection, distant spread is surprisingly rare.

PARASITIC DISEASES

Giardiasis

Infection with the protozoan parasite *Giardia lamblia* produces a generally mild malabsorption state. It is a cause of 'traveller's diarrhoea', and of diarrhoea in childhood, in people with IgA deficiency, and following gastric surgery. It has been suggested that the malabsorption state is due to heavy infestation blocking access of nutrients to the surface epithelium; however, this is unlikely, as the numbers of organisms are rarely sufficient.

Amoebiasis

Amoebiasis is a disease of the large intestine resulting from infection with the protozoan *Entamoeba histolytica.* It is worldwide in its distribution, though more prevalent in the tropics than in temperate climates. Vegetative forms are present in the large bowel in infected individuals; these are passed in the stools, encyst into a more resistant form, and may survive in food and fluid and be reingested later.

The cysts pass unharmed through the stomach; on reaching the intestine the cyst wall is dissolved, liberating the active amoebae. These secrete a cytolytic enzyme which enables them to pass through the intestinal epithelium and, in disrupting the mucosa, release red blood cells which they then ingest.

Contamination of food and water is brought about by human carriers, infected rats, or flies. Carriers may either be individuals known to have suffered an attack in the past, or be apparently healthy people, some of whom may have symptomless lesions in the bowel.

The disease can lead to discrete oval ulcers, which are characteristically 'flask-shaped' in section, or to a diffuse colitis.

Balantidiasis

Balantidiasis is a rare form of colitis caused by the ciliated protozoan *Balantidium coli.* It may be acute or chronic. Most cases are found in tropical or sub-tropical countries among debilitated, malnourished individuals. Gross and microscopic findings in the tissues are much like those in amoebiasis.

The organism is readily detected by microscopy in both the lumen and the mucosa: it is so large as to dwarf the surrounding host cells.

Schistosomiasis

Infestation of the large intestine by *Schistosoma* occurs most commonly with S. *mansoni* and *S. japonicum* but can also be found with *S. haematobium.* Humans may become infected while wading or bathing in water contaminated with the second larval stage (cercaria) of the fluke.

The cercariae penetrate the skin, enter venules, and are carried through the circulation to the portal veins in the liver, where they

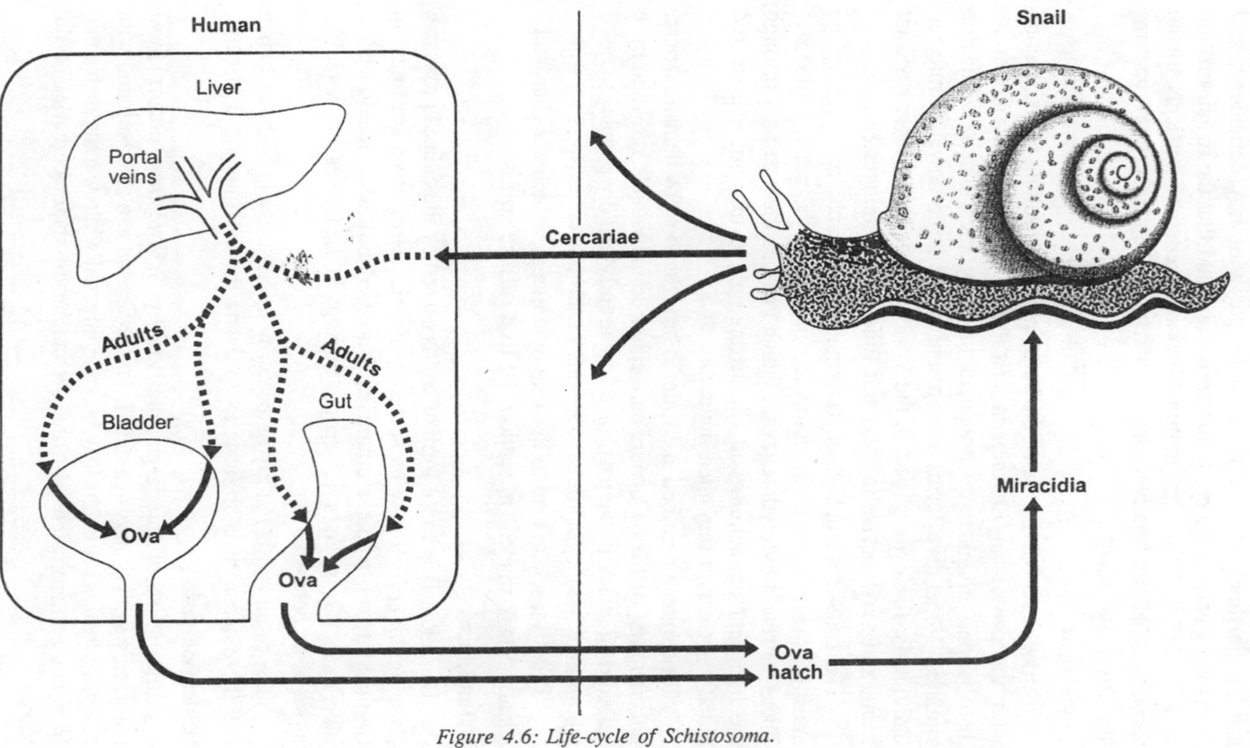

Figure 4.6: Life-cycle of Schistosoma.

mature to form the, adult flukes. The adults migrate to either the submucosal veins of the gut, or the venous plexus in the bladder, where they lay their eggs.

The ova pass through the intestinal wall into the faeces or through the bladder wall into the urine. The cycle is completed in water contaminated with egg-containing urine or faeces. The eggs hatch out, liberating miracidia (first larval stage) which infect a snail, the intermediate host within which the second larval stage of cercariae develop, later to emerge in their free-swimming form.

The pathological changes in schistosomiasis are essentially the result of an inflammatory reaction to the eggs in the tissues of the intestinal wall. Lesions are commonest in the rectum and left colon and are then nearly always due to *S. mansoni;* if the lesions are in the right side of the colon and the appendix then *S. haematobium* may be responsible.

Cryptosporidiosis

Cryptosporidiosis is caused by a coccidial organism of the genus *Cryptosporidium.* These are common parasites in a variety of reptiles, birds and mammals, but were not believed until recently to infect or, cause diarrhoea in humans. It is now appreciated that they are a frequent cause of diarrhoea in children, and they are increasingly encountered in AIDS sufferers.

Infection usually results from drinking contarninated water. A severe acute colitis with surface exudation and ulceration may be produced. Cryptosporidia cannot be recognised in stool specimens, so a biopsy or mucosal scraping is needed to make the diagnosis.

CHRONIC INFLAMMATORY DISORDERS

The term 'chronic (idiopathic) inflammatory bowel disease' embraces two conditions: Crohn's disease and ulcerative colitis. Crohn's disease most commonly affects the small bowel, but, when it involves the colon, the differential diagnosis from ulcerative colitis can be a problem. The main distinguishing features are listed in Table anywhere else in this chapter.

Crohn's Disease

- Chronic inflammatory disorder of unknown aetiology
- Small bowel most commonly affected, but any part of the gut may be involved
- Characterised by transmural inflammation with granulomas

- Thickened and fissured bowel leads to intestinal obstruction and fistulation

It was not until 1932 that Burrill Bernard Crohn and his colleagues established regional enteritis as a distinct entity. Previously, the condition had been confused with intestinal tuberculosis, then a common disease in Western countries.

The chronic inflammation and ulceration in Crohn's disease predominantly affect the terminal ileum, but all parts of the alimentary tract from the mouth to the anus may be involved and more than one site may be affected. 'Satellite' lesions can also occur in skin remote from the peri-anal area.

However, involvement outside the small and large intestine is uncommon. About two-thirds of patients have only small-intestinal involvement, about one-sixth only large-intestinal involvement, and in one-sixth of patients both small and large bowel are affected. Crohn's disease usually presents with either smallintestinal obstruction or abdominal pain which may mimic acute appendicitis; other presentations can relate to its complications.

Table 4.3: Chronic (idiopathic) inflammatory bowel disease: distinguishing features of Crohn's disease and ulcerative colitis.

Feature	*Crohn's disease*	*Ulcerative colitis*
Distribution	Commonly terminal but may occur anywhere from mouth to anus	Colon and rectum ileum,
Skip lesions	Common	Rare
Affected bowel	Thickened wall and narrowed lumen	Mucosal ulceration and dilated lumen
Extent of inflammation	Transmural	Mainly mucosal
Granulomas	Often present	Absent
Fissures and fistulae	Common	Rare
Cancer risk	Slightly raised	Significantly raised

The course of the disease is chronic, with exacerbations and remissions not always linked to therapy. Onset is usually in early adult life, with about half of all cases beginning between the ages of 20 and 30 years and 90% between 10 and 40 years. Slightly more males than females are affected.

Morphology

Intestinal involvement by Crohn's disease is frequently segmental; that is, lengths of diseased bowel are separated by apparently normal tissue. Such separated segments of disease are referred to as 'skip lesions'.

The earliest evidence of involvement visible with the naked eye is the presence of small discrete shallow ulcers with a haemorrhagic rim. These ulcers have been likened to the common aphthous ulcers of the mouth and are thus often described as 'aphthoid'; however, there is no aetiological link between the two conditions.

Later, the more characteristic longitudinal ulcers develop which progress into deep fissures. The process comes to involve the full thickness of the wall and subsequent fibrosis leads to considerable narrowing in the diseased segments. This produces a characteristic radiological sign where only a trickle of contrast medium passes through the affected segment (the 'string sign').

Where longitudinal fissures cross oedematous transverse mucosal folds, a 'cobblestone' appearance results. The mesenteric lymph nodes are enlarged by reactive hyperplasia and may also contain granulomas. Microscopy reflects the gross appearances. Inflammatory involvement is discontinuous: it is focal or patchy.

Collections of lymphocytes and plasma cells are found, mainly in the mucosa and submucosa but usually affecting all layers (transmural inflammation). The classical microscopic feature of Crohn's disease is the presence of granulomas. These consist of epithelioid macrophages and giant cells surrounded by a cuff of lymphocytes.

The giant cells are usually of the Langhans' type, but may resemble foreign body giant cells. The granulomas are distinguished from those of tuberculosis by the absence of central caseous necrosis. While they are virtually diagnostic of the condition, granulomas are found in only 60% of cases of Crohn's disease; in their absence the diagnosis must be based on a summation of the less specific histological changes.

In addition to the aggregated transmural pattern of inflammation, these changes include the finding of vertical fissure ulcers and marked submucosal oedema, lymphangiectasia, fibrosis and neuromatoid hyperplasia (enlargement and proliferation of submucosal nerves).

Complications

The complications of Crohn's disease are summarised in Table elsewhere in this chapter. Widespread involvement of the small intestine can lead to a malabsorption syndrome, but the commonest cause of malabsorption in Crohn's disease is iatrogenic. Repeated resections of small intestine can lead to a 'short bowel syndrome' in which adequate nutrition can be maintained only by intravenous or intraperitoneal alimentation.

Fistula formation is a frequent complication; deep penetration by ulcers produces fistulae between adherent loops of bowel and, particularly after surgical intervention, leads to entero-cutaneous fistulae.

Approximately 60% of patients have anal lesions. These include simple skin 'tags', fissures, and fistulae into the anal canal or peri-anal skin. Acute complications such as perforation, haemorrhage and toxic dilatation do occur but are much less frequently seen in Crohn's disease than in ulcerative colitis.

Table 4.4: Complications of Crohn's disease.

Complication	*Comment/example*
Malabsorption syndrome	Often iatrogenic ('short bowel syndrome')
Fistula formation	Causes malabsorption when loops of bowel are bypassed
Anal lesions	Skin tags, fissures, fistulae
Acute complications	Perforation (haemorrhage, toxic dilatation-rare)
Malignancy	Increased risk-adenocarcinoma
Systemic amyloidosis	Rare

In the long term, there is an increased risk of malignancy, particularly in the small intestine, but the overall risk is less than in patients with ulcerative colitis because more people with Crohn's disease have the affected areas resected.

Interestingly, there are reports of an increase in malignancy outside the digestive tract in patients with longstanding Crohn's disease. Systemic amyloidosis is a rare, long-term complication that results from excessive production of serum amyloid A protein.

Aetiology and Pathogenesis

The incidence of idiopathic inflammatory bowel disease (Crohn's disease and ulcerative colitis) shows considerable geographic variation. These diseases have a much higher incidence in northern Europe and the USA than in countries of southern Europe, Africa, South America and Asia, although increasing urbanisation and prosperity is leading to a higher incidence in parts of southern Europe and Japan. Even within Europe and the USA the incidence of Crohn's disease varies widely from around 4 up to 65 affected persons per 100 000 population.

There are, however, interesting ethnic differences: Jewish populations in Israel have a much higher incidence than Bedouin Arabs in the same locality. On the other hand, Ashkenazi Jews living in Israel have a lower incidence than those living in the United States.

Such data indicate a stronger role for environmental than genetic factors. On epidemiological grounds, both Crohn's disease and ulcerative colitis are thought to be diseases brought about by genetic susceptibility to as yet undetermined environmental agents.

In Crohn's disease it has been proposed that a genetic defect, possibly in a major recessive gene, prevents the patient from mounting a controlled and effective immune response to the causative agent. Support for a genetic role comes from a twin study in Sweden where 44% of monozygous twins had Crohn's disease compared with 4% of dizygous twins, and in 1996 a gene conferring susceptibility to Crohn's disease was identified on chromosome 16 in families with multiple affected members.

Other studies have sought a linkage to HLA types, and a higher prevalence of HLA-DR I and DQw5 has been found in Crohn's disease. However, genetic links may be obscured by the heterogeneity within Crohn's disease; clinically there are two main groups, the first comprising patients whose disease goes into lasting remission within 3 years of onset, the second comprising patients with disease persisting beyond 3 years. Clearer links might emerge if these clinical subgroups were to be considered separately.

The most clearly determined environmental influence is that of cigarette smoking. Smokers have an increased risk of developing Crohn's disease, whereas the opposite applies with ulcerative colitis. Nevertheless smoking is not incriminated as an *aetiological* agent in Crohn's disease. It has been suggested that, in genetically predisposed individuals, smoking habit will determine the type of inflammatory bowel disease that will develop.

The most likely candidates as aetiological factors are infective agents. In this regard, the defective gene on chromosome 16 has been identified as NOD2, a gene that regulates the handling of endotoxin, and thereby has a role in innate immunity to microbial infection.

Ever since a Scottish surgeon and farmer, Dalziel, recognised the similarity between a mycobacterial infection, Johne's disease, affecting his pedigree cattle and (presumed) Crohn's disease affecting some of his patients, there has been varying interest in the role of *Mycobacterium paratuberculosis* in Crohn's disease.

These mycobacteria can be identified in milk samples destined for human consumption, and slow-growing mycobacteria biochemically and genetically identical to *M. paratuberculosis* have been isolated on rare occasions from Crohn's disease patients.

However, similar organisms have also been isolated from patients with ulcerative colitis and other colonic disorders, and no specific serological response to *M. paratuberculosis* antigens can be found in Crohn's disease. Likewise, the results of tests for mycobacterial DNA by the polymerase chain reaction have also produced conflicting results, and trials of anti-mycobacterial treatment in Crohn's disease do not show any convincing improvement separate from the antiinflammatory effects of some of the regimens.

The case for *M. paratuberculosis* as an aetiological agent in Crohn's disease remains unproven. Another line of investigation has pursued the role of microvascular infarction in the aetiology of Crohn's disease. Occlusion of the microcirculation is demonstrable in affected segments of intestine and there may even be granulomatous involvement of intramural and mesenteric arteries.

Allied to this, there are the promoting effects of smoking and use of the contraceptive pill, which, together with the finding of other pro-coagulant changes in Crohn's disease patients, lend circumstantial support to microthrombosis as a cause. It has been proposed that the triggering event is measles virus infection (either wild type or vaccine strain), which in certain genetically predisposed individuals leads to chronic endothelial injury, intravascular accumulation of monocytes and platelet aggregation, followed by occlusion of the microcirculation.

This theory is even more controversial than the mycobacterial hypothesis. Public discussion of the aetiology of Crohn's disease invariably leads to inflamed opinions. The cause of inflammation, however, remains a mystery. Whatever the aetiology, there is evidence of persistent and inappropriate T-cell and macrophage activation in Crohn's disease, with increased production of pro-inflammatory cytokines, in particular interleukins 1, 2, 6 and 8, and interferon y and TNFa. Crohn's disease is characterised by sustained (chronic) inflammation accompanied by fibrosis.

The process of fibroblastic proliferation and collagen deposition may be mediated by transforming growth factor β which has certain anti-inflammatory actions, namely fibroblast recruitment, matrix synthesis and down-regulation of inflammatory cells. But it is likely that many other mediators including platelet-derived growth factor and basic fibroblast growth factor released from activated mast cells, will be implicated.

Ulcerative Colitis

- Chronic relapsing inflammatory disorder, but may have an acute fulminating presentation R Aetiology is unknown
- Affects only colon and rectum, sometimes confined to the latter
- Diffuse superficial inflammation
- Acute complications include toxic dilatation, perforation, haemorrhage and dehydration; the chronic complications are anaemia, liver disease and malignant change

In temperate climates ulcerative colitis is the commonest cause of diarrhoea associated with the passage of blood, mucus and pus. It is a non-specific inflammatory disorder of the large intestine, usually commencing in the rectum and extending proximally to a varying extent.

Unlike Crohn's disease, ulcerative colitis is confined to the large intestine. Involvement of the terminal ileum in a so-called 'backwash ileitis' is occasionally seen, but this is thought to represent chronic inflammation provoked by incompetence of the ileo-caecal valve, rather than an actual part of the disease.

Aetiology

The geographic variation in the incidence of inflammatory bowel diseases has already been remarked upon. In northern Europe and the USA the incidence of ulcerative colitis varies between 12 and 140 per 100 000 population, but lower rates occur in underdeveloped countries with warmer climates.

Part of the wide variation found in the northern, developed countries is attributable to a lack of uniformity in the inclusion of proctitis, some believing this to be ulcerative colitis confined to the rectum while others argue that it is a different disease entity. In low-incidence countries there may be diagnostic confusion with chronic infective colitis.

The consensus of opinion is in favour of a strong genetic predisposition towards ulcerative colitis; these genetic factors may operate at both the level of the host response and in the colonic mucosa. Differences in host response will be reflected in links to particular HLA types, cytokine genes and immunoglobulin marker genes. In ulcerative colitis there is an association with HLA-DR2 and with certain alleles of cytokine genes, and preferential production of IgGl compared with IgG2, the latter being increased in Crohn's disease. At the mucosal level, changes in permeability and in mucin glycoprotein composition have been found in ulcerative colitis but increased permeability may well be a consequence rather than a cause of the disease.

Other evidence of a role for genetic factors comes from increased aggregations in families, a higher concordance rate in monozygotic twins, an increased prevalence in certain ethnic groups and association with diseases that have a known genetic predisposition such as ankylosing spondylitis, psoriasis and primary sclerosing cholangitis.

There is growing evidence to indicate that ulcerative colitis is a consequence of altered autoimmune reactivity but mucosal injury could also result from inappropriate T-cell activation and indirect damage brought about by cytokines, proteases and reactive oxygen metabolites from macrophages and neutrophils. This latter mechanism of damage to the colonic epithelium has been termed 'innocent bystander' injury.

Evidence in favour of autoimmunity is the presence of self-reactive T-lymphocytes, auto-antibodies directed against colonic epithelial cells and endothelial cells, and anti-neutrophil cytoplasmic auto-antibodies (ANCA). However, these antibodies and self-reactive lymphocytes are not considered to be responsible for the tissue damage, and ulcerative colitis should not be thought of as an autoimmune disease in which mucosal injury is a direct consequence of an immunological reaction to self-antigens. Thus some of these autoimmune aspects are considered to be epiphenomena.

Inappropriate and persistent T-cell activation may lie at the centre of both ulcerative colitis and Crohn's disease. Under normal circumstances the mucosal immune system is tolerant of luminal foreign antigens, and this tolerance is dependent upon the relationship between colonic epithelium and suppressor T-cells.

Changes in epithelial cell antigen presentation consequent upon the acquired expression of class II (HLA-DR) major histocompatibility molecules activate helper T-lymphocytes and initiate a cascade of cytokine-mediated effects that induce and sustain a mucosal immune reaction. The nature of the antigen or putative triggering factors is not known, but microbial antigens from the gut flora are likely candidates. This could account for the well-known triggering of ulcerative colitis by enteric infections.

Interactions between the immune system and smoking, and the effects of stress and neuropeptide release on immune reactivity and mucosal inflammation, are capable of modulating the response to such triggering factors.

Whatever the initiating events it seems clear that the mucosal injury in ulcerative colitis is largely a consequence of polymorph accumulation in the mucosa and release of destructive proteases, nitric oxide and superoxide radicals. Polymorph emigration from mucosal vessels follows upregulation of endothelial adhesion receptors, including E-selectin, ICAM-1 and VCAM, by pro-inflammatory cytokines.

Subsequent neutrophil production of leukotriene B4 and interleukin 8 attracts more polymorphs into the inflamed mucosa and amplifies their accumulation. Increased permeability and absorption of bacterial antigens may give rise to immune complex phenomena and some of the extra-intestinal complications.

Morphology

Ulcerative colitis is continuous in its distribution. Thus the disease, which is typically maximal in the rectum, extends proximally and continuously to involve the colon. Some cases are confined to the rectum (proctitis), others to the rectum and sigmoid (distal colitis), while others may exhibit a total colitis extending into the caecum.

The disease does not involve the mucosa of the anal transitional zone or the anal canal, but a small proportion of patients do have anal tags and fissures. The ulcers are irregular in outline and orientation and become confluent; they extend horizontally to undermine adjacent, less involved, mucosa which remains as discrete islands.

Usually the ulceration remains superficial, involving mucosa and submucosa, but in severe cases there is extension into the main muscle coats and perforation is likely. There is intense hyperaemia of the intact mucosa and haemorrhage from the ulcers.

Microscopically, there is diffuse infiltration of the mucosa by mixed acute and chronic inflammatory cells. Polymorphs are seen in the interstitium, but are particularly evident as aggregates within distended crypts (crypt abscesses).

There are widespread degenerative changes in surface and crypt lining epithelium, with marked depletion of their mucin content. Crypts undergo destruction during the acute phase, and when regeneration occurs they are frequently distorted by branching or dilatation. This disturbance of the crypt pattern is a useful diagnostic pointer in quiescent cases, when the inflammatory features may have totally subsided.

Thus, in longstanding disease, rectal biopsy will reveal crypt atrophy and distortion, and there may be metaplastic features such as the acquisition of Paneth cells as a defence against the altered bowel flora. Ulcerative colitis is a recognised premalignant condition, and a few cases will reveal epithelial dysplasia.

Table 4.5: Complications of ulcerative colitis.

Complication	Comment/example
Blood loss	May be: acute (haemorrhage) chronic, leading to anaemia
Electrolyte disturbances	Due to severe diarrhoea in acute phase
Toxic dilatation	May develop insidiously
Colorectal cancer	Overall incidence 2%
Skin involvement	Pigmentation, erythema nodosum, pyoderma gangrenosum
Liver involvement	Fatty change, chronic pericholangitis, sclerosing cholangitis, cirrhosis, hepatitis
Eye involvement	Iritis, uveitis, episcleritis
Joint involvement	Ankylosing spondylitis, arthritis

Malignancy

The overall incidence of colorectal cancer in ulcerative colitis is low, around 2%, but this rises to about 10% in patients who have had the disease for 25 years. The increased risk over that for the general population warrants colonoscopic surveillance of longstanding cases. The clinical factors apparently associated with a higher cancer risk are:

- onset of the disease in childhood
- clinically severe first attack
- total involvement of the colon
- continuous rather than intermittent symptoms.

In practice, patients with extensive colitis of longer than 8-10 years duration are usually admitted into surveillance programmes and undergo regular (usually annual) colonoscopy and multiple biopsy. If high-grade (severe) dysplasia is seen, then the development of carcinoma is considered imminent and total resection is warranted.

Local complications

Haemorrhage is occasionally massive and life-threatening, but more often occurs as chronic blood loss leading to irondeficiency anaemia. In the acute phase, severe diarrhoea with a markedly increased loss of water and mucus can lead to serious electrolyte disturbances. A further hazard of the acute phase is so-called toxic dilatation.

Toxic dilatation occurs when ulceration affects large areas of the muscle coats and their viability and contractile strength is impaired. The resultant adynamic segment-commonly the transverse colon-becomes progressively distended, and the consequent thinning of the wall predisposes to perforation.

Since there are few adhesions to localise its spread, perforation into the peritoneal cavity results in generalised faecal peritonitis and a fatal outcome is likely. Frequent radiographs should be taken in the seriously ill patient, as toxic dilatation may develop insidiously.

Systemic complications

Patients with ulcerative colitis are at risk of developing systemic problems. These include:

- skin-erythema nodosum (subcutaneous inflammation) and *pyoderma gangrenosum* (sterile dermal abscesses)
- liver *pericholangitis* (inflammation around bile ducts), *sclerosing cholangitis* (fibrous constriction and obliteration of bile ducts), *cholangiocarcinoma,* and *chronic active hepatitis*
- eyes-iritis, *uveitis* and *episcleritis*
- joints-increased incidence of ankylosing *spondylitis.*

VASCULAR DISORDERS

Ischaemic injury to the intestine occurs either as a consequence of obstruction to the mesenteric arterial supply *(occlusive ischaemia)* or in circumstances where, despite patency of the vessels, the blood supply falls to a level at which the nutrition of mucosa cannot be maintained *(nonocclusive ischaemia).*

Thus occlusive ischaemia results from arterial thrombosis (usually on the basis of atherosclerosis) or thrombo-embolism originating from atrial or ventricular mural thrombosis; non-occlusive ischaemia is a consequence of systemic hypotension, vasoconstriction, viscosity disturbances, arterial narrowing, and of certain drugs, such as digitalis and cocaine.

Pathogenesis

Total vascular occlusion results in segmental anoxic or hypoxic injury, the extent of which depends on the adequacy of the collateral supply; cell death appears to ensue from a lethal ingress of calcium ions through the damaged plasma membrane.

However, much of the mucosal injury in nonocclusive ischaemia develops after the period of hypoperfusion, i.e. when normal perfusion and oxygenation have been restored. This is an example of a 'reperfusion injury' of the kind seen after myocardial and cerebral ischaemia and following iatrogenic ischaemia in organ transplantation.

Reperfusion injuries are thought to be mediated by free radical formation. These oxygen-derived free radicals are responsible for the membrane injuries which bring about mucosal disintegration in the reperfusion phase.

Acute Ischaemia

Acute ischaemia results in varying degrees of infarction of the bowel wall. Such infarcts can be classified, according to the depth of involvement, as mucosal, mural or transmural.

Mucosal infarction

Mucosal infarction is usually considered transient or reversible because the lesion can be followed by complete regeneration. However, mucosal damage leads to release of proteolytic enzymes and increased permeability to toxic substances; this can bring about further cardiovascular deterioration and gradual progression of the intestinal lesion to transmural infarction.

Mural infarction

Mural infarction reaches into the submucosa or into, but not through, the muscularis propria. The mucosa is variably ulcerated and, where intact, is haemorrhagic and elevated by marked submucosal oedema. The deeper extent of necrosis with involvement of connective tissues necessitates healing by granulation tissue formation and a more prolonged process of repair. If the patient recovers, this is likely to lead to fibrous stricture formation.

Transmural infarction

Transmural infarction of the intestine extends through the muscularis propria and is synonymous with gangrene. The bowel becomes flaccid and dilates, and the serosal aspect is deeply congested and coated in a thin layer of fibrin. The wall becomes friable and liable to perforation. Segmental infarction results either from occlusion of distal mesenteric vessels which is sufficiently widespread to impair the collateral supply, or by mechanical obstruction of the supply to a loop of intestine.

This type of involvement is amenable to surgical treatment, but many patients already have peritonitis, endotoxaemia and severe circulatory problems at the time of diagnosis, so operative results remain poor. Massive infarction, most commonly seen in the small intestine following complete occlusion of the superior mesenteric artery, has a hopeless prognosis.

Chronic Ischaemia

Chronic ischaemia leads to two main problems:

- fibrous stricture formation following segmental mural infarction
- chronic mesenteric insufficiency.

Strictures are encountered most often in the large intestine, particularly in the 'watershed' area around the splenic flexure of the colon. The patients generally present with the consequences of large bowel obstruction.

Chronic mesenteric insufficiency is used to describe a condition in which there is insufficient blood flow to the small intestine to satisfy the demands of increased motility, secretion and absorption that develop after meals. The insufficiency is usually manifest as pain (so-called *mesenteric angina),* but patients may also have diarrhoea and malabsorption.

Necrotising Enterocolitis

Necrotising enterocolitis is an uncommon condition which arises through a combination of ischaemia and infection. The disease manifests as severe abdominal pain, distension and diarrhoea. Paralytic ileus develops and progresses to intestinal infarction, sepsis and shock.

The appearances are typically those of gas gangrene, with either segmental or total involvement of the small and large intestines by coagulative necrosis and intramural gas bubble formation.

Most cases of necrotising enterocolitis are seen in neonates, where the interplay of intestinal ischaemia, bacterial colonisation and excess protein substrate in the intestinal lumen in bottle-fed babies is the main cause. In adults the disease is related to *Clostridium perfringens* infection.

Vascular Anomalies

Vascular anomalies in the gut are uncommon but enter into the differential diagnosis of gastrointestinal haemorrhage. Their classification is confused; some are congenital malformations which form part of recognised syndromes, while other, possibly identical, lesions are claimed to be acquired.

Congenital types include arteriovenous malformations and telangiectasias; acquired forms are usually termed angiodysplasias. *Angiodysplasia* of the colon is an occasional cause of blood loss from the large bowel.

This condition is more common in the elderly and can be diagnosed by mesenteric angiography.

DISORDERS RESULTING FROM ABNORMAL GUT MOTILITY

Diverticular Disease

Diverticula are herniations of mucosa into the intestinal wall. The herniations are of the pulsion type and form at sites of potential weakness, notably where lymphoid aggregates breach the muscularis mucosae. They extend through the muscularis propria at the point of entry or exit of blood vessels and bulge into the subserosa.

Diverticula can be found anywhere in the intestinal tract, but the colon, and particularly the sigmoid, is by far the commonest site. Most diverticula occur between the mesenteric and anti-mesenteric longitudinal muscle bands-the taenia coli.

The affected segment of colon shows thickening of the muscularis propria, and prominence of the mucosal folds so that they almost occlude the lumen. The disease is generally acknowledged to result from a deficiency of fibre in the diet.

Sigmoid motility is peculiarly sensitive to the bulk of the colonic contents and when this is low, due to a low-fibre diet, abnormally high intra-luminal pressures are generated which push the mucosa into the wall.

Complications

Diverticular disease presents as abdominal pain and altered bowel habit, but it is also prone to develop some serious complications, the most common being *diverticulitis.*

The faecal contents can lead to abrasion of the herniated mucosa, or a microscopic perforation in the apex of a diverticulum can occur, which allows infection by faecal organisms and the development of a suppurative diverticulitis.

This in turn can cause a peri-colic abscess and *a fistula* may form into the bladder, vagina or small intestine; more seriously, a peri-diverticular abscess may perforate and produce a generalised faecal peritonitis.

Diverticula can be the source of *haemorrhage* from the colon. This usually arises from areas of granulation tissue in an inflamed diverticulum, but the precise source is sometimes difficult to identify.

Intussusception

An intussusception is an invagination of one segment of bowel into another, thus causing intestinal obstruction. A lesion in the wall of the bowel disturbs normal peristaltic contractions, forcing the lesion and a segment of proximal bowel into a distal segment.

Several lesions can act as the apex of an intussusception, including polyps, ingested foreign bodies, a Meckel's diverticulum, an area of intramural haemorrhage, and lymphoid hyperplasia. Such hyperplasia close to the ileo-caecal valve is the cause of the ileo-colic intussusception, the most common form of this disorder.

Volvulus and Strangulation

Intestinal obstruction can result from a twist in the bowel which occludes its lumen (volvulus) or when a segment of bowel becomes trapped in a defect in either the posterior peritoneum or mesentery (internal herniation), or herniates into an inguinal or para-umbilical peritoneal sac.

The neck of the sac may then constrict the bowel and compromise its blood supply *(strangulation)*. Volvulus occurs around a 'fulcrum' such as a Meckel's diverticulum or a congenital band of fibrous tissue, or around an abnormally long mesentery. About two-thirds of cases affect the small intestine; most of the remaining one-third affect the sigmoid colon.

TUMOURS

Paradoxically, the small intestine, with its vast surface area and a higher cell turnover rate than any other tissue in the body, is an uncommon site for primary neoplasms. For example, benign epithelial neoplasms (adenomas) and adenocarcinomas are distinctly rare in the small intestine, yet in the large bowel represent a very common form of neoplasia.

The low incidence of carcinoma means that other neoplasms, such as endocrine cell tumours and lymphomas, assume more importance in the small intestine where they are relatively more common than in the large bowel.

Polyps

A polyp is simply a protuberant growth and there is thus a wide variety of histological types. These can be broadly divided into *epithelial* and *mesenchymal* polyps (of which the latter are distinctly uncommon), and into benign and malignant categories.

Even epithelial polyps are rare in the small intestine and some, such as metaplastic polyps, are confined to the large bowel. Thus, the following account is confined to large-intestinal polyps.

Benign Epithelial Polyps

Benign epithelial polyps fall into four categories: adenomas, and inflammatory, hamartomatous and metaplastic polyps.

Table 4.6: Polyps of the large intestine.

Type of polyp	*Benign*	*Malignant*
Epithelial	Neoplastic • adenoma Inflammatory (e.g. in inflammatory bowel disease) Hamartomatous • juvenile polyp • Peutz-Jeghers syndrome or Metaplastic (or hyperplastic)	Polypoid adenocarcinomas Carcinoid polyps
Mesenchymal	Lipoma Lymphangioma Haemangiomas Leiomyoma	Sarcomas Lymphomatous polyps Fibromas

Adenomas

The most important of the epithelial polyps are the neoplastic polyps; these, being derived from a secretory epithelium, are termed adenomas. Adenomas are very common; there is an increase in incidence with age so that at 60 years they are found in about 20% of the population. There are two main histological types-tubular (75%) and villous (10%); the remaining 15% are intermediate in pattern and are designated *tubulo-villous*. Tubular adenomas are generally small (usually less than 10 mm in diameter), and macroscopically resemble a raspberry.

Most have a stalk (pedunculated) and a minority have a broad base (sessile). Microscopically, they consist of numerous cross-sectioned crypt profiles lined by mucussecreting epithelium showing varying degrees of dysplasia. Villous adenomas are usually sessile; they are often over 20 mm in diameter and some extend over a wide area as a thick, carpet-like growth.

Microscopically, they consist of elongated villi in a papillary growth pattern; the villi are again lined by columnar epithelium showing dysplasia. Large adenomas may secrete copious electrolyte-rich mucus, resulting in hypokalaemia and acute renal failure, but their real importance lies in their propensity for malignant change. However, not all adenomas are polypoid. Flat adenomas, defined as adenomas whose height is less than twice the thickness of the adjacent normal mucosa, are increasingly recognized and may serve as an alternative source of colorectal carcinomas.

Inflammatory polyps

These usually arise in the context of inflammatory bowel disease, and represent excessive reparative and regenerative tissue formed in the aftermath of mucosal ulceration. In most cases there is a preponderance of granulation or mature fibrovascular tissue, so their categorisation as epithelial is somewhat debatable.

Hamartomatous polyps

These rare polyps may be solitary, like the majority of socalled 'juvenile' polyps, or be multiple and occur throughout the gastrointestinal tract, as in *Peutz Jeghers syndrome.*

Metaplastic (or hyperplastic) polyps

These polyps are of unknown histogenesis, but the surface cells are hypermature compared to normal epithelium. They are common lesions, being found with increasing age, and are most frequently situated in the rectum. Microscopically they are sessile with elongated crypts, but the majority show no dysplasia.

Their characteristic feature is the 'serrated' appearance of the cells lining the upper crypt and at the surface. In contrast to adenomas, these polyps have a low malignant potential.

Malignant Epithelial Polyps

Examples of malignant epithelial polyps are polypoid carcinomas and carcinoid polyps arising from entero-endocrine cells. Some adenocarcinomas develop as protuberant growths and appear endoscopically as polyps, hence the term 'polypoid carcinoma'.

The vast majority of adenocarcinomas, however, arise within pre-existing adenomas and these constitute the bulk of 'malignant polyps'. A very small minority of polyps are neoplasms derived from enteroendocrine cells; such carcinoid polyps have a low malignant potential and only give rise to metastases late in their course. Thus, complete local removal is usually curative.

Benign Mesenchymal Polyps

Mesenchymal polyps are uncommon. The benign forms are lipomas, haemangiomas, lymphangiomas and fibromas. Smooth muscle and stromal tumours are less likely to present as polyps, and are of uncertain malignant potential.

Malignant Mesenchymal Polyps

Malignant varieties include the sarcomas equivalent to the benign tumours, and lymphomatous polyps.

The Adenoma-carcinoma Sequence

Adenomas are probably the precursors of most, if not all, colorectal cancers. Evidence in favour of a link comes from a number of sources, but one of the strongest associations is illustrated by the condition of *familial adenomatous polyposis* (FAP).

FAP is a rare autosomal disease carried by either parent and transmitted as a Mendelian dominant. Both sexes are equally affected. Adenomas, mainly in the large intestine but also in the small, develop during the second and third decades and subsequently undergo malignant change, with an almost inevitable progression to cancer by the age of 35.

The gene responsible for FAP is on the long arm of chromosome 5; interestingly, a somatic mutation has been identified on chromosome 5 in cases of sporadic (non-inherited) colorectal cancer.

Epidemiological support comes from the marked geographic variation in the prevalence of adenomas, and a strong correlation with the incidence of colorectal carcinoma in the same countries.

Adenomas and carcinomas are frequently found together in a resected segment of bowel. Such patients have an increased risk of developing a second cancer, compared with patients having carcinoma alone. Histologically, the finding of residual adenomatous tissue in many cancers, and the observation of early invasive malignancy developing in adenomas, is further supportive evidence of a link.

Examination of adenomas showing early malignancy has demonstrated an association with increasing size, villous growth pattern and more severe degrees of dysplasia, although flat adenomas more frequently show high-grade dysplasia in spite of their small size.

Molecular pathology of the adenoma-carcinoma sequence

In no other tumour system are the genetic events underlying the development of carcinoma as clearly understood as they are in colorectal cancer. In general, these genetic defects are:

- activation of oncogenes
- loss or mutations of tumour suppressor genes

- defective genes of the *DNA* repair pathway leading to genomic instability.

The oncogenes most frequently altered in colorectal cancer are *c-Ki-ras* and *c-myc*. Point mutations in *Ki-ras* mean that the protein can no longer hydrolyse bound *GTP* to *GDP* Persistence of *GTP-ras,* the active form of the protein, results in continual signalling of cell division.

Over-expression of *c-myc* is a feature of most colorectal cancers; *c-myc* encodes a nuclear phosphoprotein which is required for *DNA* synthesis, and increased expression may well be followed by increased cellular proliferation.

Tumour suppressor genes appear to be very important in colorectal carcinoma. *FAP* results from point mutations in a tumour suppressor gene, *APC,* localised on chromosome 5q, and subsequent deletion of the accompanying normal allele results in loss of tumour suppressor function that leads to colorectal cancer.

Mutations and deletions of the APC gene, and in other tumour suppressor genes, have also been identified, in sporadic (i.e. non-hereditary) colorectal cancer. Other genes implicated are MCC (mutated in colorectal cancer), DCC (deleted in colorectal cancer), *c-yes, bcl-2* and *p53* genes. *bcl-2* is a key inhibitor of apoptosis; over-expression renders the cell more resistant to degrees of damage which would normally result in apoptosis and elimination of the cell.

As a consequence 'faulty' cells may remain in the stem cell pool. The *p53* gene product is a nuclear protein which can apply a checkpoint in the G, phase of the cell cycle and allow time for successful DNA repair or divert the cell towards apoptosis and elimination. While mutations of tumour suppressor genes have been readily identifiable, they are unlikely to be the main mechanism leading to loss of function.

Much more likely is that age-related and cancer-specific hypermethylation of the promoter regions of critically important suppressor genes is the key event. By this mechanism, acquired *epigenetic* events may be more relevant to colorectal cancer than purely genetic lesions.

Mutation or loss of function of the *p53* gene is not the only way in which DNA repair can be compromised. Highly conserved genes have been discovered which recognise mismatched nucleotides in complementary DNA strands and orchestrate the enzymes that effect repairs.

Defects in these genes and the ensuing replication errors are manifest as microsatellite instability. Alterations in two mismatch repair genes, hMLH1 and hMSH2, have been identified in most kindreds with hereditary non-polyposis colorectal cancer. Similar alterations in these and other 'housekeeper' genes are found in sporadic cancers with around 15% of cases showing high microsatellite instability. Finally, deletion of the *nm23* gene may be related to an increased metastatic potential.

The sequence of these genetic events in causing colorectal cancer is not as critical as the accumulation of changes, but the different prevalences of mutations and deletions between premalignant lesions and invasive carcinoma does suggest that there is a preferred order.

Colorectal Cancer

- Common malignancy in developed countries
- All are adenocarcinomas
- Increased risk in patients with adenomatous polyps and longstanding ulcerative colitis
- Dukes' staging, based on local extent and metastatic status, is the best guide to prognosis

Cancer of the colon and rectum is one of the commonest forms of malignancy in developed countries. For example, it accounts for about 10% of all cancer registrations in the United Kingdom, where the death rate is second only to that of lung cancer, with gastric cancer a close third. The incidence appears to be rising.

Aetiology

Apart from the role played by inherited genetic factors, and a few cases developing in the unstable mucosa of ulcerative colitis, the most important factor in the aetiology of colorectal cancer appears to be environmental. Epidemiological evidence indicates that this is dietary.

Diet affects the bacterial flora of the large bowel, the bowel transit time, and the amount of cellulose, amino acids and bile acids in the bowel contents. It is known that certain kinds of bacteria, the nuclear dehydrogenating clostridia (NDC), can act on bile acids to produce carcinogens. Similarly, bacterial transformation of amino acids may result in carcinogen (or co-carcinogen) production.

On the other hand, a high content of fermentable cellulose leads to high levels of volatile fatty acids which appear to be 'protective' in that they provide nutrition and aid maturation of the epithelial cells. Thus, the type of diet that has been linked to colorectal cancer is a high-fat, high-protein, low-fibre diet.

High fat leads to an increase in bile salt production and higher load of faecal bile acids to react with NDC; high protein favours the transformation of amino acids by bacteria; low fibre reduces volatile fatty acids and prolongs intestinal transit so that there is more time for bacterial action on the contents and more prolonged contact between any carcinogen generated and the mucosa. These factors, more than anything else, account for the high incidence of colorectal cancer in developed countries.

Clinicopathological features

Approximately 50% of cancers occur in the rectum, where they are equally divided between the upper, middle and lower thirds; about 30% occur in the sigmoid colon and the rest are equally distributed in the ascending, transverse and descending colon. This anatomical distribution is of practical importance, as about 50% of large bowel cancers can be reached with the examining finger and 80% with the sigmoidoscope.

In the rectum, the majority of cancers are of the ulcerating type and usually present with rectal bleeding. The stenosing type is more common in the descending colon and sigmoid, where it usually produces obstruction relatively early because of the narrowing of the lumen and the solid consistency of the faeces at this site.

Polypoid and larger fungating cancers are more common in the right colon, where they tend to give rise to recurrent occult bleeding; the patient may present late with iron-deficiency anaemia or change in bowel habit.

Microscopically the cancers are adenocarcinomas, showing varying degrees of mucin production and differentiation. To a limited extent, the degree of differentiation (grade) determines the outlook for the patient after surgery, but a much more valuable guide to prognosis is the completeness of excision and the extent of spread.

If microscopic examination of the resection margins (especially the circumferential margin) establishes that all the tumour has been removed and the operation has been potentially curative, then the extent of spread through the bowel wall and the presence of lymph node metastases are the major prognostic determinants.

The extent of spread is given by the Dukes' stage. Unfortunately, only about 70% of patients with colorectal cancer undergo a potentially curative operation; in about 15-25% of patients only a palliative operation is possible because they have widespread peritoneal deposits or liver secondaries, and the remainder are totally inoperable.

However, with technical advances, patients formerly considered inoperable are undergoing resection of liver metastases, so that the number of operations for 'cure' will increase.

APUD Cell Tumours

The endocrine cells of the gut are part of a diffuse system present throughout many tissues which utilises amino acids, or derivatives of amino acids, as chemical messengers mediating paracrine and neurocrine effects. They are known by the acronym APUD (amine precursor uptake and decarboxylation) cells and may be divided into two broad categories.

- *Enterochromaffin cells*. These are cells found in small groups at the bases of the intestinal crypts which are named for their staining after chromate fixation. They secrete 5-hydroxytryptamine (5-HT) and kallikrein, and give rise to the classical carcinoid tumours.
- *Entero-endocrine cells*. More dispersed single cells are found scattered in the crypt and villous epithelium, and in the bowel wall. They are non-chromaffin, and secrete a multiplicity of gut regulatory peptides.

  These are generally referred to as entero-endocrine cells. Although the cells are capable of producing more than one peptide, when neoplasms develop they are identified by their major product and are therefore designated as gastrinoma, somatostatinoma, etc.

  Most of these neoplasms, which are rare, arise in the pancreas rather than in the intestine.

The great majority of APUD cell tumours of the gastrointestinal tract are carcinoid tumours ('argentaffinomas') of mid-gut origin and are found in the appendix and ileum. Those in the appendix are generally small (less than 20 mm diameter), situated at or near the tip, and are discovered incidentally in specimens removed for abdominal pain.

Such tumours can be considered benign, and no further treatment is necessary. However, larger tumours in the appendix and carcinoids of the ileum exhibit a tendency to spread to regional lymph nodes and the liver, and must be considered as tumours of low-grade malignancy.

Mid-gut carcinoids produce varying amounts of 5-HT, which exerts local effects but is inactivated in the liver by monoamine oxidases to form 5-hydroxyindole acetic acid (5-HIAA), and this is excreted in the urine. The local effects comprise diarrhoea and borborygmi (excessive bowel sounds) because 5-HT stimulates intestinal contractility.

Once metastases have formed in the liver, the products (5-HT and kinins) are released into the hepatic veins and can affect the right side of the heart and the lungs before oxidation takes place in the pulmonary vasculature; this results in the *carcinoid syndrome*. The patient develops flushing of the face, cyanosis, and stenosis or incompetence of the pulmonary and tricuspid valves.

The heart shows smooth muscle proliferation within the endocardium; this is thought to result from bradykinin stimulation of mesenchymal cells which undergo differentiation to muscle cells. The development of carcinoid tumours and their effects are summarised in Figure elsewhere in this chapter.

Lymphomas

Lymphomas are the commonest form of malignancy in the small intestine but are rare in the large bowel. Mention has already been made of the development of malignant lymphoma in coeliac disease, but this accounts for only a small proportion of the total; the majority of cases in developed countries have no predisposing cause.

In the Middle East and South Africa, however, lymphoma of the small intestine frequently follows alpha heavy chain disease, a condition in which there is an initially benign proliferation of plasma cells secreting incomplete immunoglobulins.

The non-coeliac-associated lymphomas are most commonly of B-cell lineage and of centrocytic or centroblastic types. They appear as plaques or polypoid masses and may be multiple, and give rise to abdominal pain, obstruction (either directly or by intussusception), and anaemia through intestinal blood loss.

APPENDIX

The appendix can be the site for carcinoid tumours, adenocarcinomas and lymphomas, but these are rare compared with the frequency of non-specific suppurative inflammation.

Appendicitis

- Common cause of the 'acute abdomen'
- Inflammation often precipitated by obstruction due to faecolith, lymphoid hyperplasia or tumour
- Complications include peritonitis, portal pyaemia and hepatic abscesses

Aetiology

Several factors are claimed to predispose to acute inflammation of the appendix, including faecoliths (hard pellets of faeces arising from dehydration and compaction) and food residues, lymphoid hyperplasia (as occurs in childhood and with some viral infections), diverticulosis of the appendix, and the presence of a carcinoid tumour. Specific inflammations can also affect the appendix, and very occasional cases are due to *Yersinia pseudo tuberculosis,* typhoid, tuberculosis and actinomycosis. The appendix is also involved by ulcerative colitis and Crohn's disease.

Pathogenesis

Acute inflammation commences in the mucosa following a breach in the epithelium which permits infection by bowel flora. Infection leads to mucosal ulceration and a polymorph response, with exudation of cells and fibrin into the lumen.

Further spread involves all the layers of the appendix and eventually causes a peritonitis over the serosal aspect. The build-up of fluid exudate within the wall increases tissue pressure and this, together with toxic damage to blood vessels and thrombosis, can lead to superimposed ischaemia. In this way the distal part of the appendix can become gangrenous and perforate.

Complications

Complications of acute appendicitis include those arising as a result of perforation, such as generalised peritonitis, abscess and fistula formation, and the consequences of blood spread, suppurative pyelophlebitis (inflammation and thrombosis of the portal vein), liver abscess and septicaemia.

The inflammation may become chronic, or obstruction to the neck of the appendix may lead to mucus retention causing *a mucocele.* This does not often give rise to clinical problems but, on rare occasions, may rupture and disseminate mucus-secreting epithelial cells into the peritoneal cavity.

ANUS AND ANAL CANAL

Normal Structure and Function

The anal canal begins at the upper border of the internal sphincter at the level of the insertion of the puborectalis portion of levator ani (the so-called anorectal ring), and extends down to the groove between the terminal ends of the internal and external sphincters. It is 30-40 mm long.

The upper part of the canal is lined by rectal-type glandular mucosa, the lower part by non-keratinising squamous epithelium. The upper end of the squamous portion is clearly delineated by the pectinate (or dentate) line. Proximal to this is a narrow zone of 'transitional' mucosa, consisting of columnar epithelium with multilayered small basal cells, which merges with the rectal-type mucosa of the upper segment. The sensory nerves of the anal canal and the muscle sphincters are of vital importance in the control of defecation.

DISEASES OF THE ANUS AND ANAL CANAL

Fissures, fistulae and abscesses are common anal conditions that arise either in isolation or as part of Crohn's disease. Anorectal tuberculosis is *very* rare in the United Kingdom, but is common in countries with a high incidence of pulmonary tuberculosis. Lesions of syphilis and other sexually transmitted diseases may occur at the anus.

Haemorrhoids ('piles')

Haemorrhoids are varicosities resulting from dilatation of the internal haemorrhoidal venous plexus. The mechanisms involved in their formation are not clearly understood, although chronic constipation with straining at stool is most commonly invoked. As such they are largely a consequence of the low-residue 'Western' diet and are relatively uncommon in developing countries.

Haemorrhoids present with rectal bleeding as streaks of blood on the outside of the stool. They may prolapse through the anal verge and can undergo secondary inflammation, thrombosis and infarction, when they become acutely painful.

Tumours

Warts

Warts (condyloma acuminata) are the commonest benign neoplasm of the anus. They are often multiple and are almost always attributable to human papillomavirus (HPV) infection. Their high incidence in homosexual males suggests venereal transmission through anal intercourse. There is also an increased risk of anal carcinoma.

Carcinoma

There are three main categories of carcinoma corresponding to the three kinds of epithelium found in the anal canal:

- adenocarcinoma in the upper part
- squamous carcinoma in the lower part
- 'basaloid' carcinoma arising from the transitional zone.

Squamous carcinomas are the predominant tumours at the anal verge and arising in peri-anal skin. They appear as ulcerated lesions with rolled margins, and cause pain or bleeding.

They spread upwards into the lower rectum, outwards to involve the sphincters, and via lymphatics to involve the lateral pelvic and inguinal nodes. Squamous carcinomas have a higher incidence in homosexual males.

Some are known to have developed in pre-existing viral warts (condyloma acuminata), and a relationship between HPV infection and the development of squamous carcinoma, akin to that seen in the uterine cervix, therefore seems likely.

Melanoma

The anus and anal canal are also rare sites for a malignant melanoma.

5

PATHOLOGY OF RESPIRATORY SYSTEM

Respiratory diseases, particularly lung infections, cause most damage in developing countries where, together with gastrointestinal infection, they account for most deaths. Out of a global total of 55.69 million deaths in 2000, 3.86 million were due to acute lower respiratory tract infections, 1.66 million to tuberculosis, 2.94 million to HIV/AIDS, 1.21 million to lung cancer and 3.54 million to a variety of other respiratory diseases, mainly chronic obstructive pulmonary disease (2.52 million).

Respiratory disease is also a common cause of death in the industrialised nations, however, accounting for about 14% of deaths in each sex. There is also considerable morbidity due to respiratory diseases: it is estimated that, in the UK, about 40% of absence from work is the result of such diseases, approximately 85% of which are transient infections of the upper respiratory tract. Most respiratory illness is due to environmental factors, especially smoking; genetic factors have a minor role.

NORMAL STRUCTURE AND FUNCTION

The respiratory system extends from the nasal orifices to the periphery of the lung and the surrounding pleural cavity. From the nose to the distal bronchi, the mucosa is lined by mainly pseudostratified ciliated columnar epithelium with mucus-secreting goblet cells; this is respiratory mucosa. A portion of the larynx is covered with stratified

Table 5.1: Major aetiological factors in respiratory disease.

Aetiological factor	*Disease*
Genetic	Cystic fibrosis α_1-Antitrypsin deficiency Some asthma
Environmental	
Smoking	Lung cancer Chronic bronchitis and emphysema Susceptibility to infection
Air pollution	Chronic bronchitis Susceptibility to infection
Occupation	Pneumoconiosis Asbestosis, mesothelioma and lung cancer
Infection	Influenza Measles Bacterial pneumonias Tuberculosis

squamous epithelium. The co-ordinated rhythmic beating of the cilia in the surface of the respiratory mucosa wafts mucus containing dust particles from the depths of the lung up to the larynx. From there the mucus can be either expectorated or swallowed.

Nasal Passages and Sinuses

The nasal passages and sinuses are in continuity and are lined with respiratory mucosa. The hairs in the nose trap large particles of foreign material, thereby filtering the air.

The air is also warmed and humidified as it passes through the nasal cavity. The middle ear, also lined with respiratory epithelium, connects with the nasal cavity via the Eustachian tube.

Larynx

The larynx connects the trachea to the pharynx. Consisting of a complicated system of cartilages and muscles, it allows air into the trachea, with the epiglottis preventing the passage of food into the lungs, and also produces sound for speaking.

Part of the larynx, including the vocal cords and epiglottis, is cove-

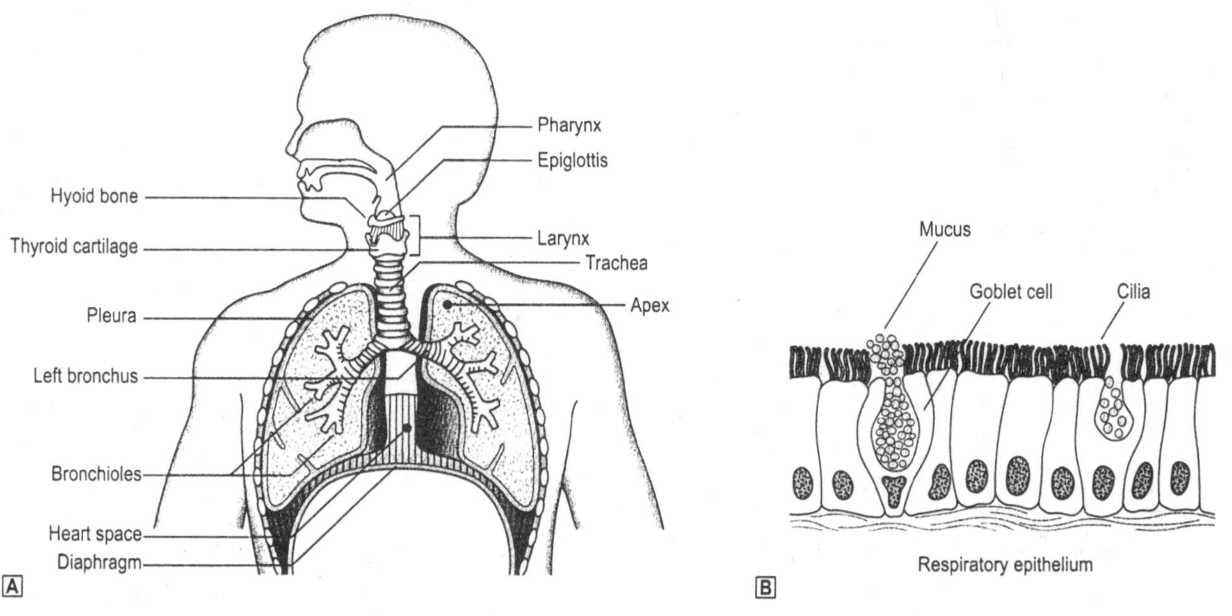

Figure 5.1: The respiratory system.

Pathological basis of respiratory signs and symptoms.

Sign or symptom	*Pathological basis*
Sputum	
• clear or mucoid	Excess secretion from bronchial mucous glands in, for example, asthma and chronic bronchitis
• purulent	Inflammatory exudate from respiratory tract infection
• with blood	Extravasation of red cells due to cardiac failure, pulmonary infarction or ulceration of respiratory mucosa (e.g. by tumour)
Cough	Physiological reflex response to presence of mucus, exudate, tumour or foreign material
Wheezing	
• on inspiration	Narrowing of larynx, trachea or proximal bronchi (e.g. by tumour)
• on expiration	Distal bronchial narrowing (e.g. asthma)
Dyspnoea	Decreased oxygen in the blood from impaired alveolar gas exchange, left heart failure or anaemia
Cyanosis	Increased non-oxygenated haemoglobin, e.g. circulatory bypassing of lungs in congenital heart diseases or impaired alveolar gas exchange
Pleuritic pain	Irritation of the pleura due to pulmonary inflammation, infarction or tumour
Pleural effusion	
• transudate (low protein)	Cardiac failure Hypoalbuminaemia (e.g. cirrhosis, nephrotic syndrome)
• exudate (high protein)	Pleural inflammation Tumour
Clubbing	Often accompanies carcinoma of lung and pulmonary fibrosis, as well as, less commonly, cirrhosis and chronic inflammatory bowel disease
Weight loss	Protein catabolic state induced by chronic inflammatory disease (e.g. tuberculosis) or tumours

Auscultation signs	
• crackles	Sudden inspirational opening of small airways resisted by fluid or fibrosis
• wheezes	Generalised or localised airway narrowing
• pleural rub	Pleural surface roughened by exudate
Percussion signs	
• dullness	Solidification of lung by exudate (pneumonia) or fibrosis Pleural effusion
• hyper-resonance	increased gas content of thorax due to pneumothorax or emphysema

red with non-keratinising squamous epithelium similar to that lining the oral cavity, pharynx and oesophagus.

Lungs

The lungs are divided into *lobes:* the right lung has three lobes (upper, middle, lower); the left lung has only two lobes (upper and lower). Each lung is formed of ten anatomically defined *bronchopulmonary segments*. Each segment is supplied by a segmental artery and bronchus, but the veins draining adjacent segments often anastomose before they reach the hilum.

The lungs develop from an outpouching of the anterior wall of the primitive foregut at about the fifth week of development. From this tube, two lateral outgrowths appear which eventually form the right and left lungs. These outgrowths are surrounded by mesenchyme from which forms the connective tissue of the respiratory tree.

Thus the lungs, like the gastrointestinal tract, develop from endoderm, and developmental abnormalities such as cysts can therefore be lined by either respiratory or gastrointestinal mucosa. The larynx forms at the proximal end of the trachea and is partially lined with squamous epithelium.

The lower respiratory tract consists of the trachea, bronchi, bronchioles, alveolar ducts and alveoli. The structure of each portion differs. The *respiratory tree* is designed to transport clean, humidified air into distal airways and alveoli, where the waste product of metabolism (CO_2) is exchanged for O_2. *Bronchioles* branch until they form terminal bronchioles less than 2 mm in diameter.

The respiratory system distal to the terminal bronchiole is called the *acinus* or *terminal respiratory unit,* where gas exchange occurs. Small airways, defined as having an internal diameter of less than 2 mm, consist of terminal and respiratory bronchioles.

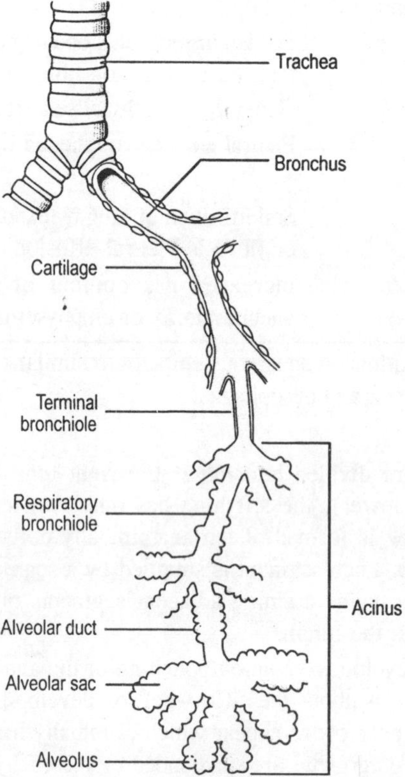

Figure 5.2: Structure and nomenclature of the lower respiratory tract.

Respiratory bronchioles are involved with gas exchange, having alveoli in their walls. A group of 3-5 respiratory acini is called a *lobule*. The *alveoli* are lined by flattened type I pneumocytes with occasional type II pneumocytes; the latter are rounded cells with surface microvilli and osmiophilic (affinity for osmium stain) lamellated inclusions in their cytoplasm.

Type II cells secrete surfactant, and replicate quickly after injury to alveolar walls. Beneath these alveolar cells lie a basement membrane and some interstitial matrix, including elastin fibres, separating the airspaces from the capillary wall. The structure of the alveolar-capillary membrane permits rapid and efficient diffusion of oxygen and carbon dioxide.

The *pleura* consists of a double layer of fibrous connective tissue lined by mesothelial cells. A thin film of fluid lubricates the two layers,

Table 5.2: Structure of the respiratory tree.

Part of respiratory tract	*Structure*
Trachea	Anterior C-shaped plates of cartilage with posterior smooth muscle. Mucous glands
Bronchi	Discontinuous foci of cartilage with smooth muscle. Mucous glands
Bronchioles	No cartilage or submucosal mucous glands. Clara cells secreting proteinaceous fluid. Ciliated epithelium
Alveolar duct	Flat epithelium. No glands. No cilia
Alveoli	Type I and II pneumocytes

allowing easy movement of the lungs against the thoracic cage wall. The lungs and pleura are enclosed within the chest by the diaphragm, ribs and intercostal muscles, vertebral column and sternum.

Blood Supply and Lymphatic Drainage

The lungs are perfused *by a dual arterial blood supply*. The trunk of the *pulmonary artery* arises from the right ventricle, splits into main right and left pulmonary arteries and thence follows the airways. The *bronchial arteries* arise from the descending thoracic aorta and supply oxygenated blood to lung parenchyma around the hilum.

Pulmonary veins take all the blood from the lungs back to the left atrium. Theoretically the obvious benefit of a dual blood supply is that, should a pulmonary artery branch become blocked (e.g. due to pulmonary embolism), the structure of the lung can remain intact, as it is still supplied with nutrients from the bronchial arteries.

In practice this rarely happens because most pulmonary infarcts are peripheral, whereas bronchial arteries supply only hilar regions. Pulmonary veins course along the interlobular septa with *lymphatics*. The lymphatics drain into the thoracic duct and thence into the left subclavian vein.

Control of Respiration

Respiration is controlled by the *respiratory centre* in the medulla oblongata, and the carotid bodies situated at the carotid bifurcations. The medullary centre senses any change in CO_2 concentration in the cerebrospinal fluid, and modifies respiration by nervous stimulation of respiratory muscles and the diaphragm.

The partial pressure of O_2 in the blood is monitored by the *carotid bodies,* which can then stimulate the respiratory centre through the glossopharyngeal nerves. Carotid bodies can become hyperplastic in response to chronic arterial hypoxaemia, such as occurs in:

- high altitude dwellers
- pulmonary emphysema
- diffuse pulmonary fibrosis
- kyphoscoliosis with chronic hypoventilation
- Pickwickian syndrome (gross obesity with chronic hypoxaemia)

Gas Exchange

Air is drawn into the lungs by contraction of the diaphragm and intercostal muscles, creating a negative intrapleural pressure. On relaxation of these muscles, air is expelled as the lungs contract under the action of gravity and the elasticity in the lung connective tissue.

The stiffness of the lungs, or *compliance*, is a measure of change in volume per unit change in pressure, and is therefore a measure of compressibility; for example, in pulmonary fibrosis the lungs cannot be easily compressed and therefore the compliance is decreased.

Clearly, gas exchange occurs only in alveoli that are both perfused and ventilated. Ventilation of non-perfused alveoli increases the 'dead space', that proportion of inspired air not involved with gas exchange. Perfusion of non-ventilated alveoli leads to physiological right-to-left shunting of non oxygenated blood as it passes through the pulmonary circulation.

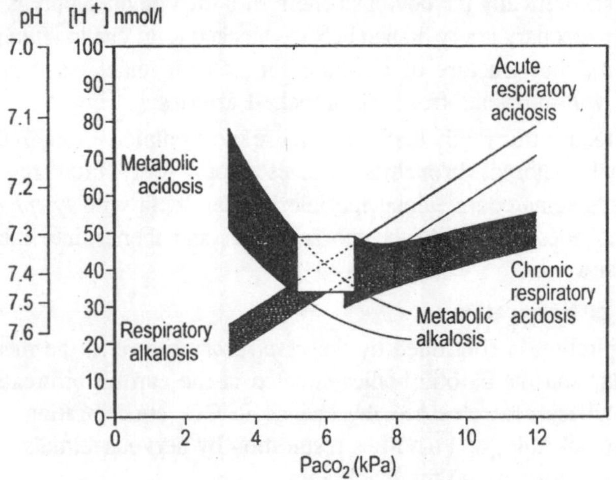

Figure 5.3: Acid-base imbalance.

Acid-base Balance

Normal acid-base balance in blood is dependent on both efficient alveolar ventilation and perfusion, with consequent successful gas exchange. This leads to the normal partial pressures of O_2 and CO_2 in arterial blood (Pao_2 and $Paco_2$), and a normal blood pH. Various metabolic disease states lead to disturbances in acid-base balance. If the disease becomes chronic, compensatory mechanisms by both the lungs and kidneys operate in an attempt to restore blood pH.

MEASUREMENT OF LUNG CAPACITY AND FUNCTION

In normal quiet respiration under diaphragmatic drive, only a relatively small proportion of the *total lung capacity* (TLC) is inhaled and exhaled; this is the *tidal volume (TV)*. TLC is made up of the amount of air totally exhaled after maximum inspiration (the *vital capacity* or VC) and the *residual volume (RV)*. TLC, RV, TV and VC are all easily measured in the laboratory using helium dilution techniques.

Pulmonary Function Tests

In addition to calculating volume parameters, some techniques also assess pulmonary function. *Spirometry* measures the amount of exhaled air per second. The maximum volume of air blown from the lungs within the first second after a previous maximum inspiration is called the *forced expiratory volume* (FEV_1).

This figure, highly reproducible in each individual, is governed by the state of major intrathoracic airways (trachea and bronchi). It is also dependent on the patient's age, sex and size; for example, the small lungs of a child obviously cannot expel as much air as those of an adult. The total amount of air expired after maximum inspiration is the *vital capacity (VC)*.

The ratio FEV_1:VC compensates to a degree for the variability of lung size. It is possible to inhale more rapidly than exhale because, during inspiration, forces on the airways tend to open them further; during expiration, opposite forces tend to close the airways and thus restrict airflow. For a given lung volume, the *expiratory flow rate* reaches a peak (PEFR), which is again a measure of airways resistance.

An assessment of the ability of the lungs to exchange gas efficiently can be made by measuring the *transfer factor* for carbon monoxide (T_{CO}). Air containing a known concentration of carbon monoxide is inhaled; the breath is held for 15 seconds and then exhaled. The amount of carbon monoxide absorbed is a measure of pulmonary gas exchange.

T_{CO} is dependent on the concentration of blood haemoglobin, which has a strong affinity for carbon monoxide. Diseases that diffusely affect the alveolar-capillary membrane (such as any diffuse pulmonary fibrosis) will result in a low Tco.

Recently the level of nitric oxide (NO) in exhaled air has been added as a useful test; increased levels have been associated with asthma and other causes of bronchial irritation, while decreased levels have been found in cigarette smokers, patients with pulmonary hypertension and during treatment with corticosteroids.

Obstructive and Restrictive Defects

There are two major groups of patients in whom the above pulmonary function tests are of great value: those with *obstructive defects (e.g.* asthma) and those with *restrictive defects (e.g.* pulmonary fibrosis). Restrictive diseases are those that restrict normal lung movement during respiration. Both types of lung disease show a contrasting pattern of pulmonary function tests.

In obstructive airways disease, RV and TLC are mildly increased due to hyperinflation of the lung distal to diseased airways. Clearly, in asthma, the results of pulmonary function tests will depend on the clinical state of the patient, whether in an acute attack of asthma or in remission.

These tests are of most value in the follow-up of patients. They can also give an indication as to the possible benefits of treatment; for example, observing the improved FEV_1:VC and PEFR after treatment with a bronchodilator would be a measure of the reversibility of the airways obstruction.

RESPIRATORY FAILURE

Respiratory failure can occur as a result of:

- ventilation defects
- perfusion defects, if diffuse or extensive, e.g. cardiac failure or multiple pulmonary emboli
- gas exchange defects, if diffuse and severe, e.g. emphysema or diffuse pulmonary fibrosis.

Ventilation defects may be:

- nervous, e.g. due to narcotics, encephalitis, a spaceoccupying lesion, poliomyelitis, motor neurone disease, etc.
- mechanical, e.g. due to trauma, kyphoscoliosis, muscle disease, pleural effusion, gross obesity (Pickwickian syndrome).

Table 5.3: Respiratory function tests and their diagnostic significance.

Test	*Diagnostic significance*
Peak expiratory flow rate (PEFR)	Reduced with obstructed airways or muscle weakness
Forced expiratory volume in 1 second (FEV_1)	Reduced with obstructed airways, pulmonary fibrosis or oedema, or muscle weakness
Vital capacity (VC)	Reduced with reduction in effective lung volume (fibrosis or oedema), chest wall deformity (kyphoscoliosis), or muscle weakness
Forced expiratory ratio (FEV,:VC)	Low in obstructive defects Normal or high in restrictive defects
Carbon monoxide transfer (T_{CO})	Reduced in pulmonary fibrosis, oedema, embolism and anaemia
Exhaled nitric oxide (NO)	Increased in asthma, bronchiectasis and infections Decreased in pulmonary hypertension, cigarette smokers and after treatment with corticosteroids

The effects of respiratory failure include impaired clearance of CO_2 from the lungs, resulting in hypercapnia, and impaired absorption of O_2 from the air, resulting in hypoxaemia. The patient is typically dyspnoeic, cyanosed and lapsing into coma. Hypercapnia (high blood CO_2 concentration) is associated with a bounding pulse and warm, moist extremities.

DISEASES OF INFANCY AND CHILDHOOD

Respiratory diseases of infancy and childhood are predominantly infectious; such diseases, together with diarrhoea, are the primary cause of death in childhood in the developing world. Rarely disease may arise as a result of either developmental abnormalities or immaturity.

Developmental Abnormalities

Developmental abnormalities include:

- tracheo-oesophageal fistula
- congenital diaphragmatic hernia with pulmonary hypoplasia

- bronchogenic and alveolar cysts
- pulmonary sequestration
- congenital lobar emphysema.

Tracheo-oesophageal fistula

Embryologically, the oesophagus and the trachea begin as a single tube; the trachea then buds off to form the pulmonary tree. In a tracheo-oesophageal fistula, the oesophagus ends in a blind pouch; the trachea then usually connects to the stomach via a fistula.

On ingestion of food, the upper pouch quickly fills and overflows into the pulmonary tree, with choking and coughing, leading to aspiration pneumonia. Treatment is by surgery, usually after a period of feeding via gastrostomy.

Congenital diaphragmatic hernia with pulmonary hypoplasia

This presents as neonatal respiratory distress due to herniation of the stomach and loops of bowel into the thorax; usually the left diaphragm is defective. Surgical correction to normal thoracic and abdominal anatomy is essential at the earliest possible opportunity. However, even after this there is still a considerable mortality from the associated severe pulmonary hypoplasia, usually of the left lung.

Bronchogenic and alveolar cysts

These occur in the lung, lined either by bronchial elements such as cartilage, smooth muscle and ciliated respiratory epithelium (bronchogenic cysts), or by simple flattened alveolar type epithelium (alveolar cysts). Usually, such cysts are asymptomatic, although complications may occur.

Pulmonary sequestration

A sequestered piece of lung is a mass of abnormal lung that does not communicate anatomically with the tracheobronchial tree; it is supplied by an anomalous artery, usually from the aorta. Sequestered pieces of lung are found most often around the left lower lobe. Histology shows a multilobulated cystic mass with fibrosis and variable inflammation. An endogenous lipid pneumonia may result.

Congenital lobar emphysema

This condition is characterised by overdistension of a lobe due to intermittent bronchial obstruction. Symptoms arise due to pressure effects caused by the massively distended lobe. Usually, the left upper lobe is affected. The pathogenesis is thought to be abnormal bronchial cartilage allowing inspiration of air but not expiration.

Extrabronchial compression by enlarged lymph nodes may cause a similar clinical picture. Treatment is surgical removal of the diseased lobe.

Immaturity

Diseases due to immaturity include:

- hyaline membrane disease or idiopathic respiratory distress syndrome
- bronchopulmonary dysplasia.

Hyaline membrane disease or idiopathic respiratory distress syndrome

- Complication of prematurity (less than 36 weeks gestation)
- Due to deficiency of pulmonary surfactant
- Tachypnoea, dyspnoea, expiratory grunting, cyanosis
- Diffuse alveolar damage with hyaline membranes
- Associated with maternal diabetes, multiple pregnancy, caesarean section, amniotic fluid aspiration
- Many similarities to adult respiratory distress syndrome (ARDS)

Hyaline membrane disease (HMD) is almost always seen in premature infants of birth weight less than 2.5 kg. Infants are usually of less than 36 weeks gestation, and the incidence of HMD rises as the gestational age decreases. Other associated factors include maternal diabetes, birth by caesarean section, multiple births and difficult deliveries complicated by amniotic fluid aspiration.

Clinical features

After a few hours of relatively normal respiration, symptoms of tachypnoea and dyspnoea with expiratory grunting appear. Cyanosis quickly follows, with worsening respiratory distress. Hypoxaemia refractory to high concentration of inhaled oxygen is one hallmark of the disease, a finding also characteristic of adult respiratory distress syndrome (ARDS).

Pathogenesis

The pathogenesis is thought to be due to a deficiency of surfactant. This is secreted by type II pneumocytes, and normally lines distal airways; it reduces surface tension, thereby allowing airway opening during inspiration. Without normal quantities of surfactant, airways need greater effort to open, leading to respiratory distress.

Morphology

At autopsy the lungs are heavy, purple and solid, and sink in water. Histology shows unopened alveoli with hyaline membranes lining alveolar ducts. Pulmonary lymphatics are dilated. As in ARDS, if the infant survives, resolution follows within the next few days, although pulmonary fibrosis may occur in a minority of cases. Treatment is with oxygen and artificial ventilation.

Bronchopulmonary Dysplasia

Bronchopulmonary dysplasia is the term used to describe the picture of lung organisation after HMD. Often, infants have been previously treated with high levels of oxygen, and it is not clear whether bronchopulmonary dysplasia is a separate disorder, solely related to oxygen toxicity, or merely a result of organisation after HMD.

Certainly, the features are almost identical to those seen with organisation of ARDS; there is interstitial fibrosis with peribronchial fibrosis, and features of pulmonary hypertension; airways may show extensive squamous metaplasia.

NASAL PASSAGES, MIDDLE EAR AND SINUSES

- Inflammatory diseases, e.g. rhinitis, are very common
- Nasal polyps are either inflammatory or allergic
- Malignant tumours are rare

Inflammatory Disorders

Rhinitis (the common cold) is caused by many different viruses, especially rhinoviruses, although respiratory syncytial virus (RSV), parainfluenza viruses, coronaviruses, coxsackieviruses, echoviruses and bacteria, such as *Haemophilus influenzae,* may also be implicated. Rhinitis may also be caused by inhaled allergens as in 'hay fever'; the inflammatory reaction is mediated via type I and type III hypersensitivity reactions.

Nasal polyps may result from either chronic infective inflammation or chronic allergic inflammation. They consist of polypoid oedematous masses of connective tissue infiltrated with chronic inflammatory cells, especially plasma cells; eosinophils may be numerous if allergy is the cause.

Sinusitis is inflammation of the paranasal sinuses; it may be acute or chronic. If the drainage orifice is blocked by inflamed swollen mucosa, an abscess may follow. Cranial osteomyelitis, meningitis or cerebral abscess may then result from sinusitis by direct extension.

Otitis media is infection of the middle ear, often associated with generalised upper respiratory tract infection (URTI). The Eustachian tube may become swollen and blocked, leading to trapping of exudate in the middle ear. Eardrum perforation may ensue, followed by drainage of the effusion. More serious complications include mastoiditis, meningitis and brain abscess.

Tumours

Tumours of the nasal passages and sinuses are uncommon. They may be:

- benign: haemangioma, squamous papilloma, juvenile angiofibroma
- malignant: squamous cell carcinoma, adenocarcinoma, plasmacytoma.

Haemangioma and *squamous papilloma* are benign lesions, the former often presenting with troublesome epistaxis (nosebleeds). Some squamous papillomas may be caused by human papillomavirus.

Juvenile angiofibromas are rare and occur exclusively in males, usually during adolescence. They are extremely vascular, and surgical removal can be difficult. These tumours contain androgen receptors, explaining the male preponderance.

Squamous cell carcinoma may be well differentiated, producing keratin, or very poorly differentiated. The latter may contain many lymphocytes and have been misnamed 'lympho-epitheliomas'. Such tumours are rare in the US but account for 18% of all cancers in China; evidence suggests the Epstein-Barr virus is involved in its aetiology and pathogenesis.

Adenocarcinoma of the nasal passages and sinuses occurs more frequently in people who have worked in woodwork and furniture industries. These tumours may present clinically up to 40 years after initial exposure.

Plasmacytomas are tumours composed of plasma cells. They can occur as part of multiple myeloma or as isolated lesions without systemic disease.

LARYNX

- Laryngitis may be infective, allergic or irritative
- *Polyps* and papillomas are benign lesions
- Squamous cell carcinoma, typically in male smokers

Inflammatory Disorders

Laryngitis may occur in association with viral or bacterial inflammation of trachea and bronchi; this is laryngotracheobronchitis. *Diphtheria* was once a common, and serious, bacterial cause of laryngitis, leading to the formation of a fibrinopurulent membrane that could cause airway obstruction.

Now, as a result of immunisation in infancy with diphtheria toxoid, the disease is rare. *Epiglottitis* is caused by capsulated forms of *Haemophilus influenzae* type B. The epiglottis becomes inflamed and greatly swollen, leading to airway obstruction.

Treatment is by intubation, although, rarely, tracheostomy may be necessary; antibiotics are also given to treat the infection. *Allergic laryngitis* occurs after inhalation of an allergen. There may be gross oedema leading to airway obstruction.

Irritative laryngitis may be due to cigarette smoke or mechanical factors, e.g. endotracheal intubation. *Laryngeal polyps* often develop in singers and are thus sometimes referred to as 'singer's nodes'.

Even when only a few millimetres in diameter they can alter the character of the voice. They consist of oedematous myxoid connective tissue covered with squamous mucosa with amyloid-like material in the stroma.

Tumours

Laryngeal tumours may be:

- benign: papilloma
- malignant: squamous cell carcinoma.

Papilloma may be caused by types of human papillomavirus. Papillomas consist of papillomatous squamous epithelium covering fibrovascular cores of stroma. They may be multiple and recurrent, especially in children, but are usually single in adults.

Such papillomas can extend into the trachea and bronchi. Squamous *cell carcinoma* of the larynx typically affects males over 40 years of age and is associated with cigarette smoking. There may also be an increased risk in asbestos workers. As in squamous epithelium of the cervix, neoplasia is thought to be preceded by a phase of dysplasia.

The dysplasia, especially if low grade, may be reversible on withdrawal of causative factors. Most laryngeal carcinomas arise on the vocal cords, although they may arise above, in the pyriform fossa, or below, as upper tracheal carcinomas.

The lesions ulcerate, fungate and invade locally, later causing metastases in regional lymph nodes and beyond. Symptoms are hoarseness of voice and, later, pain, haemoptysis and dysphagia. Treatment is by resection and/or radiotherapy.

THE LUNGS

Respiratory Infections

The lungs have an exposed internal surface area of approximately 500 m^2. It is therefore not surprising that respiratory infections are relatively common, with the World Health Organization projecting such infections to continue as one of the global leading causes of death and disability. Countering the threat of pathogens are the defence mechanisms, any abnormality in which will predispose to infection. Such abnormalities include:

- loss or suppression of the cough reflex, e.g. in coma, anaesthesia, neuromuscular disorders, or after surgery
- ciliary defects, e.g. in immotile cilia syndromes, or loss of ciliated cells with squamous metaplasia
- mucus disorders, e.g. excessive viscosity as in cystic fibrosis or chronic bronchitis
- acquired or congenital hypogammaglobulinaemia, e.g. with decreased IgA in the mucus
- immunosuppression, e.g. with loss of B- and/or T-lymphocytes
- macrophage function inhibition, e.g. in people who smoke or are hypoxic
- pulmonary oedema with flooding of the alveoli.

Infections can be classified as *primary,* with no underlying predisposing condition in a healthy individual, or *secondary,* when local or systemic defences are weakened. The latter are by far the most common types of respiratory infection in developed countries, and are becoming yet more important with the spread of AIDS.

Bronchitis

- Characterised by cough, dyspnoea, tachypnoea, sputum
- Usually viral
- Often superimposed on chronic obstructive pulmonary disease

In acute bronchitis, the trachea and larynx are involved as well as the lungs, and the disease is then known as *acute laryngotracheobronchitis* (or 'croup'). The disease is more severe in children, with symptoms of cough, dyspnoea and tachypnoea.

Viruses are usually the cause, especially respiratory syncytial virus (RSV), although *Haemophilus influenzae* and *Streptococcus pneumoniae* are frequent bacterial causes. Exacerbations of acute bronchitis are common in chronic obstructive airways disease, and cause a sudden deterioration in pulmonary function with cough and the production of purulent sputum. Acute bronchitis may be caused by direct chemical injury from air pollutants, such as smoke, sulphur dioxide and chlorine.

Chronic bronchitis is a clinical term defined as cough and sputum for 3 months in 2 consecutive years; it is discussed below under diffuse obstructive airways disease.

Bronchiolitis

- Often with bronchopneumonia
- Can be primary in infants
- Causes dyspnoea and tachypnoea
- Usually viral, especially respiratory syncytial virus (RSV)

Primary bronchiolitis is an uncommon respiratory infection caused by viruses, especially RSV, in infants. Symptoms are of acute respiratory distress with dyspnoea and tachypnoea. Most cases resolve within a few days, although a minority may develop bronchopneumonia.

Follicular bronchiolitis with lymphoid aggregates and germinal centres, compressing the airway, can occur in rheumatoid disease.

Bronchiolitis obliterans is characterised by polypoid masses of organising inflammatory exudate and granulation tissue extending from alveoli into bronchioles; it may occur in viral infections, especially RSV, after inhalation of toxic fumes, with extrinsic allergic alveolitis, in pulmonary fibrosis, after aspiration, and with collagen vascular diseases.

Pneumonia

- Alveolar inflammation
- Protein-rich exudate
- Polymorphs and later lymphocytes and macrophages
- Lobar or bronchopneumonia

Pneumonia is usually due to infection affecting distal airways, especially alveoli, with the formation of an inflammatory exudate. It may be classified according to several criteria.

The two anatomical patterns, lobar and bronchopneumonia, can result from infection by one of several types of bacteria, some of which have been mentioned above. There are also several other pathogens that cause distinct types of pneumonia.

Bronchopneumonia

- Patchy consolidation
- Centred on bronchioles or bronchi

Table 5.4: Classifications of pneumonia.

Criterion	*Type*	*Example/comment*
Clinical circumstances	Primary	In an otherwise healthy person
	Secondary	With local or systemic defects in defence
Aetiological agent	Bacterial	*Streptococcus pneumoniae, Staphylococcus aureus, Mycobacterium tuberculosis,* etc.
	Viral	Influenza, measles, etc.
	Fungal	*Cryptococcus, Candida, Aspergillus,* etc.
	Other	*Pneumocystis carinii, Mycoplasma,* aspiration, lipid, eosinophilic
Host reaction	Fibrinous Suppurative	According to dominant component of exudate
Anatomical pattern	Bronchopneumonia Lobar pneumonia	Most widely used classification before identifying aetiological agent

- Usually in infancy or old age
- Usually secondary to pre-existing disease

Bronchopneumonia has a characteristic patchy distribution, centred on inflamed bronchioles and bronchi with subsequent spread to surrounding alveoli. It occurs most commonly in old age, in infancy and in patients with debilitating diseases, such as cancer, cardiac failure, chronic renal failure or cerebrovascular accidents.

Bronchopneumonia may also occur in patients with acute bronchitis, chronic obstructive airways disease or cystic fibrosis. Failure to clear respiratory secretions, such as is common in the post-operative period, also predisposes to the development of bronchopneumonia.

Causative organisms may be low-virulence pathogens, especially in an immunosuppressed patient, and as such would not cause similar disease in a young, healthy individual. Typical organisms include staphylococci, streptococci, *Haemophilus influenzae*, coliforms and fungi. Patients often become septicaemic and toxic, with fever and reduced consciousness.

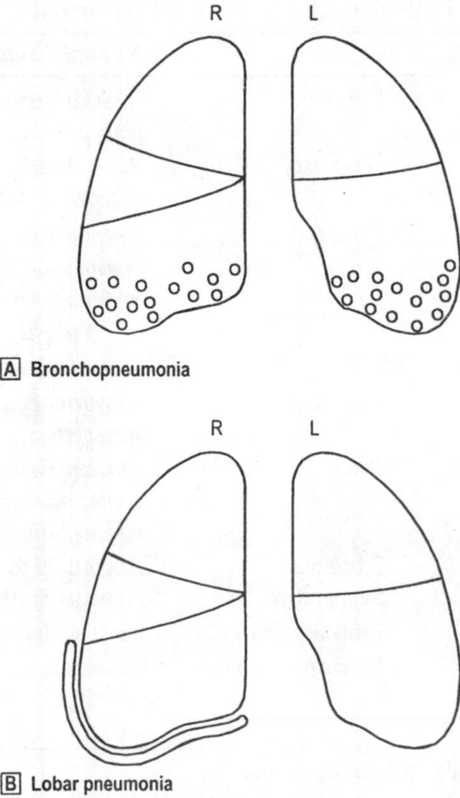

Figure 5.4: Distribution of lesions in lobar and bronchopneumonia.

The areas of affected lung can be identified clinically by hearing crackles (crepitations) on auscultation. Affected areas of the lung tend to be basal and bilateral, and appear focally grey or grey-red at postmortem. The inflamed lung parenchyma can be demonstrated by gently pressing on an affected area; normal lung recoils like a sponge, whereas pneumonic lung offers little resistance.

Histology shows typical acute inflammation with exudation. With antibiotics and physiotherapy, the areas of inflammation may resolve, or heal by organisation with scarring.

Lobar Pneumonia

- Affects a large part, or the entirety, of a lobe
- Relatively uncommon in infancy and old age
- Affects males more than females

- 90% due to Streptococcus *pneumoniae* (pneumococcus)
- Cough and fever with purulent or 'rusty' sputum

Pneumococcal pneumonia typically affects otherwise healthy adults between 20 and 50 years of age; however, lobar pneumonia caused *by Klebsiella* typically affects the elderly, diabetics or alcoholics. Symptoms include a cough, fever and production of sputum.

The sputum appears purulent and may contain flecks of blood, so-called 'rusty' sputum. Fever can be very high (over 40°C), with rigors. Acute pleuritic chest pain on deep inspiration reflects involvement of the pleura. As the lung becomes consolidated, the chest signs are dullness to percussion with increased whispering pectoriloquy, and bronchial breathing. The dullness recedes with resolution of the exudate.

The pathology of lobar pneumonia is a classic example of acute inflammation, involving four stages:

1. *Congestion.* This first stage lasts for about 24 hours and represents the outpouring of a protein-rich exudate into alveolar spaces, with venous congestion. The lung is heavy, oedematous and red.

2. *Red hepatisation.* In this second stage, which lasts for a few days, there is massive accumulation in the alveolar spaces of polymorphs, together with some lymphocytes and macrophages. Many red cells are also extravasated from the distended capillaries. The overlying pleura bears a fibrinous exudate. The lung is red, solid and airless, with a consistency resembling fresh liver.

3. *Grey hepatisation.* This third stage also lasts a few days and represents further accumulation of fibrin, with destruction of white cells and red cells. The lung is now grey-brown and solid.

4. *Resolution.* This fourth stage occurs at about 8-10 days in untreated cases, and represents the resorption of exudate and enzymatic digestion of inflammatory debris, with preservation of the underlying alveolar wall architecture. Most cases of acute lobar pneumonia resolve in this way.

Special Pneumonias

Special pneumonias may be subclassified into those occurring in normal (non-immunosuppressed) hosts, and those occurring in immunosuppressed hosts.

In Normal Hosts

Special pneumonias in normal (non-immunosuppressed) hosts may be due to:

- viruses, e.g. influenza, RSV, adenovirus and mycoplasma

- Legionnaires' disease.

Viral and mycoplasma pneumonia

The clinical course is varied depending on the extent and severity of the disease. In fatal cases, the lungs appear heavy, red and consolidated, as in adult respiratory distress syndrome (ARDS). Histology shows interstitial inflammation consisting of lymphocytes, macrophages and plasma cells. Hyaline membranes of fibrinous exudate are prominent. The alveoli may be relatively free of cellular exudate.

Mycoplasma pneumonia tends to cause a more low-grade chronic pneumonia, with interstitial inflammation and fewer hyaline membranes. The chronic nature of the disease may result in organisation of the inflammation and pulmonary fibrosis.

Influenza viruses can cause an acute fulminating pneumonia with pulmonary haemorrhage; the clinical course may be rapidly fatal.

Legionnaires' disease

Since the first well-described outbreak in 1976, in a group of American Legion conventioneers, this disease has become increasingly recognised; 201 cases were reported in 1996 in the United Kingdom. It is caused by a bacillus, *Legionella pneumophila,* transmitted in water droplets from contaminated air humidifiers and water cisterns.

Patients may be previously well, although a proportion have an underlying chronic illness, such as heart failure or carcinoma. Symptoms include cough, dyspnoea and chest pain, together with more systemic features, such as myalgia, headache, confusion, nausea, vomiting and diarrhoea. About 5-20% of cases are fatal depending on the age of the population affected. At autopsy the lungs are very heavy and consolidated.

In Immunosuppressed Hosts

When immunosuppression affects a patient, the lungs are prone to disease by unusual organisms that are nonpathogenic in non-immunosuppressed individuals; these are known as 'opportunistic' infections. In any immunosuppressed patient, the onset of fever, shortness of breath and cough, together with pulmonary infiltrates, is an ominous event.

Common offending 'opportunistic' agents include:

- Pneumocystis carinii
- other fungi, e.g. *Candida, Aspergillus*
- viruses, e.g. cytomegalovirus, measles.

Pneumocystis carinii

Alveoli are filled with a bubbly pink exudate. Round or crescent-

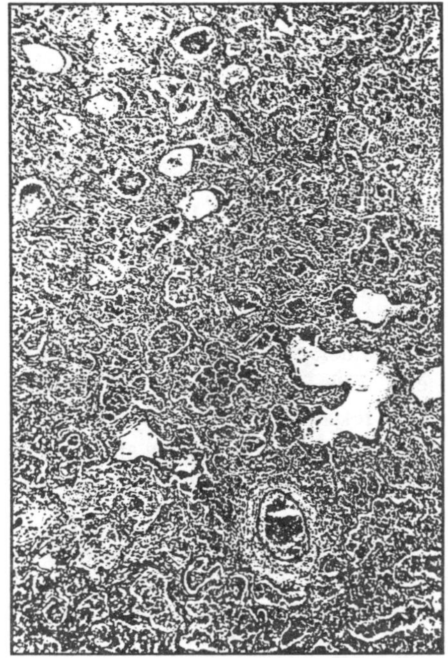

Figure 5.5: Viral pneumonia.

shaped organisms are seen using a silver impregnation stain. There may also be diffuse alveolar damage.

Fungi

Both *Candida* and *Aspergillus* species can cause widespread areas of necrosis. Micro-abscesses contain the characteristic fungal filaments (hyphae).

Viruses

Viral infection may produce diffuse alveolar damage. Characteristic intranuclear inclusions are seen with infections by cytomegalovirus (CMV). Measles pneumonitis produces widespread giant pneumocytes with squamous metaplasia of bronchi and bronchioles.

HIV lung disease

At the end of 2001, the World Health Organization estimated that there were approximately 40 million people globally with HIV/AIDS, of whom 5.0 million were infected in 2001, including 800 000 children. Since the beginning of this epidemic, it has been estimated that 60 million people have been infected, over 20 million of whom have died.

Infection with HIV leads to progressive immunosuppression terminating in the development of AIDS.

The lung is frequently involved with infections, the commonest globally being tuberculosis, although combinations of common bacteria, *Pneumocystis* carinii, viruses and even fungi are commoner in AIDS seen in Western society. Pulmonary disease accounts for up to 70% of AIDS-defining illnesses and is the cause of death in at least a third of all AIDS patients.

Non-infective Pneumonias

Bronchiolitis obliterans/organising pneumonia (BOOP)

BOOP is a clinicopathological syndrome; it is a reaction of the lung to a variety of agents. This is analogous to ARDS, which is another reaction of the lung in response to a different set of insults. Clinically patients with BOOP present with a dry cough, fever, headache and general malaise; dyspnoea increases over days or weeks, leading to respiratory failure.

There is often a dramatic response to high-dose corticosteroid treatment. Histology of BOOP shows loose granulation tissue in alveolar ducts with a patchy interstitial inflammatory infiltrate and type II pneumocyte hyperplasia. Causes of BOOP include a variety of infections, inhalation of fumes, aspiration, drug reactions and collagen vascular disease, although in most cases the cause is not found.

Aspiration pneumonia

Aspiration pneumonia occurs when fluid or food is aspirated into the lung, resulting in consolidation and secondary inflammation. Clinical situations where patients are at risk include sedation, operations, coma, stupor, laryngeal carcinoma and severe debility.

The parts of the lung affected vary according to the patient's posture: lying on the back, the affected area is the apical segment of the lower lobe; lying on the right side, the posterior segment of the upper lobe is affected. Often, such areas of aspiration pneumonia contain anaerobic organisms, and a lung abscess containing foul material may ensue.

Lipid pneumonia

Lipid pneumonia may be endogenous, associated with airway obstruction causing distal collections of foamy macrophages and giant cells. This is often seen distal to bronchial carcinoma or an inhaled foreign body. Alternatively, lipid pneumonia may be exogenous, due to aspiration of material containing a high concentration of lipid.

Such materials include liquid paraffin or oily nose drops. Vacuoles of lipid are ingested by foreign-body giant cells; there may be some interstitial fibrosis.

Eosinophilic pneumonia

Eosinophilic pneumonia is characterised by numerous eosinophils in the interstitium and alveoli. There may be plugging of proximal airways by mucus, as in asthma, or by aspergilli, as in bronchopulmonary aspergillosis.

Recurrent bronchial inflammation can lead to destruction of the wall with replacement by granulation tissue and giant cells; this is *bronchocentric granulomatosis.*

In addition, eosinophilic pneumonia may be seen when microfilaria migrate through the pulmonary circulation. It may also be idiopathic, associated with blood eosinophilia in Loffler's syndrome.

Pulmonary Tuberculosis

- Lung is commonest site for tuberculosis
- Chronic alcoholism, diabetes mellitus, immunosuppression (especially HIV/AIDS), etc. are predisposing conditions
- Often reactivation of primary or secondary lesion
- A major cause of death in developing countries

Pulmonary tuberculosis (TB) is the leading cause of death globally from a single infectious agent; it has been estimated that a third of the world's population has been infected with TB. The number with active disease is approximately 22 million, and the World Health Organization reported 8.9 million new cases in 1995, 95% of whom were in the developing world. About 1.66 million people die annually from TB.

Disease, however, only occurs in about 10070 of cases of infection, when the balance between host resistance and the pathogenicity of the bacteria tips in favour of the latter. TB is therefore the principal cause of HIV-related death in Africa and the Far East with 33% of people living with HIV/AIDS being co-infected with TB.

In 1990, 4.2% of TB cases were attributed to HIV infection; this rose to 11% by the year 2000. Before the advent of antituberculous treatment, therapy was aimed at improving host resistance using special diets and bed rest together with a change in socio-economic factors such as improved living conditions.

Now therapy is aimed at killing the organism using combination antibacterial chemotherapy, and immunisation against infection using BCG (bacille Calmette-Guerin).

Clinicopathological Features

Clinical and pathological features of pulmonary tuberculosis are extremely variable, and depend on the extent, stage and activity of the disease. Symptoms may vary from insidious weight loss with night sweats and a mild chronic cough, to rampant bronchopneumonia with fever, dyspnoea and respiratory distress ('galloping consumption'). Most early cases of primary tuberculosis are clinically silent.

Primary tuberculosis

The lungs are usually the initial site of contact between tubercle bacilli and humans. The focus of primary infection, which is usually asymptomatic, is called a Ghon complex.

The pulmonary lesion is usually about 10 mm in diameter, and consists of a central zone of caseous necrosis surrounded by palisaded epithelioid histiocytes, the occasional Langhans' giant cell, and lymphocytes. Similar granulomas are seen in lymph nodes that drain the affected portion of the lung.

In almost all cases, a primary lesion will organise, leaving a fibrocalcific nodule in the lung, and there will be no clinical sequelae. However, tubercle bacilli may still be present within such scarred foci and may persist as viable organisms for years. In a few cases, complications may occur, especially if the individual is immunocompromised.

Secondary tuberculosis

As indicated above, most secondary TB represents reactivation of old primary infection. These lesions are nearly always located in the lung apices, sometimes bilaterally, and are about 30 mm in diameter at clinical presentation.

Histologically, typical granulomas are seen, most having central zones of caseous necrosis. Progression of the disease depends on the balance between host sensitivity and organism virulence. Most lesions are converted to fibrocalcific scars, a frequent finding in the lungs of elderly people at autopsy. However, as in primary TB, many complications can ensue.

Miliary tuberculosis

Miliary TB may be a consequence of either primary or secondary TB in which there is severe impairment of host resistance. The disease becomes widely disseminated, resulting in numerous small granulomas in many organs. Lesions are commonly found in the lungs, meninges, kidneys, bone marrow and liver, but no organ is exempt.

The granulomas often contain numerous mycobacteria, and the

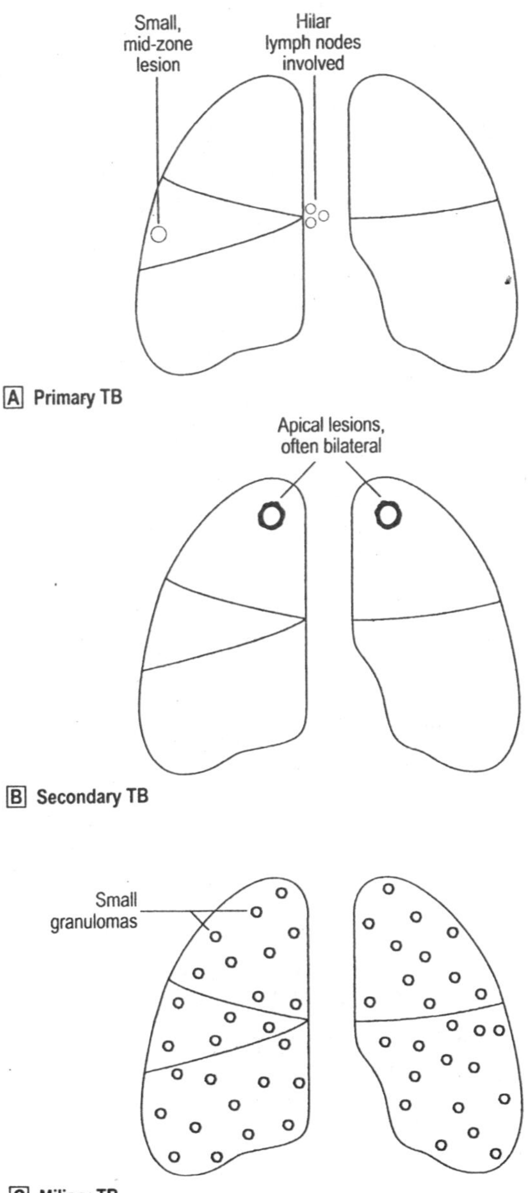

Figure 5.6: Types of pulmonary tuberculosis.

Mantoux test is frequently negative (see below). This is an acute medical emergency necessitating prompt treatment with antituberculous chemotherapy if a fatal outcome is to be averted.

Host Resistance to Tuberculosis and the Tuberculin (Mantoux or Heaf) Test

A delicate balance exists between the properties of the tubercle bacillus and host (human) resistance. Tuberculosis is the classical infective example of the type IV delayed hypersensitivity reaction. Killing is mediated by cytotoxic T-lymphocytes, with recruitment of macrophages responding to the secretion of cytokines, such as migration inhibiting factor (MIF), and subsequent macrophage arming.

This process takes time; sensitivity to tubercle bacilli becomes detectable only about 2-4 weeks after inoculation. At this time, a challenge with tubercle bacillus antigen (the *Mantoux, Heaf* or *tuberculin test*) will give a positive reaction.

Antigenicity and virulence are probably related to the lipid properties of the bacillus cell wall; hence hypersensitivity can usually be induced by immunisation with BCG, a vaccine made from non-virulent tubercle bacilli.

It follows that, in a primary infection, there is no specific hypersensitivity to tubercle bacilli and the inflammatory reaction is relatively mild with little caseous necrosis. In secondary tuberculosis, sensitised T-cells recognise the new threat and, mediated by lymphokines, recruit macrophages to form large granulomas; caseous tissue necrosis is extensive.

The disease becomes disseminated when resistance becomes lowered. Nevertheless, even when host resistance is strong, tubercle bacilli remain extremely difficult to eradicate, and may survive and replicate within the same macrophages recruited as their executioners.

VASCULAR DISEASE OF THE LUNGS

Vascular disease of the lungs may be caused by:

- damage to vessel walls, e.g. arteritis
- obstruction, e.g. emboli
- variations in intravascular pressure, e.g. pulmonary arterial or venous hypertension.

Damage to Vessel Walls

- Arteritis with ischaemia and local necrosis, e.g. Wegener's

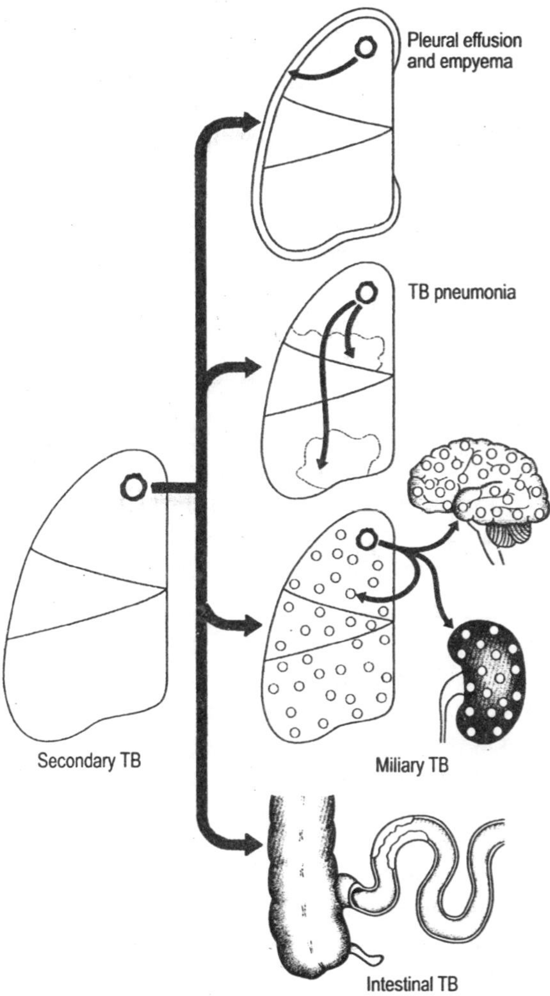

Figure 5.7: Complications of pulmonary tuberculosis.

granulomatosis, Churg-Strauss syndrome

- Goodpasture's syndrome with anti-glomerular basement membrane antibody

Diseases of the lungs due to vessel wall damage are uncommon. Most are thought to be immunologically mediated, e.g. *Goodpasture's syndrome;* in this disease, circulating antiglomerular basement membrane antibody binds to the cross-reacting antigens on the pulmonary basement membrane leading to pulmonary haemorrhage.

Wegener's granulomatosis is a necrotising vasculitis affecting the lungs, upper respiratory tract and kidneys, with the formation of a necrotising glomerulonephritis. The aetiology is unknown. Pulmonary involvement is characterised by large areas of necrosis associated with a necrotising granulomatous vasculitis affecting veins and arterioles.

Churg-Strauss syndrome (allergic angiitis and granulomatosis) may lead to similar necrotising granulomas in the lungs. There is often a history of bronchial asthma. The kidneys and upper respiratory tract are not involved.

Obstruction

- Due to thrombus, air, fat, cancer cells, epithelial squames in amniotic fluid
- Blockage may lead to a pulmonary infarct
- Multiple emboli can cause pulmonary arterial hypertension
- Risk factors for thrombo-embolism include immobilisation, pregnancy, oral contraceptives, malignancy (especially pancreatic), cardiac failure, and the post-operative recovery phase

Thrombo-embolism

Thrombo-embolism is the commonest pulmonary vascular lesion. Most emboli are thrombotic, originating in veins: typical sites are the deep pelvic veins or the deep veins of the calf.

Depending on the size, emboli may lodge in various sites in the pulmonary arterial tree. Symptoms will be related to the volume of lung tissue deprived of blood:

- A saddle embolus at the bifurcation of the left and right pulmonary arteries usually causes sudden death or severe chest pain with dyspnoea and shock. Most patients die within a few hours.
- Occlusion of one main pulmonary artery also frequently leads to death. Alternatively, there may be severe chest pain and shock, mimicking myocardial infarction.
- Occlusion of a lobar or segmental artery causes chest pain and may lead to distal lung infarction, especially in the presence of raised pulmonary venous pressure, as in left ventricular failure or mitral stenosis.
- Multiple small emboli occluding arterioles result in gradual occlusion of the pulmonary arterial bed; this leads to pulmonary arterial hypertension. The effects are discussed below.

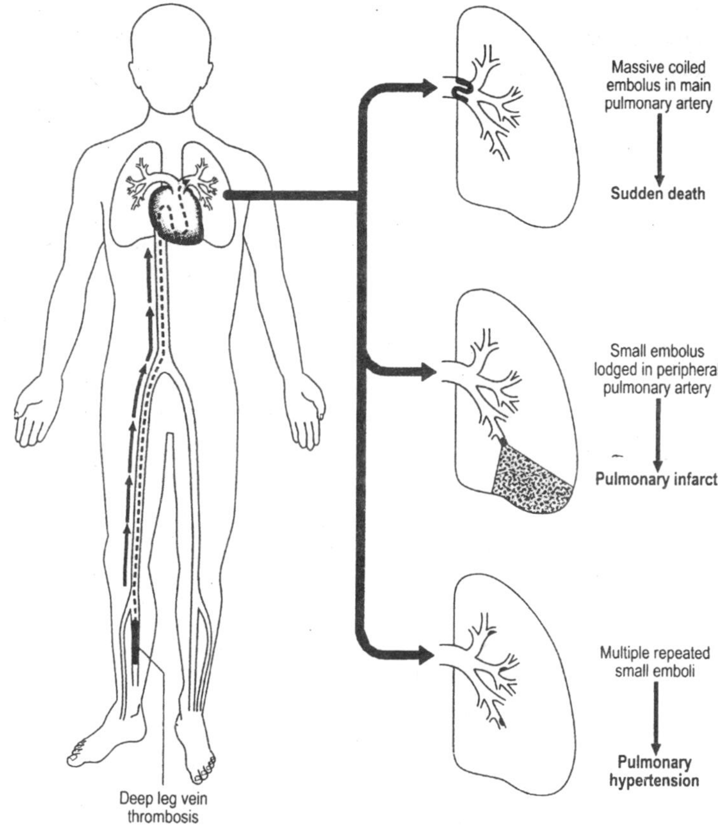

Figure 5.8: Pathogenesis of pulmonary thrombo-embolism.

Clearly, prevention of deep vein thrombosis is of major importance. Encouragement of improved venous flow in deep leg veins is effected by early ambulation of patients after operations, the use of tight elastic stockings, and leg exercises.

Prophylactic anticoagulation is also used in some high-risk patients. Treatment of a major pulmonary embolus includes fibrinolytic agents and even surgical embolectomy. Such heroic measures must be tempered by the fact that patients with a pulmonary embolus have about a 30% chance of developing further emboli. Some patients experiencing repeated pulmonary embolism have an inherited thrombotic tendency.

Fat Emboli

Fat emboli may occlude pulmonary arterioles, leading to breathlessness and sudden death. Such emboli result from fractures of bones containing fatty marrow, or from massive injury to subcutaneous fat. Globules of lipid enter the torn veins and thereby lead to embolism. Marrow tissue may also be seen within pulmonary vessels.

Air Emboli

Air emboli occur occasionally during childbirth or with abortion. Bubbles in the circulation can also occur when dissolved nitrogen comes out of solution, for example in divers during rapid decompression (Caisson disease or 'the bends'). These micro-emboli can cause tiny infarcts in several organs, including muscle, bone, brain and lung.

Amniotic Fluid Emboli

Amniotic fluid emboli may occur during delivery or abortion. Flakes of keratin and vernix from fetal skin are seen in pulmonary arterioles.

Tumour Emboli

Tumour emboli are, of course, very common; this is an important mechanism in the development of metastases.

Variations in Intravascular Pressure

Several disorders are associated with changes in intravascular pressure:

- venous congestion and pulmonary oedema
- pulmonary veno-occlusive disease
- pulmonary hypertension and 'cor pulmonale'
- pulmonary arterial hypertension with a right-to-left shunt.

Venous congestion and pulmonary oedema

Pulmonary oedema can result from:

- increased venous hydrostatic pressure
- injury to the alveolar-capillary wall
- lowered plasma oncotic pressure (a rare cause of pulmonary oedema)
- blockage of lymphatic drainage.

An initial increase in venous hydrostatic pressure leads to pulmonary venous congestion. Common causes are:

- left ventricular failure
- mitral stenosis
- mitral incompetence.

Secondary pulmonary venous hypertension follows, with congestion of alveolar wall capillaries. Fluid is then forced out of the venous circulation into the alveoli to form pulmonary oedema. However, this occurs only after the normal lymphatic drainage capacity has been exceeded; lymphatic flow can increase by about 10-fold before the onset of pulmonary oedema.

If lymphatic drainage is blocked, for example by cancer cells, then pulmonary oedema will occur more readily. The lungs are heavy, congested and wet. Airways contain bubbly fluid. In chronic congestion, recurrent alveolar haemorrhages lead to the accumulation of haemosiderin-laden macrophages (heart-failure cells) with some interstitial fibrosis, so-called 'brown induration of the lung'.

Clinically, there is dyspnoea with a cough, producing bubbly fluid. Auscultation reveals fine crackles in the chest due to air bubbling through numerous fluid-soaked airways. There is respiratory impairment with hypoxaemia. The boggy lungs are prone to secondary infection.

Pulmonary Veno-occlusive Disease

Pulmonary veno-occlusive disease is rare; it leads to chronic venous congestion with interstitial fibrosis and many haemosiderin-laden macrophages in alveolar spaces. The left heart is normal, and disease is caused by internal thickening and occlusion of pulmonary veins in the septa.

The aetiology is largely unknown, although some cases have been reported in association with drugs and radiotherapy. Symptoms are of progressive dyspnoea and 'cor pulmonale'.

Pulmonary Hypertension and 'cor pulmonale'

Pulmonary hypertension may be:

- pre-capillary, e.g. pulmonary emboli, left-to-right shunts, primary pulmonary hypertension
- capillary, e.g. fibrosing alveolitis, chronic obstructive airways disease
- post-capillary, e.g. left ventricular failure, mitral stenosis
- chronic hypoxaemia, e.g. Pickwickian syndrome, kyphoscoliosis, poliomyelitis.

All the above mechanisms lead to 'cor pulmonale' or heart failure caused by respiratory disease, which is manifested by pulmonary hypertension and right ventricular hypertrophy.

Pre-capillary pulmonary hypertension may be:

- Due to multiple *pulmonary emboli:* numerous tiny emboli block arterioles leading to eventual obliteration of the vascular bed
- Due to *left-to-right shunts,* such as cardiac septal defect: blood shunts from the high-pressure left heart to the right heart,

causing an increase in its volume and pressure on the pulmonary arterial tree

- Primary or of *unknown cause:* this disease tends to affect young women. The cause of primary pulmonary hypertension is uncertain, but may include: ingestion of drugs and toxins (the appetite suppressant, Aminorex, and plant alkaloid, *Crotalaria spectabilis,* are known to cause pulmonary hypertension); overactivity of the sympathetic nervous system leading to vasoconstriction; or 'occult' showers of tiny pulmonary emboli.

  Exhaled nitric oxide (NO) levels are lower in patients with pulmonary hypertension than in normal controls; giving NO by inhalation to such patients leads to pulmonary vasodilatation. Other vasodilators that may give some success include prostacyclins, calcium-channel blockers and adenosine. Patients with severe disease refractory to medical management should be considered for surgery such as atrial septostomy and lung transplantation.

Capillary pulmonary hypertension is due to disease in the pulmonary vascular bed. Examples include fibrosing alveolitis, or honeycomb lung from any cause. Severe chronic obstructive airways disease may also cause pulmonary hypertension and 'cor pulmonale'.

Post-capillary pulmonary hypertension is due to high pressure in the pulmonary venous system causing secondary back pressure into the arterial tree. Examples include mitral stenosis, left ventricular failure from any cause, and the rare pulmonary veno-occlusive disease.

Any cause of *chronic hypoxaemia* may lead to pulmonary hypertension, including living at high altitude. The Pickwickian syndrome is characterised by chronic hypoxaemia and pulmonary hypertension caused by poor respiration associated with gross obesity.

Obviously, the gross and microscopic pathology in each instance is determined by the underlying cause. There are also relatively constant changes seen in the pulmonary arterial tree, including muscular hypertrophy, intimal proliferation, capillary dilatation and necrotising arteritis.

Pulmonary Arterial Hypertension with Right-to-Left Shunt

In patients with a congenital atrial septal defect, often asymptomatic, who subsequently develop pulmonary hypertension, the raised right intra-atrial blood pressure causes blood to flow through the defect into the left atrium (right-to-left shunt). This has two important consequences:

- *Paradoxical embolism.* Venous emboli usually impact in the pulmonary arteries. If there is a right-to-left shunt there is a risk of venous emboli bypassing the pulmonary arteries and entering the systemic arterial circulation, thus causing infarcts in the brain, kidneys, spleen, etc.
- *Impaired oxygenation.* Diversion of venous blood through the atrial septal defect from right to left causes dilution of the blood in the left atrium with blood that has not been oxygenated by passage through the lungs. This exacerbates the impaired oxygenation that already exists in patients with lung disorders associated with pulmonary hypertension.

OBSTRUCTIVE AIRWAYS DISEASE

Obstructive airways disease falls into two major groups:

- localised
- diffuse.

Localised Obstructive Airways Disease

- Obstruction by tumour or foreign body
- Causes distal collapse or over-expansion
- May be complicated by distal lipid or infective pneumonia
- Usually normal pulmonary function tests

Localised obstructive airways disease is caused by mechanical factors, for example a foreign body obstructing an airway. The area involved is usually small with little respiratory embarrassment, but tissue damage may occur. When a bronchus or bronchiole becomes obstructed, the distal lung usually collapses.

Numerous lipid-laden macrophages may fill the alveolar spaces distal to the obstruction, with possible secondary infection leading to bronchopneumonia. Bronchiectasis may result if the obstruction is not relieved. Occasionally, the lung distal to an obstruction may become over-expanded, perhaps due to a valve effect caused by the obstruction.

The obstruction is usually by a carcinoma or inhaled foreign body. Clinical symptoms are related to the underlying pathology and to secondary obstructive events. A localised wheeze may be heard over the lesion. Bronchoscopy usually identifies the problem, and the treatment is surgical. Rarely, a foreign body may partially obstruct the trachea; in this situation, there is profound respiratory distress with stridor.

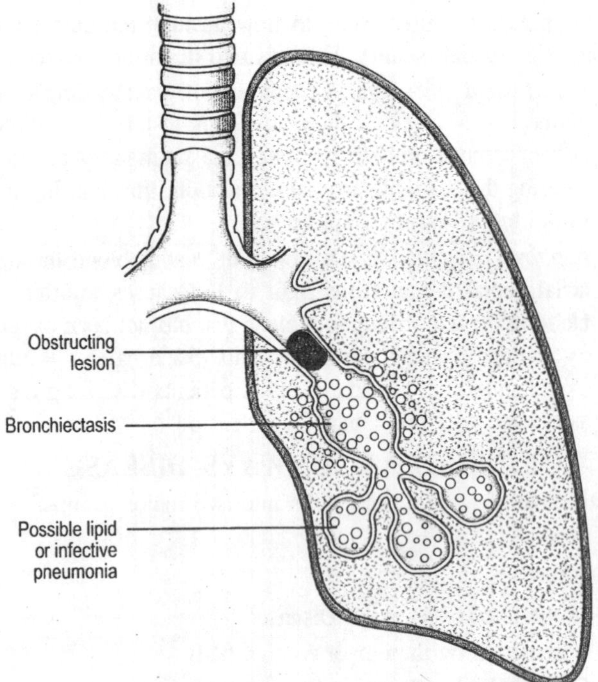

Figure 5.9: Bronchial obstruction.

Diffuse Obstructive Airways isease

- Reversible and intermittent, or irreversible and persistent
- Centred on bronchi and bronchioles
- 'Obstructive' pulmonary function tests
- Usually many airways involved, therefore a diffuse disease

Diffuse obstructive airways disease is due to reversible or irreversible abnormalities in numerous bronchi and/or bronchioles. There is, therefore, significant respiratory impairment causing chronic airflow limitation and a characteristic obstructive pattern of pulmonary function tests:

- reduced vital capacity (VC)
- reduced FEV_1:VC ratio
- reduced peak expiratory flow rate (PEFR).

The major diseases are:

- chronic bronchitis and emphysema or chronic obstructive pulmonary disease (COPD)
- asthma

- bronchiectasis.

Chronic bronchitis and emphysema (COPD) almost always co-exist to some degree. Together they rank fifth in the global burden of disease; in the UK COPD affects approximately 6% of men and 4% of women over the age of 45.

Chronic bronchitis is a clinical term defined as chronic cough and sputum for at least 3 months each year for 2 consecutive years. Emphysema is an *anatomical* term defined as permanent enlargement of airspaces distal to the terminal bronchioles, together with destruction of their walls.

Chronic Bronchitis

- Defined clinically as cough and sputum for 3 months in 2 consecutive years
- Mucus hypersecretion with bronchial mucous gland hypertrophy
- Respiratory bronchiolitis
- Most cases caused by smoking

Aetiology

There is no doubt that chronic bronchitis is almost always entirely due to cigarette smoking. In the United Kingdom, before the Clean Air Act of 1956, urban air pollution was a significant factor.

However, the incidence of chronic bronchitis over the last 10 years has remained steady in spite of everreducing air pollution; the only change has been a small reduction in male chronic bronchitis, undoubtedly resulting from less cigarette smoking in males. In the USA, COPD is the fourth leading cause of death, claiming -120 000 lives annually.

Clinical factors

Chronic bronchitis typically affects middle-aged men who are heavy smokers. Clinical episodes are associated with recurrent, low-grade bronchial infections caused by bacteria such as *Haemophilus influenzae* and *Streptococcus pneumoniae,* or viruses such as respiratory syncytial virus and adenovirus.

Treatment is with antibiotics and physiotherapy and, sometimes, short-term use of oxygen therapy. There may also be a reversible element to the airways obstruction due to local bronchial irritation causing bronchoconstriction; bronchodilators, such as salbutamol, are therefore also used in the treatment of an attack of chronic bronchitis.

Over time, the obstructive airways disease becomes progressively more severe and is accompanied by hypercapnia, hypoxaemia and cyanosis.

Such patients have been called 'blue bloaters'. 'Pink puffers' are those with more emphysema than bronchial obstruction; they therefore hyperventilate to produce a relatively normal blood gas profile.

However, it must be emphasised that most patients have *a mixture* of chronic bronchitis and emphysema, and therefore fall between the above two extremes, showing degrees of hypercapnia, hypoxaemia and hyperventilation. Eventually, right heart failure (cor pulmonale) or respiratory failure ensues.

Morphology

The earliest abnormality in chronic bronchitis is thought to be a respiratory bronchiolitis, affecting airways of less than 2 mm in diameter. This may lead to destruction of the wall and surrounding parenchymal elastin, with the development of centrilobular emphysema.

The reduced airway tension and mural weakness, together with mucus plugging, lead to obstructive clinical features. Bronchioles are so numerous that bronchiolar obstruction must be extensive and widespread to give clinical symptoms.

Bronchial abnormalities are mainly mucus hypersecretion with chronic inflammation; these features produce the typical cough and sputum. Irritation and inflammation in the bronchial epithelium can produce squamous metaplasia with loss of ciliated cells.

The metaplastic squamous epithelium may become dysplastic from persistent injury by smoking, and may even become malignant (squamous cell carcinoma of bronchus).

Emphysema

- Defined anatomically as enlargement of alveolar airspaces with destruction of elastin in walls
- Frequent association with chronic bronchitis

There are various types of emphysema. Although each category has a precise anatomical definition, it must be emphasised that in advanced cases there is usually a *mixed* picture, and an accurate classification in an individual patient is therefore not possible.

Suffice to say that all forms of pulmonary emphysema show destruction of distal lung parenchyma.

Centrilobular Emphysema

Centrilobular (centriacinar) emphysema involves airspaces in the centre of lobules. This lesion is commonest in men, and is closely associated with cigarette smoking, although mild centrilobular emphysema may be seen in patients with coal-worker's pneumoconiosis. In addition,

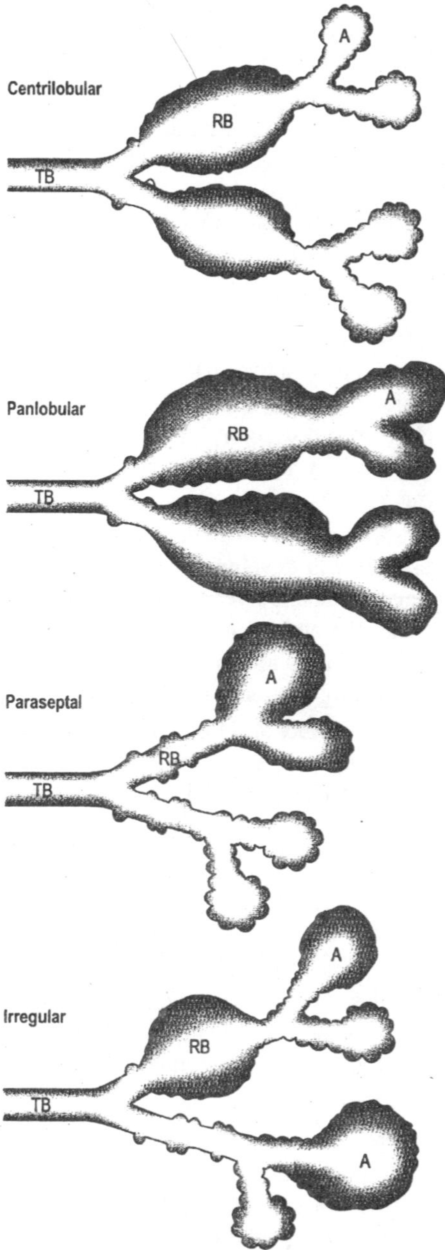

Figure 5.10: Classification of emphysema.

a recent judgement in Britain stated coal mine dust to be a cause of centrilobular emphysema in the absence of coal-worker's pneumoconiosis. The lesions are most common in the upper lobes.

As noted above, a respiratory bronchiolitis is also frequently present, together with some large airways disease such as is seen in chronic bronchitis. Dust-laden macrophages and chronic inflammatory cells are often seen in the walls of dilated airways in this type of emphysema.

Although the pathogenesis is unknown, it is suggested that respiratory bronchiolitis is the precursor lesion of centrilobular emphysema, with local destruction of airway walls and elastin in adjacent lung parenchyma.

Panlobular Emphysema

Panlobular (panacinar) emphysema involves all airspaces distal to the terminal bronchioles. Usually, lower lobes are affected, the bases being most severely involved. Grossly, the lungs appear overdistended and voluminous. The aetiology and pathogenesis of panlobular emphysema is largely unknown.

However, 70-80% of patients with *a,-antitrypsin (a, AT) deficiency* in the homozygous state will develop this type of respiratory disease, usually before the age of about 50 years. a_1AT is an acute phase serum protein which inhibits the actions of collagenase, elastase and other proteases, including trypsin. One action of a_1AT is to inhibit enzymes released from dying neutrophils and macrophages.

Any stimulus, such as smoking, that leads to increased numbers of inflammatory cells in the lung will lead to alveolar wall destruction (emphysema) in patients with α_1AT deficiency. The enzyme deficiency is inherited as an autosomal dominant trait, and the homozygous deficiency state is said to affect about 1 in 3630 Caucasians; the defect is even rarer in black people.

Paraseptal Emphysema

Paraseptal (distal acinar) emphysema involves airspaces at the periphery of the lobules, typically adjacent to pleura. There is often adjacent scarring and fibrosis. The dilated airspaces can become large and, if over 10 mm in diameter, are termed bullous. Upper lobes are more frequently involved.

Irregular Emphysema

Irregular emphysema irregularly involves the respiratory acinus. This type is almost always associated with scarring and there is almost certainly an overlap with paraseptal emphysema. The pathogenesis is thought to be air trapping caused by fibrosis; this irregular pattern of emphysema is therefore commonly present around old healed tuberculous scars at lung apices.

Other Pathological Types

In addition to the four anatomical types of pulmonary emphysema discussed above, some other categories exist.

Bullous emphysema. This is not a separate category of emphysema but refers merely to the presence of balloon-like foci of emphysema over 10 mm in diameter. Cases of emphysema with bullae should, where possible, be classified into one of the four anatomical types discussed above.

Bullae are prone to rupture, causing spontaneous pneumothorax. They are typically subpleural and apical.

Interstitial Emphysema

This refers to inflation of the interstitium of the lung by air, and is most commonly due to traumatic rupture of an airway or spontaneous rupture of an emphysematous bulla. Interstitial emphysema may spread to the mediastinum or subcutis, giving the characteristic spongy crepitus on palpation.

Senile emphysema. This is also a misnomer, as there is no destruction of alveolar walls. Alveolar surface area decreases, and alveolar ductular size increases, progressively after the age of 30 years, leading to the overdistended, apparently voluminous lungs seen at autopsy in aged patients. This process is one of normal senile involution and is not a disease.

Clinical Features

About one-third of lung capacity must be destroyed before clinical symptoms of emphysema appear. In cases of 'pure' emphysema without chronic bronchitis, overventilation leads to relatively normal levels of Paco2 and Pao2 at rest (so-called 'pink puffers'). The progressive dyspnoea leads to weight loss and right heart failure.

Cough and sputum are related to the degree of associated 'chronic bronchitis'. The chest is overinflated and hyper-resonant with loss of the area of cardiac dullness to percussion. Pulmonary function tests show a characteristic obstructive picture with a relatively normal Tco, reflecting the presence of normal alveolar-capillary walls in the remaining lung parenchyma.

In typical cases of 'chronic bronchitis and emphysema' (COPD), recurrent pulmonary infections are associated with increased dyspnoea and purulent sputum. If respiratory failure accompanies an episode of 'chronic bronchitis', short-term oxygen therapy is used. However, there are grave doubts about the benefits of long-term oxygen therapy in the management of severe obstructive airways disease, as patients needing this treatment are unlikely ever to be free from the cumbersome equipment required.

Asthma

Increased irritability of bronchi causes bronchospasm

- Paroxysmal attacks
- Overdistended lungs
- Mucus plugs in bronchi
- Enlarged bronchial mucous glands

Asthma is defined as increased irritability of the bronchial tree with paroxysmal narrowing of the airways, which may reverse spontaneously or after treatment. Asthma is increasingly common in many countries, but it is a relatively rare cause of death.

There are five major clinical categories of asthma:

- atopic
- non-atopic
- aspirin-induced
- occupational
- allergic bronchopulmonary aspergillosis.

Each type has different predisposing factors, and is mediated in different ways. However, the resulting clinical symptoms and pathology are similar to those seen in atopic asthma. Any important differences are outlined below.

Atopic Asthma

Atopic asthma is triggered by a variety of environmental agents, including dust, pollens, foods and animal danders, e.g. faecal pellets from housedust mites. There is often a family history of asthma, hay fever or atopic eczema. Patients with atopic asthma may also suffer from atopic disorders such as hay fever or eczema.

Increased levels of endogenous nitric oxide (NO) produced by a variety of cells in the respiratory tract have been found in exhaled air from asthmatics when compared with normal controls; whether NO is merely a marker of airway irritation or has a more fundamental role in the pathogenesis of asthma is not known.

Recently the gene labelled ADAM33 (a disintegrin and metalloproteinase) has been identified that may underlie the variation in bronchial hypersensitivity between individuals. Bronchoconstriction is mediated by a type I hypersensitivity reaction; bronchoconstriction leads to the clinical effects of wheezing, tachypnoea and dyspnoea.

Rarely, symptoms persist for days (status asthmaticus), leading to respiratory failure and even death. Release of histamine and slow-reacting substance of anaphylaxis (SRS-A) leads to bronchoconstriction, increased vascular permeability and mucus hypersecretion. Eosinophil chemotactic factor of anaphylaxis (ECF-A) attracts numerous eosinophils to the bronchial walls.

Platelet activating factor (PAF) leads to the aggregation of platelets with the release of further histamine and 5-hydroxytryptamine (5-HT) from their granules. The results of the hypersensitivity reaction are:

- bronchial obstruction with distal overinflation or atelectasis (collapse)
- mucus plugging of bronchi
- bronchial inflammation
- Curschmann's spirals: whorls of shed epithelium within mucus plugs
- Charcot-Leyden crystals: crystals within aggregates of eosinophils
- mucous gland hypertrophy
- bronchial wall smooth muscle hypertrophy
- thickening of bronchial basement membrane.

Bronchial inflammation may extend into bronchioles and cause local obstruction, leading to centrilobular emphysema.

Non-atopic Asthma

Non-atopic asthma is associated with recurrent respiratory tract infections, especially in chronic bronchitis, and does not appear to be immunologically mediated. Testing for allergens by skin patching is negative. Bronchoconstriction may be due to local irritation in patients with unusually reactive airways.

Aspirin-induced Asthma

Patients with this form of asthma may also have recurrent rhinitis with nasal polyps, and skin urticaria. The mechanism of induction of asthma by aspirin is unknown but may involve locally decreased prostaglandins or increased leukotrienes leading to airway irritability.

Occupational Asthma

Occupational asthma is induced by hypersensitivity to an agent inhaled at work. Inhaled agents may act as nonspecific stimuli precipitating an asthmatic attack in those with hyper-reactive airways, or they may act as agents capable of inducing asthma and airway hyper-reactivity.

There are many different occupationally inhaled agents that can cause asthma. The mechanism of airway reaction is thought to be a combination of type I and type III hypersensitivity.

In the United Kingdom, if asthma can be proved to be the result of an agent inhaled at work, the patient is entitled to statutory compensation.

Allergic Bronchopulmonary Aspergillosis

Allergic bronchopulmonary aspergillosis causes asthma and is due to inhalation of spores of the fungus *Aspergillus fumigatus,* inducing an immediate type I and delayed immune complex type III hypersensitivity reaction. Mucus plugs in bronchi contain the hyphae of aspergilli.

Pathogenesis of Asthma

As noted above, some forms of asthma are mediated by type I and type III hypersensitivity reactions, yet in others the mechanisms are unknown. One hypothesis that would explain all types of asthma is that patients have bronchial β-receptors relatively insensitive to catecholamines; thus, bronchi are partially constricted in the non-challenged resting state, and do not dilate well to β-agonists, such as adrenaline (epineph-rine).

In addition to reacting to specific agents, these hyper-reactive airways also react to nonspecific factors, such as cold, exercise and emotional stress. Why this should happen remains a mystery.

Bronchiectasis

Results from bronchial obstruction with distal infection and scarring, or severe infection alone

- Destruction of alveolar walls, especially interstitial elastin, with fibrosis of lung parenchyma Airways then dilate, as surrounding scar tissue (fibrosis) contracts
- Secondary inflammatory changes lead to further destruction of airways
- Symptoms are a chronic cough with dyspnoea and production of copious amounts of foul-smelling sputum
- Complications include pneumonia, lung abscess, emphysema, remote abscesses, amyloid, pulmonary fibrosis and cor pulmonale

Bronchiectasis is characterised by permanent dilatation of bronchi and bronchioles.

Aetiology

Bronchiectasis is almost always associated with bronchial obstruction and severe inflammation. Even in rare congenital abnormalities, such as Kartagener's syndrome (immotile cilia syndrome), the cause of the bronchiectasis is nearly always severe distal inflammation leading to lung fibrosis, then dilatation of airways and damage to their walls.

Clinical Features

Usually, the lower lobes are affected, leading to pooling of bronchial secretions with further infection. Symptoms are usually a chronic cough with expectoration of large quantities of foul-smelling sputum, sometimes flecked with blood.

Patients may have finger-clubbing. Recurrent respiratory tract infections result from the inability of the patient to clear pooled secretions. Infective processes may remain localised to the bronchi, or spread.

Complications include:

- pneumonia
- empyema
- septicaemia
- meningitis
- metastatic abscesses, e.g. in brain
- amyloid formation.

Recurrent infection and inflammation lead to further airway necrosis and destruction of lung tissue. Depending on the extent of disease, cor pulmonale may result. Secondary amyloidosis may occur systemically.

Morphology

There is dilatation of bronchi and bronchioles, with inflammatory infiltration, especially polymorphs, during acute exacerbations. The inflammation and associated fibrosis extend into the adjacent lung tissue. The dilated bronchi and bronchioles can appear cylindrical, saccular or fusiform; these terms are purely descriptive of the variable morphology and are of no aetiological or prognostic significance.

INTERSTITIAL DISEASES OF THE LUNG

- Increased tissue in the lung causing increased stiffness and therefore decreased compliance

- Restrictive lung defect
- Alveolar-capillary wall is the site of lesion
- Acute or chronic clinical picture
- Numerous different causes giving similar ultimate pathology

Interstitial diseases of the lung imply increased amounts of tissue within the lung. Therefore, a chest X-ray will show increased lung density, and the lung will be stiff with reduced compliance. This leads to a restrictive respiratory defect of pulmonary function:

- reduced T_{CO}
- reduced VC
- reduced FEV_1
- relatively normal FEV_1:VC ratio
- relatively normal PEER.

Diseases may be grouped into acute and chronic categories on the basis of clinical history and histological findings.

Each disorder shows a basic pattern of either acute alveolar injury or chronic pulmonary fibrosis; many diseases also display their own characteristic features, allowing the specific aetiology to be identified.

Acute Interstitial Diseases

Acute interstitial diseases are characterised by a short history of dyspnoea, tachypnoea and respiratory distress. There is diffuse alveolar damage with alveolar exudation, formation of hyaline membranes and type II pneumocyte hyperplasia. Examples include:

- adult respiratory distress syndrome (ARDS)
- drug and toxin reactions
- radiation pneumonitis
- diffuse intrapulmonary haemorrhage.

Adult Respiratory Distress Syndrome

- Diffuse alveolar damage with hyaline membranes
- Many different clinical conditions, all associated with severe injury to alveolar-capillary walls
- Fatal in 40% of cases
- Causes acute respiratory distress with tachypnoea, dyspnoea, pulmonary oedema and arterial hypoxaemia refractory to O_2 therapy

Aetiology

Adult respiratory distress syndrome (ARDS) is a medical catastrophe; it can affect people of any age who are victims of:

- shock, e.g. haemorrhagic, cardiogenic, septic, anaphylactic, endotoxic
- trauma, e.g. direct pulmonary trauma, or multisystem trauma
- infections, e.g. viral or bacterial pneumonia
- gas inhalation, e.g. NO_2, SO_2, smoke, Cl_2
- narcotic abuse, e.g. heroin, methadone
- ionising radiation
- gastric aspiration
- disseminated intravascular coagulation
- oxygen toxicity.

ARDS came to prominence during the Vietnam War when it was found that many soldiers were dying of respiratory failure during the first few days of recovery from severe wounds; most had suffered shock from blood loss, but this had been successfully treated by medical officers at the battleground. Clinically, there is respiratory distress with tachypnoea, dyspnoea and hypoxaemia refractory to oxygen therapy.

Pathogenesis

All the clinical situations listed above deliver a massive insult to alveolar-capillary walls, leading to diffuse alveolar damage. In many cases, the exact pathogenesis is unknown; in others, there may be O_2 toxicity, in which damage is thought to be caused by free radicals, such as superoxides and peroxides. Polymorphs are also thought to be important in the pathogenesis, with release of enzymes and activation of complement.

Morphology

In the acute stages the lungs are heavy, oedematous and congested with areas of haemorrhage. Histology shows hyaline membranes lining alveolar ducts and alveoli, together with pulmonary oedema and extravasation of red cells. Resolution occurs via resorption of the oedema, and ingestion of red cells and hyaline membranes by alveolar macrophages; there is then regeneration of type II pneumocytes, which later differentiate to type I flattened pneumocytes.

Prognosis

About 40% of patients die within the first few days despite intensive therapy. Most of the survivors progress to full recovery with resolution of the inflammation and restoration of the normal alveolar architecture; however, a small number heal by organisation, leading to pulmonary fibrosis.

Drug and Toxin Reactions

Cytotoxic drugs, such as busulphan and bleomycin, lead to a low-grade alveolitis with healing by interstitial fibrosis and type II pneumocyte hyperplasia; many of the latter have atypical hyperchromatic nuclei with prominent nucleoli. These features are characteristic of lung disease caused by cytotoxic agents.

Paraquat is a potent herbicide acting by release of hydrogen peroxide and the superoxide free radical. It is therefore understandable that ingestion of this toxin leads to diffuse alveolar damage. Pulmonary symptoms occur after about 5-7 days because the drug remains highly concentrated in the lungs for several days after ingestion.

Once pulmonary symptoms develop, the condition is rapidly progressive. The pathological findings are very similar to those seen in ARDS, with prominent fibroblastic proliferation in alveolar spaces.

Radiation Pneumonitis

The clinical effects of radiation toxicity to the lungs are highly dependent on the dose given, the volume of lung irradiated and the length of treatment. If heavily exposed, a picture of diffuse alveolar damage is seen. If exposure is less severe and occurs over a longer period, progressive pulmonary fibrosis is seen with the typical restrictive defect of pulmonary function.

Diffuse Intrapulmonary Haemorrhage

Goodpasture's syndrome is characterised by haemoptysis, haematuria, anaemia and pulmonary infiltrates. Most cases have circulating anti-glomerular basement membrane antibody in their blood. This antibody causes glomerulonephritis, and also acts on alveolar membranes leading to pulmonary haemorrhage.

Idiopathic pulmonary haemosiderosis is a rare condition presenting most often in children. Clinically, patients may present with recurrent episodes of intra-alveolar haemorrhage associated with haemoptysis, cough and dyspnoea; alternatively, they may present with insidious pulmonary fibrosis. The more acute form shows evidence of diffuse alveolar damage, with type II pneumocyte hyperplasia.

Chronic Interstitial Diseases

Chronic interstitial diseases give a clinical history lasting months or years with slowly increasing respiratory insufficiency, dyspnoea, cough and finger-clubbing. There is interstitial fibrosis, infiltration with lymphocytes and macrophages, and microcyst formation. Examples include:

- fibrosing alveolitis (idiopathic pulmonary fibrosis)
- pneumoconioses
- sarcoidosis
- Langerhans' cell granulomatosis (histiocytosis X)
- alveolar lipoproteinosis
- diffuse malignancies
- rheumatoid disease.

Fibrosing alveolitis

- Progressive chronic pulmonary fibrosis of unknown aetiology
- Probably arises as a low-grade smouldering 'alveolitis'
- Progressive dyspnoea and fatigue leading to respiratory failure and/or cor pulmonale
- Finger- and toe-clubbing
- Results in end-stage lung fibrosis (honeycomb lung)

Fibrosing alveolitis is a progressive chronic pulmonary fibrosis of unknown aetiology, although approximately 20% of patients give a history of occupational exposure to metals and wood dusts.

Clinical Features

Most patients are aged over 60 years and present with increasing dyspnoea and a dry cough. Men are affected twice as often as women. The disease progresses to respiratory failure, with or without cor pulmonale, within about 5 years. Fatigue and considerable weight loss may occur, raising the clinical suspicion of malignancy.

Examination often shows finger- and toe-clubbing; auscultation of the chest reveals dry crackles, reflecting the opening and closing of fibrotic airspaces. Signs of right ventricular strain or failure may be present.

Pathogenesis

The pathogenesis of fibrosing alveolitis is unknown. Pulmonary function tests show the characteristic restrictive pattern.

Morphology

The lungs show abnormally large and irregular airspaces separated by coarse fibrous septa (honeycomb lung). The subpleural regions of the lower lobes are predominantly affected.

Histology shows interstitial fibrosis with hyperplasia of type II pneumocytes lining airspaces; varying numbers of chronic inflammatory cells are seen. This pattern of histology is known as *usual interstitial pneumonitis*. Alveolar macrophages may be seen in unusually large numbers, with relatively little interstitial fibrosis; this pattern is known as *desquamative interstitial pneumonitis*.

Its significance is that some benefit may be gained in treating these patients with corticosteroids. Small airways may be filled with granulation and loose connective tissue, an appearance known as *bronchiolitis obliterans*.

It is merely a histological observation and is seen in some other clinical situations, including extrinsic allergic alveolitis, certain viral infections, aspiration pneumonitis and collagen vascular diseases.

Pneumoconioses

- Lung disease caused by inhaled dusts
- Dusts may be inorganic (mineral) or organic
- Reaction may be inert, fibrous, allergic or neoplastic
- Co-existing disease may aggravate the reaction

When exposed to dust the lung can respond in several ways. Such a reaction may be:

- inert, e.g. simple coal-worker's pneumoconiosis
- fibrous, e.g. progressive massive fibrosis, asbestosis, silicosis
- allergic, e.g. extrinsic allergic alveolitis
- neoplastic, e.g. mesothelioma, lung carcinoma.

The distribution of lung disease depends on the physical properties of each separate type of dust, which determine where the particles settle in the lung. Particles of less than 2-3 mm in diameter reach distal alveoli, but larger particles are trapped in the nose or excreted by the mucociliary staircase.

Exceptions to this rule are asbestos fibres, some of which may be up to 100 mm long yet can eventually settle in terminal respiratory units. This is because, although very long, asbestos fibres are very thin (about 0.5 mm in diameter).

Dust particles are phagocytosed by alveolar macrophages, which then collect and drain into peribronchiolar lymphatics and thence to hilar lymph nodes. Not surprisingly, lesions caused by dust in the lungs are also often present in the sinuses of hilar lymph nodes.

X-ray appearances are related to the degree of associated fibrosis and to the atomic number of the dust involved; for example, tin, with an atomic number of 56, will give a more dense 'abnormal' radiograph than carbon, of atomic number 12, given the same amount of particles inhaled.

Coal-worker's Pneumoconiosis

In coal-worker's pneumoconiosis (CWP), coal dust is ingested by alveolar macrophages (dust cells), which then aggregate around bronchioles; the degree of black pigment in the lung (anthracosis) is related to the amount of inhaled carbon. The consequences of coal-dust inhalation are variable, ranging from trivial to lethal.

Anthracosis is simply the presence of coal-dust pigment in the lung. It is not associated with disability. *Macular CWP* consists of focal aggregates of dust-laden macrophages in and around the walls of respiratory bronchioles, pulmonary arterioles and pulmonary veins.

Similar cells are seen in lymphatics and hilar lymph nodes. No significant scarring is present, although there is often some local dilatation of respiratory bronchioles representing mild centrilobular emphysema, which has now been recognised as a consequence of coal-dust inhalation rather than always a result of concomitant cigarette smoking.

Nodular CWP is a progression from the macular stage; nodules less than 10 mm in diameter are seen in a background of more extensive macular CWP Again, there is no significant scarring and little functional respiratory impairment. *Progressive massive fibrosis (PMF)* is represented by large, irregular nodules with scarring; they are greater than 10 mm in diameter and can be massive.

These fibrotic black nodules may show central liquefaction and, when cut at autopsy, exude viscid jet-black liquid. They may contract, leading to adjacent irregular emphysema. Large nodules are usually mid-zonal or in upper lobes, and may be bilateral. The associated emphysema is always severe, often with the formation of bullae.

Progression of the disease leads to further scarring and lung destruction. Honeycomb lung with respiratory failure, or cor pulmonale, are terminal features. *Caplan's syndrome* is characterised by the presence of large pigmented necrobiotic nodules in patients with CWP This occurs in the presence of severe seropositive rheumatoid disease, although lung nodules may precede the development of systemic features. The nodules may regress.

It is known that in a group of miners working at the same pit for the same length of time, some will develop PMF and die, while others develop little respiratory impairment. The reasons why only some miners develop PMF are unknown. Theories include:

- the amount of concurrently inhaled silica or quartz
- superimposed infection with tubercle bacilli or atypical mycobacteria

- hypersensitivity reactions caused by the death of pulmonary macrophages
- fibrosis mediated by immune complexes.

However, none of these theories is proven, and some investigators believe that the determining factor for development of PMF is merely the amount of coal dust inhaled. Whatever the cause, the progression of CWP to PMF is an ominous event.

Silicosis

Silicates are inorganic minerals abundant in stone and sand. Consequently, any industrial worker involved in the grinding of stone or sand will be at risk from silicosis.

Small particles of silica less than 2 mm in diameter enter the terminal respiratory units where they are ingested by alveolar macrophages. However, in contrast to pure coal dust, silicates are toxic to macrophages, leading to their death with release of proteolytic enzymes and the undigested silica particles.

The enzymes cause local tissue destruction and subsequent fibrosis; the silica particles are ingested by other macrophages and the cycle repeats itself. Nodules tend to form in the lungs after many years of exposure. With progressive fibrosis and increasing numbers of nodules, respiratory impairment increases.

Pulmonary function tests show a restrictive defect like any other chronic interstitial lung disease. Some patients develop reactivation of tuberculosis. The lungs show scattered minute nodules of hard, fibrous tissue with surrounding irregular emphysema. Advanced cases show the typical features of end-stage diffuse pulmonary fibrosis, together with numerous silicotic nodules.

Asbestosis

The name 'asbestos' is derived from a Greek word meaning 'inconsumable', and, indeed, asbestos has been used for its fire-resistant qualities for many centuries. Asbestos is used for insulation and the manufacture of brake linings and other friction materials.

There are several types of asbestos: amphiboles are the fibres that cause pulmonary disease in humans, and of these crocidolite (Cape blue asbestos) is probably the most dangerous. Asbestos fibres, although 5-100 mm long, are only 0.25-0.5 mm in diameter, and therefore may collect in the alveoli at lung bases.

Many become coated in acid mucopolysaccharide and encrusted with haemosiderin to form 'asbestos bodies', appearing as characteristic beaded structures. However, most fibres are detectable only by electron microscopy.

The first symptoms of asbestosis are dyspnoea and a dry cough; finger-clubbing is common. The typical late inspiratory crackles indicate significant diffuse pulmonary fibrosis. Lower lobes are more severely affected. Asbestos bodies in the sputum help to differentiate asbestosis from fibrosing alveolitis.

Histology shows the features of pulmonary fibrosis and honeycomb lung, together with asbestos bodies. Patients with asbestosis may also develop large areas of fibrosis resembling progressive massive fibrosis in coalminers, but without the coal-dust pigment. These patients have almost all been exposed to significant amounts of silica as well as asbestos.

Extrinsic Allergic Alveolitis (Hypersensitivity Hneumonitis)

In pneumoconiosis caused by organic dusts, the disease results from the individual being already sensitised (hypersensitive) to the inhaled antigen. Many antigens can cause allergic lung disease; these include: cotton fibres, causing byssinosis; sugar cane fibres, causing bagassosis; and bird faeces, causing bird fancier's lung.

The best known and most typical example of extrinsic allergic alveolitis is *farmer's lung*. In this disorder, a fungus present in poorly stored, mouldy hay is inhaled by whoever disturbs the hay. If the individual is already sensitised to the organism, a type III immune complex hypersensitivity reaction follows.

One of the earliest features is a bronchiolitis. Later, chronic inflammatory cells are seen in the interstitium, together with non-caseating granulomas in airways. These may either resolve on withdrawal of the antigen, or organise, leading to pulmonary fibrosis.

Clinically, there is acute dyspnoea and cough a few hours after inhalation of the antigen. Corticosteroid treatment helps to ameliorate the inflammatory reaction and to prevent the onset of pulmonary fibrosis.

Sarcoidosis

Sarcoidosis of the lung is a common cause of interstitial lung disease. The lung is often involved by this disease; only lymph nodes are involved with greater frequency. The typical, non-caseating granulomas are usually found in, or close to, small lymphatics.

They then heal by organisation, leading to pulmonary fibrosis. Granulomas also occur in the walls of small airways and blood vessels, especially veins. Clinical symptoms are variable depending on the extent of the disease. The aetiology is unknown. A Kveim test, in which the subcutaneous injection of sterile sarcoid tissue homogenate induces granulomas in affected patients, is a useful diagnostic procedure, as is the serum level of angiotensin converting enzyme (ACE) which is raised in 33-50% of patients with sarcoidosis.

Langerhans' Cell Granulomatosis

Langerhans' cell granulomatosis (previously known as *histiocytosis X)* is a disease of unknown cause characterised by the proliferation of Langerhans' cells; these are specialised histiocytes containing characteristic racquet-shaped cytoplasmic inclusions (Birbeck granules) visible only by electron microscopy.

Infiltrates are seen in the pulmonary interstitium, where they may heal by resolution, or organise, leading to pulmonary fibrosis. Pulmonary Langerhans' cell granulomatosis is confined to the lung in 80% of cases, with a mortality rate of approximately 7%. However, systemic spread to bone marrow or lymph nodes carries a poorer prognosis.

Alveolar Lipoproteinosis

Alveolar lipoproteinosis (or proteinosis) is a rare condition characterised by the accumulation of eosinophilic material within alveoli. It may complicate other interstitial diseases, notably desquamative interstitial pneumonitis, and occur also following acute exposure to high levels of silica dust.

However, in most instances the aetiology is unknown and the pathogenesis is uncertain. Symptoms include dyspnoea and cough, when gelatinous material may be expectorated.

Diffuse Malignancies

Diffuse malignancies invading the lung may lead to pulmonary fibrosis if a desmoplastic (fibroblastic) response is prominent. *Lymphangitis carcinomatosa* is the spread of tumour throughout the pulmonary lymphatics; a chest X-ray may show diffuse increase in density. Bronchiolo-alveolar cell carcinomas may spread widely throughout the lungs, possibly through the airways, and lead to diffuse pulmonary involvement.

Rheumatoid Disease

It has been estimated that the lung and/or pleura may be affected in 10-15⁰70 of patients with rheumatoid disease. Usually, such patients have severe rheumatoid disease and are seropositive, with vasculitis and subcutaneous nodules. Pulmonary disease may precede the development of systemic features. The lung may show diffuse pulmonary fibrosis, contain rheumatoid nodules and, if coal-worker's pneumoconiosis is also present, show features of Caplan's syndrome.

The pleura may be involved and show fibrosis; pleural effusions are also relatively common. Small airways disease is common, showing either a follicular bronchiolitis with lymphoid aggregates and germinal centres around bronchioles, or bronchiolitis obliterans.

LUNG TUMOURS

Lung tumours may be primary or secondary. Both are common.

Primary Carcinoma of the Lung

- Most common primary malignant tumour in the world
- Directly related to cigarette smoking
- Associated with occupational exposure to carcinogens
- Overall 5-year survival rate of 4-7%
- Squamous cell, small cell, adenocarcinoma, and large cell undifferentiated types

Over 90% of primary lung tumours are carcinomas. Lung cancer is the leading cause of death from cancer in the world, with the worst overall prognosis, typically around 5% 5-year survival. This is due to the aggressive natural history of the disease, only about 10% of cases being operable at diagnosis.

Another reason for the dismal prognosis is that by far the best chance of a cure is by complete surgical resection. However, intensive chemotherapy regimens are beginning to show some benefit for patients with small cell lung cancer.

About one-third of all cancer deaths in males in the United Kingdom are due to lung cancer. The disease is also increasing in incidence among women; it now ranks as the commonest lethal cancer in females in the United Kingdom.

Typically, patients are aged between 40 and 70 years; the disease rarely affects those less than 30 years of age.

Aetiology

Major risk factors for the development of lung cancer are:

- cigarette smoking
- occupational hazards, e.g. inhalation of asbestos and other dusts, radioactive gases
- pulmonary fibrosis.

Cigarette smoking

There is now overwhelming evidence implicating cigarette smoking as the major risk factor for the development of lung cancer. The rise in the incidence of lung cancer over the last century has closely paralleled the increase in cigarette smoking.

For example, in 1941 about 5000 deaths occurred from lung cancer in England and Wales; the figure had risen to 35 000 in 1984, falling to 31 500 in 1992 and 30 914 in 1996. In 1978, male deaths from lung cancer in England and Wales peaked at 26 771; this figure fell slightly to 26 041 in 1984, falling further to 21 291 in 1992 and dropping again to 19 838 in 1996.

At the same time the prevalence of cigarette smoking has fallen and more people are giving up smoking than ever before, the biggest decrease occurring in professional men. The increase in lung cancer in women since World War II is undoubtedly due to more women smoking cigarettes; 9996 women died from lung cancer in England and Wales in 1986, rising to 11 076 in 1996.

There are progressive changes in the bronchial mucosa associated with smoking. Carcinoma is preceded by squamous metaplasia and, subsequently, dysplasia. Squamous metaplastic and dysplastic cells are seen far more commonly in the sputum of smokers than in that of non-smokers. The number of shed abnormal cells is also in proportion to the number of cigarettes smoked daily.

Occupational Hazards

There are several occupational hazards associated with an increased incidence of lung cancer. The most important are:

- *Asbestos.* There is a significantly increased risk of lung cancer in those exposed occupationally to asbestos. If an individual also smokes, the risk is greatly increased, possibly 20-100-fold. A latent period of about 20 years is usual between exposure and the development of carcinoma. Adenocarcinoma is the most common tumour.
- *Other inhaled dusts.* There is no evidence that lung cancer is associated with coal-worker's pneumoconiosis. However, a significant proportion of haematite miners die from lung cancer.
- *Radioactive gases.* In the 19th century, the Schneeberg mines in Saxony produced rock rich not only in numerous metals but also in radon; many of the workers died from lung cancer.

Survivors of the atomic bombs dropped on Japan in 1945 showed an increased incidence of lung cancer, presumably related to radiation.

- *Other factors.* There is an increased risk of lung cancer in workers in industries involved with nickel, chromates, mustard gas, arsenic, and coal-tar distillates.

Fibrosis

Some peripheral lung cancers (usually adenocarcinomas) apparently arise in areas of fibrous scarring, e.g. wounds, old tuberculous foci or infarcts. The theory is that metaplastic and dysplastic changes occur in pneumocytes within the scar.

Such ideas have recently been challenged, the so-called 'scar cancers' being considered carcinomas with a pronounced central desmoplastic (fibroblastic) reaction. Despite this argument, there is undoubtedly a significant increase of lung adenocarcinoma in patients with pulmonary fibrosis and honeycomb lung.

Clinical Features

Weight loss, cough and haemoptysis are common presenting features. Weight loss is often severe and may be due to humoral factors from the tumour. Dyspnoea and chest pain are also common; the latter is often pleuritic and due to obstructive changes.

Patients may present with, or ultimately develop, metastases; common sites include lymph nodes, bone, brain, liver and adrenals. Paraneoplastic effects are common and are due to ectopic hormones: ACTH and ADH from small cell lung carcinomas, PTH from squamous cell carcinomas. Finger-clubbing and hypertrophic pulmonary osteoarthropathy are common.

Morphology

Most tumours arise from bronchi close to the hilum; usually an upper lobe or main bronchus is involved. Ulceration is common, so the sputum may be bloodstained and contain malignant cells which can be detected cytologically. Distally, the lung may be consolidated with foamy macrophages, the usual result of proximal bronchial obstruction.

Some adenocarcinomas may arise peripherally. Small peripheral tumours are most amenable to surgery if detected before the development of metastases.

Histological Classification

There are four major types of lung cancer, classified according to their appearance on light microscopy; their approximate incidences are:

- squamous cell carcinoma (SgCC): 20-30%
- small cell lung carcinoma (SCLC) (including oat cell carcinoma) and bronchial carcinoids: 15-2070
- adenocarcinoma (AC): 30-40%
- large cell undifferentiated carcinoma (LCUC): 10-15%.

The lung cancers are discussed below according to this classification, but it should be noted that LCUC probably represents a group of squamous and adenocarcinomas that are too poorly differentiated to categorise as such by light microscopy.

In fact, using electron microscopy it can be seen that many SqCC and AC are mixtures, composed of glandular and squamous cells; sometimes, a few cells with neuro-endocrine granules characteristic of SCLC are also seen.

This is not entirely surprising as it is now thought that all lung cancers arise from a primitive stem cell that gives rise to the numerous varied cells seen in the mature respiratory tree.

Squamous cell carcinoma

This is the type of lung cancer most closely associated with cigarette smoking. The tumours are almost always hilar, and are thought to arise from squamous metaplasia through grades of dysplasia. There is often haemorrhage and necrosis with cavitation. Tumours may be well, moderately or poorly differentiated. SqCC tends to metastasise locally to hilar lymph nodes; distant metastases are a later feature.

Small cell lung carcinomas

Also known as 'oat cell' carcinoma because the small nuclei are thought to resemble oat grains, SCLC usually arise in a hilar bronchus. Unlike SqCC, they metastasise very early, producing widespread bulky secondary deposits. Sometimes, the primary tumour can be small and difficult to find. The histology is of a highly cellular tumour composed of small cells with hyperchromatic nuclei and indistinct nucleoli.

The cells are very delicate and the chromatin may appear smudged. Electron microscopy shows a few dense core secretory granules in the cytoplasm, suggesting that the tumour originates from bronchial endocrine or APUD cells. Similar granules are seen in cells of *bronchial carcinoid* tumours, although in far greater numbers.

It is for this reason that SCLC and bronchial carcinoid are thought to represent types of bronchial neuro-endocrine carcinoma; SCLC is aggressive and highly malignant, while bronchial carcinoid is slowgrowing and of low-grade malignancy. An intermediate type of bronchial neuro-endocrine carcinoma is also recognised which has some features of SCLC and some of bronchial carcinoid.

Bronchial carcinoids are either central or peripheral, and may have a partial capsule. Histologically, they show packets or trabeculae of round cells with bland regular nuclei.

Adenocarcinomas. These are usually peripheral. There is a significant association with diffuse pulmonary fibrosis and honeycomb lung, especially if due to asbestosis. There is a suspicion that AC may arise in discrete areas of scarring such as old infarcts or fibrotic tuberculous foci, but it is also likely that the scar is a product of the adenocarcinoma.

Two growth patterns are seen. A discrete nodule in the periphery with pleural tethering is the more common. A few cases, however, show multifocal and bilateral diffuse tumour, so-called *bronchiolo-alveolar cell carcinoma*.

In the latter case, the tumour cells creep along alveolar walls. It is not clear whether the multifocal nature of the disease is due to multiple pulmonary tumours or spread by the movement of air or through intrapulmonary lymphatics.

Against the latter explanation is the fact that hilar lymph nodes are often uninvolved. Adenocarcinomas arise from glandular cells, such as mucous goblet cells, Clara cells and type II pneumocytes. The histology may, therefore, be of a mucus-secreting AC, forming glands and tubules, or of an AC without significant mucus production. A premalignant stage of pulmonary adenosis is recognised.

Large cell undifferentiated carcinomas

Usually central, these are highly aggressive and destructive lesions with necrosis and haemorrhage. Histologically, there is gross nuclear pleomorphism with numerous bizarre mitoses. No squamous or glandular differentiation is seen on light microscopy, although such evidence is often found ultrastructurally.

Staging and treatment

As with all tumours, the stage of the tumour at presentation is of great prognostic significance. The only hope of survival is complete surgical resection, usually only possible with small peripheral tumours without metastases.

As previously indicated, SCLC has almost always metastasised at the time of diagnosis and is therefore not amenable to surgery. Combination chemotherapy can induce remission in SCLC, but only in

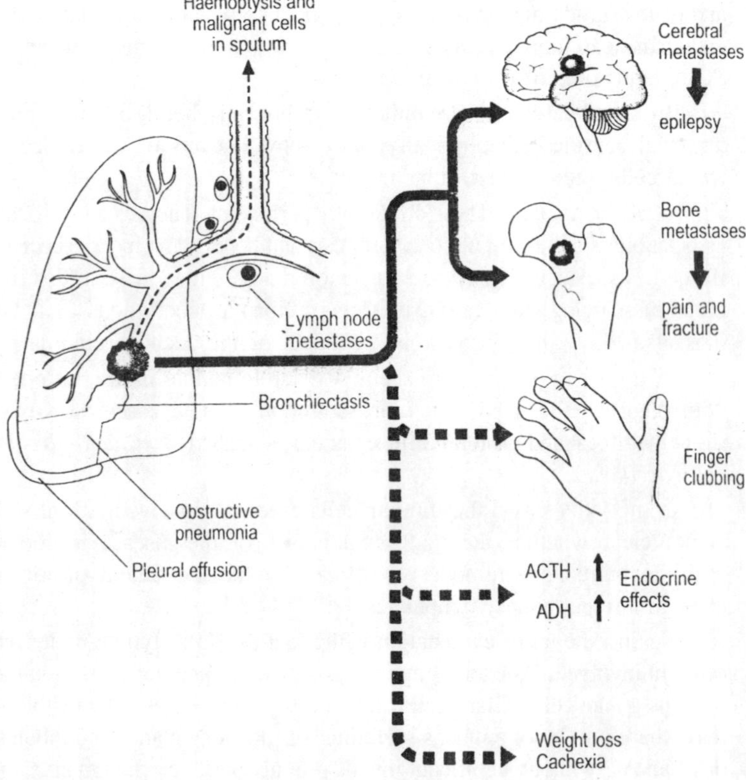

Figure 5.11: Clinical features and complications of primary lung cancer.

a few patients is this sustained.

Other Primary Tumours

Primary tumours other than carcinomas are rare. They can be classified as:

- benign, e.g. bronchial gland adenomas, benign mesenchymal tumours
- malignant, e.g. sarcomas, adenoid cystic carcinomas, combined tumours, lymphomas.

Benign Tumours

Adenomas may arise from bronchial mucous glands. They present as polypoid or sessile lesions in a bronchus. Symptoms are related to obstruction. *Benign mesenchymal tumours* may arise anywhere that mesenchyme (connective tissue) occurs. Thus neurofibromas, lipomas, etc. may be found in the lung.

More common is the chondroma or adenochondroma; this is probably a hamartoma. The lesion is hard, white and well circumscribed, and is discovered as an isolated 'coin' lesion on chest X-ray. It is composed of nodules of cartilage with infoldings and clefts lined with bronchial or bronchiolar epithelium.

Malignant Tumours

Malignant mesenchymal tumours (sarcomas) are extremely rare. *Primary pulmonary lymphomas* are rare tumours presenting as pulmonary disease with or without hilar lymph node involvement, but without clinical evidence of disease elsewhere. HIV/AIDS patients have an increased incidence of pulmonary lymphomas.

They are almost always composed of small B-lymphocytes that may show some plasma cell differentiation (lymphoplasmacytoid cells); monotypic immunoglobulin may be secreted into the blood. These tumours arise from bronchus- and bronchiole-associated lymphoid tissue.

Benign reactive lymphoid hyperplasia is the major differential diagnosis; this can be seen with infection, especially in children, or in association with connective tissue disorders, especially rheumatoid disease.

Malignant lymphoma of the lung is a slowly progressive disorder leading to respiratory impairment or, eventually, systemic disease. *Lymphomatoid granulomatosis* is a rare lymphoma of Tlymphocytes which destroys blood vessels, leading to large cavitating lesions on X-ray. The central nervous system, skin and kidneys are also often involved.

Secondary Lung Tumours

Secondary lung tumours are more common than primary tumours, although a patient presenting first with a lung tumour is more likely to have a primary. Metastases may arise from blood or lymphatic spread. Usually, discrete nodules are seen scattered throughout both lungs; however, the lymphatics may be diffusely involved, leading to the appearance of *lymphangitis carcinomatosa.*

Sarcomas, carcinomas and lymphomas can lead to pulmonary metastases. Carcinomas that commonly give rise to lung secondaries include those from the breast, kidney and gastrointestinal tract.

PLEURA

- Proteinaceous fluid, blood, lymph or air may form collections
- Inflammation is common, causing sharp localised chest pain (pleurisy)
- Pleurisy seen with pneumonia, pulmonary infarction, TB,

connective tissue disease, etc.

- Pleural plaques and mesothelioma are related to asbestos
- Secondary tumours usually from lung or breast carcinomas

The pleura is composed of connective tissue lined with mesothelial cells forming two apposing surfaces; the *visceral pleura* covers the lungs and the *parietal pleura* covers the thoracic cage wall, diaphragm, heart and mediastinum.

EFFUSIONS AND PNEUMOTHORAX

Various fluids (effusions) and air (pneumothorax) can collect between the two layers of pleura. Patients with pleural effusions or pneumothorax suffer shortness of breath and respiratory distress; these symptoms can be relieved by draining the fluid or air from the pleural cavity.

Clinically, an effusion is dull to percussion; this is in contrast to a pneumothorax, which is hyperresonant. To investigate the possibility that a pleural effusion might be due to primary or metastatic neoplasia, it is essential to perform a cytological examination of the cells within the fluid, with possible pleural biopsy.

At autopsy, effusions are usually obvious, but a pneumothorax can be demonstrated only by seeing bubbles of air escaping when the pleural cavity is opened under water.

INFLAMMATORY DISORDERS

Inflammation of the pleura (pleuritis or pleurisy) is common. It can be seen with:

- connective tissue disease: rheumatic fever, rheumatoid disease, systemic lupus erythematosus (SLE)
- infections: any pneumonia, tuberculosis, lung abscess
- pulmonary infarcts
- lung neoplasms.

The inflammation is nearly always accompanied by an effusion. Symptoms are usually of sharp, localised chest pain, worse on breathing. Treatment is of the underlying disorder causing the pleurisy. Depending on the degree of inflammation, pleurisy may resolve or organise to leave an area of fibrosis, sometimes with dystrophic calcification.

Pleural plaques are markers of asbestos exposure. They are asymptomatic patches of thickened fibrotic pleura on the diaphragm and posterior thoracic wall. Histologically, they consist of hyaline acellular connective tissue with a few inflammatory cells at the periphery.

Diffuse pleural fibrosis and *pleural effusions* may both be related to asbestos exposure in the absence of lung cancer, mesothelioma or asbestosis.

TUMOURS

Benign tumours of the pleura are rare. The *solitary fibrous* tumour is composed of a tangled network of fibroblast-like cells in a collagenous stroma. It grows as a solitary lump in the pleura, sometimes becoming very large. Hypertrophic pulmonary osteoarthropathy is a frequent association.

Malignant tumours are most often secondary deposits from primary lung adenocarcinomas, breast carcinomas or, less commonly, ovarian carcinomas. These secondary deposits may grow into the interlobar fissures, thus mimicking a mesothelioma.

Mesothelioma

Primary malignant mesothelioma is strongly associated with occupational exposure to asbestos, especially fibres such as crocidolite ('blue' asbestos) and amosite ('brown' asbestos). These fibres have a diameter of 0.25-0.5 mm, even though they may be well over 5.0 mm long. Other non-asbestos fibres of similar diameter, such as volcanic silicate erionite in Turkey, may also cause mesothelioma.

The latent interval between exposure and the development of mesothelioma is often about 30 years. The tumour begins as nodules in the pleura which extend as a confluent sheet to surround the lung and extend into fissures. The chest wall is often invaded, with infiltration of intercostal nerves, giving severe intractable pain.

Lymphatics may be invaded, giving hilar node metastases. Histology is varied; most commonly the appearance is of a mixed epithelial and spindle cell tumour. Rarely, pure epithelial or spindle cell (sarcomatous) mesotheliomas can occur.

Special histological techniques are often necessary to distinguish between mesothelioma and adenocarcinoma. There is no treatment for malignant mesothelioma, and the symptoms of chest pain and dyspnoea become worse until death, usually within two years of diagnosis.

6

PATHOLOGY OF EXCRETORY SYSTEM

NORMAL STRUCTURE AND FUNCTION OF THE KIDNEYS

The kidneys contribute to the body's biochemical homeostasis by:

- eliminating metabolic waste products
- regulating fluid and electrolyte balance
- influencing acid-base balance.

These vital functions are effected by the filtration of blood plasma in the glomeruli and subsequent processing of the filtrate by the tubules to eventually produce urine. The kidneys also produce the following hormones:

- *prostaglandins,* which are thought to affect salt and water regulation and influence vascular tone
- *erythropoietin,* which stimulates red cell production
- *1,25-dihydroxycholecalciferol,* which enhances calcium absorption from the gut and phosphate reabsorption by the renal tubules
- *renin,* which acts on the angiotensin pathway to increase vascular tone and aldosterone production.

The kidneys have a large functional reserve; the loss of one kidney produces no ill-effects. However, in renal disease waste products can accumulate, causing a condition known as *uraemia.* If the glomerular filters become excessively leaky, large protein molecules are lost in the

Pathological basis for urinary tract symptoms and signs

Symptom or sign	*Pathological basis*
Proteinuria	Increased permeability of the glomerular basement membrane
Uraemia	Renal failure
Haematuria	Severe glomerular injury (red cell casts on urine microscopy)
	Renal tumours or trauma Bladder tumours or trauma
Urinary casts	
• Hyaline casts	Formed in tubules as a result of protein loss from glomeruli
• Granular casts	Formed in tubules from aggregates of inflammatory cells
• Red cell casts	Formed in tubules from red cells in filtrate from severely damaged glomeruli
Hypertension	Renal ischaemia releasing renin
Oliguria or anuria	Severe renal failure (acute or chronic), obstruction or dehydration
Polyuria	Excessive fluid intake (e.g. beer) Osmotic diuresis (e.g. diabetes mellitus)
	Impaired tubular concentration (e.g. diabetes insipidus)
Renal (ureteric) colic	Calculus, blood clot or tumour in ureter
Oedema	Hypoalbuminaemia due to albumin loss in urine (nephrotic syndrome)
Dysuria	Stimulation of pain receptors in urethra due to inflammation

urine *proteinuria*. If the glomeruli are severely damaged, erythrocytes pass through causing *haematuria.*

The basic unit of the kidney is the *nephron;* each comprises a glomerulus connected to a tubule. Each kidney contains approximately 1 million nephrons. These form in the embryonic metanephros, after the physiological involution of the pronephros and mesonephros.

The ureter, calyceal system and collecting ducts form from the ureteric bud arising from the original duct of the pronephros-the Wolffian duct. These two separately derived structures must fuse; failure results in developmental abnormalities.

The kidneys are in the retroperitoneum; the upper poles lie beneath the 12th rib. There is considerable movement with respiration which must be controlled to avoid tearing when the kidneys are biopsied. Each adult kidney weighs approximately 150 g and has a smooth encapsulated surface.

Deep clefts occasionally divide the surface into several lobes, a developmental abnormality of no pathological significance. The medial aspect of each kidney is indented to form the hilum, where the renal artery and vein and the ureter join with the organ.

The cut surface reveals a clearly defined outer cortex and an inner medulla. The medulla comprises the pyramids, which show striations converging into the 8-11 papillae projecting into the calyceal system. Columns of cortical tissue extend between the pyramids towards the hilum.

The cortex and cortical columns contain glomeruli and the proximal and distal convoluted tubules. The medulla contains very thin tubules, the loops of Henle, and the collecting ducts.

Glomerular Structure and Function

The formation of urine begins in the glomeruli, where the filtration of approximately 800 litres of plasma each day results in 180 litres of filtrate, most of which is reabsorbed in the tubules. Each glomerulus consists of a complex tuft of capillaries projecting into Bowman's space. The glomerular capillary comprises:

- endothelial cells
- basement membrane
- epithelial cells.

All components of the capillary wall contribute to the *filtration barrier,* which has two major mechanisms:

1. charge-dependent filtration that normally retains proteins in the plasma due to:
    - polyanionic glycoproteins in the cell membranes of the endothelial and epithelial cells
    - polyanionic proteoglycans in the glomerular basement membrane (GBM).
2. size-dependent filtration due to:
    - network of collagen IV
    - slit diaphragm of epithelial cells.

The capillary tuft is supported by relatively inconspicuous *mesangial cells,* which proliferate and become more prominent in some diseases. The mesangial cells contain actin and other contractile proteins and are attached to the glomerular basement membrane directly or through microtubules where the capillary abuts on the mesangium.

Contraction of the mesangial cell therefore pulls on the glomerular basement membrane and will alter the configuration and calibre of the capillary. Glomeruli have a lobulated architecture which is very difficult to appreciate normally, but becomes pronounced in some renal diseases.

Glomerular endothelial cells are fenestrated; they have small 'windows', allowing the plasma direct contact with the underlying basement membrane. Functionally the endothelial cells:

- play an important role in the charge-dependent filtration barrier because of podocalyxin, a polyanionic sialoglycoprotein in the luminal aspect of the cell membrane
- synthesise, release and bind coagulation factors
- participate in antigen presentation along with monocytes and macrophages by expressing Class II histocompatibility antigens on their surface
- synthesise and release a relaxing factor.

The *basement membrane* is also an important filtration component of the capillary wall. The basement membrane proteoglycans (particularly heparan sulphate) are anionic and thus carry a negative charge. They also contribute to the charge-dependent filtration that normally retains proteins in the plasma.

The basement membrane contains type IV collagen, of which six subtypes have been detected; these are relevant in two conditions, Goodpasture's disease and Alport's disease. It is thought that the collagen fibrils make a three-dimensional network which, in addition to the slit diaphragm of the epithelial cells, contributes to the sizedependent filter.

The effective pore size is estimated to be 4.0 nm for uncharged molecules; those of 1.8 nm traverse the membrane with relative ease. Albumin, which is 3.5 nm and negatively charged, is impeded by the charge-dependent system.

The external aspect of the basement membrane is covered by the epithelial cells. These have long cellular processes (foot processes) which envelop the capillary loops. Slit diaphragms occur where two foot processes meet and are thought to be the limiting aspect of the size-dependent filter. These structures are not well understood but may represent a modified cell junction.

The epithelial cells:

- synthesise the glomerular basement membrane mainly
- are important in the charge-dependent filtration system because of podocalyxin, a polyanionic sialoglycoprotein in the luminal aspect of the cell membrane
- possess important specific adhesion molecules in the abluminal membrane including nephrin, shown to be relevant in glomerular damage not associated with inflammation; e.g. minimal change disease
- display C3b receptor along the entire cell membrane
- have coated pits in which a 330 kD glycoprotein (megalin) has been found to be important in experimental glomerulonephritis analogous to membranous glomerulonephritis
- function as a pericyte and have receptors for vasoactive substances and work in conjunction with the mesangial cells.

Blood enters and leaves the glomerular capillaries by arterioles. Thus, in contrast to all other systemic capillaries in which there is a fall in pressure towards the venous end, the pressure remains high in the glomerular capillary throughout its length-a feature which is essential to efficient filtration.

Juxtaglomerular Apparatus

At the vascular pole of the glomerulus is the juxtaglomerular apparatus. This cluster of specialised cells secretes renin, one of the hormones produced by the kidney. Renin is released in response to:

- reduced blood volume
- low sodium concentration in distal tubular fluid
- sympathetic nervous stimulation
- renal ischaemia.

Renin acts on precursor molecules to form, ultimately, angiotensin II which, among other effects, stimulates the zona glomerulosa of the adrenal cortex to produce aldosterone.

In turn, aldosterone acts on the distal renal tubular epithelium to increase the reabsorption of sodium. The glomerular filtrate, which is isotonic with the plasma, has to be substantially modified osmotically so that water and electrolytes are conserved and the waste metabolites are concentrated for elimination as urine.

This process occurs as the filtrate flows through the tubules, each segment having specific roles.

Tubular Structure and Function

In the *proximal convoluted tubule* 60-80% of the sodium in the filtrate is selectively reabsorbed. Amino acids, potassium and phosphate, together with all of the glucose, are also actively reabsorbed. All of these substances are osmotically active, and as a consequence 60-80% of the water in the filtrate moves passively from the lumen of the proximal convoluted tubule into the blood in the peritubular capillaries.

The high level of metabolic activity of the proximal convoluted tubule cells renders them vulnerable to ischaemia and toxins. The *loop* of *Henle* is the next part of the nephron through which the now reduced volume of filtrate must pass. The loop of Henle is responsible for the development of a high osmotic pressure within the medulla by a process known as the countercurrent system.

The active transfer of sodium from the tubular fluid into the interstitium by the cells of the ascending limb is the essential factor in the countercurrent mechanism. This transfer creates a hypertonic environment in the interstitium of the medulla, with the highest osmotic pressures in the depths of the medulla. The *distal tubule is* continuous with the ascending limb of the loop of Henle.

Where it comes close to the vascular pole of the glomerulus, there is a specialised arrangement of closely packed cells known as the *macula densa.* The convoluted part of the distal tubule is fairly short and soon empties into the collecting duct.

The final adjustment to the sodium concentration in the tubular fluid is made in the distal convoluted tubule, where sodium is exchanged for potassium and hydrogen ions under the influence of aldosterone. The cells of the distal convoluted tubule also de-aminate amino acids to produce ammonia, which passes into the lumen and combines with hydrogen ions to produce ammonium salts.

Thus, the distal tubule plays an important role in acid-base balance. The *collecting ducts* receive modified filtrate from the distal convoluted tubules and pass through the medulla. The epithelial cells of the collecting ducts are selectively permeable to water under the influence of antidiuretic hormone (ADH).

Thus, as the tubular fluid passes through the hypertonic renal medulla, ADH released from the posterior pituitary allows water to be osmotically reabsorbed, producing a hypertonic urine.

Renal Papillae and Urinary Reflux

The collecting ducts open onto the surface of the renal papillae projecting into the calyces. The shape of the duct orifice is relevant to the development of pyelonephritis. Two patterns have been described:

- In the *mid-zone papillae,* the ducts open obliquely onto the surface of the papilla. In the event of urinary reflux from the bladder, these duct orifices will close under the increased pressure in the pelvicalyceal system.
- In contrast, those in the *polar papillae* have no valve effect and remain widely patent, thus allowing the refluxed urine and any bacteria within it to be transmitted into the parenchyma of the kidney.

Physiological Changes

During Pregnancy

During pregnancy the size and weight of the kidneys increases and the glomeruli are enlarged. These changes are reflected in the raised glomerular filtration rate and renal plasma flow which reach a peak by 16 weeks and persist until the end of pregnancy.

Ageing

The weight of the kidneys begins to fall abruptly after the age of 60 years. Gradual shrinkage of the tubules commences at about 40 years. Arteries display intimal thickening, with progressive reduplication of elastic laminae.

Small arteries develop medial hypertrophy and hyalinosis. The number of sclerosed or scarred glomeruli increases with age, thus reducing renal reserve. Drugs that are usually excreted by the kidneys must, therefore, be used with caution in the elderly to avoid toxic accumulation.

URINARY TRACT DISEASE

Clinicopathological Features

Diseases of the urinary tract can present with a variety of features, alone or in combination. As the kidneys are so often affected by a primary disease elsewhere in the body, a simple urine examination (e.g. colour, glucose, protein, haemoglobin) is routine practice in patients being investigated for a variety of disorders.

Investigation

The investigation of patients with known or suspected urinary tract disease is multidisciplinary. Urine and blood analyses are essential; imaging, biopsies and cystoscopy are optional depending on the nature of the clinical problem. Tests with the greatest general clinical utility are urine testing for glucose (to exclude uncontrolled diabetes mellitus),

Table 6.1: Investigation of patients with urinary tract disease.

Investigation	*Diagnostic utility*
Urine analysis Volume Specific gravity Culture Protein content Glucose Haemoglobin Microscopy (casts, etc.)	Determination of urine production rate and concentrating power of the kidneys; investigation of urinary tract infections; urinary protein indicates integrity of glomerular filter; exclusion of diabetes mellitus; investigation of glomerular or tubular lesions
Blood analysis Urea Creatinine Electrolytes	Determination of integrity of renal function; glomerular filtration rate can be calculated from urinary and plasma creatinine concentration and urine flow rate
Imaging Plain X-ray Ultrasound Contrast urography Angiography	Determination of kidney size and symmetry; investigation of suspected tumours, cysts, etc.; detection of calculi; position and integrity of ureters
Renal biopsy Histology Electron microscopy Immunofluorescence	Diagnosis of glomerular, tubular and interstitial renal diseases-
Cystoscopy	Investigation of haematuria and other symptoms; biopsy of bladder lesions

protein (to determine the permeability characteristics of the glomerular basement membrane), and determination of the blood concentrations of urea and/or creatinine, the latter being a more reliable indicator of renal function.

Renal biopsy is performed only when justified by the clinical circumstances, because of the attendant risk of haemorrhage. The biopsy is examined by light microscopy with additional information revealed by immunofluorescence and electron microscopy. Accurate information about the incidence of diseases of the urinary tract is available from transplant and dialysis registries.

However, two important factors conspire to make the true incidence of renal disease almost impossible to ascertain. First, not all countries have registries for the accurate recording of cases. Second, transplantation and dialysis registries record severe and end-stage disease only, making no allowance for mild and subliminal disease. Clinical experience suggests that the prevalence of post infectious glomerulonephritis is much higher in Africa and India than in Europe and North America.

CONGENITAL DISEASES

Approximately 10% of individuals have a congenital abnormality of the urinary tract. Some are hereditary.

Congenital renal diseases may be:

- malformations related to the volume of renal tissue formed or its differentiation
- anatomical abnormalities of position of vascular or ureteric connections
- metabolic lesions such as enzyme defects which affect tubular transport (e.g. cystinuria and renal tubular acidosis).

Conditions Affecting the Volume of Renal Tissue

Bilateral agenesis of the kidneys (Potter's syndrome) is not compatible with independent life. It occurs in 0.04% of all pregnancies. Children with this condition have a characteristic appearance-low-set ears, a receding chin, wide-set eyes and a 'parrot beak' nose. There is always a reduced volume of amniotic fluid (oligohydramnios) due to the absence of fetal urine.

The majority of such cases are stillborn. The most likely cause is a failure of the ureteric bud to develop; there are developmental abnormalities also of other tissues derived from the mesonephros, e.g. bladder and genitalia. However, the commonly associated spinal cord abnormalities and pulmonary hypoplasia suggest that the defect is more generalised.

Unilateral agenesis of a kidney is infrequent. The opposite kidney undergoes marked hypertrophy and is subsequently prone to infections and trauma. Children with this condition often do not survive long because of associated multiple developmental abnormalities, including congenital heart disease, spina bifida and meningomyelocele.

In *renal hypoplasia,* the kidney is abnormally small but not otherwise malformed. Hypoplastic kidneys are prone to infection or stone formation.

Disorders of Differentiation

Renal dysplasia is a cause of a cystic kidney, which may present in childhood as an abdominal mass requiring surgical excision if only to exclude a malignant tumour (e.g. nephroblastoma). The lesion is characterised by islands of undifferentiated mesenchyme or cartilage within the parenchyma. If the lesion is unilateral, the prognosis is good.

Anatomical Abnormalities

Ectopic kidneys form in an abnormal site, usually the pelvis and may be associated with intestinal malrotation. Thf principal clinical importance lies in their presenting as suspicious pelvic mass, and in the risk of infection. due tc the ureteric kinking that often accompanies this condition. *Horseshoe kidney* results from fusion of the two nephrogenic blastemas during fetal life.

The majority are fused at the lower pole. The condition is not rare and renal function is usually normal. There may be a susceptibility to infection and stone formation. *Reduplication of vessels* or *ureters* is not uncommon, achieving clinical significance either when an anomalous polar artery passing anterior to the ureter causes ureteric obstruction, or during renal transplantation.

Metabolic Abnormalities

Cystinuria results from defective tubular reabsorption of several amino acids including cystine, lysine, ornithine and arginine. The precise enzyme defect is unknown, but some patients also have impaired intestinal transport. Cystine crystals are found in the urine and calculi may develop.

The disease is inherited as an autosomal recessive condition. Cystinuria is quite distinct from cystinosis. *Renal tubular acidosis* type I is probably due to a defect in the enzyme system which enables hydrogen ions to be exchanged for bicarbonate in the proximal tubule. There is loss of bicarbonate and failure to acidify and concentrate the urine.

Renal function is otherwise good, but there is a tendency to form stones and develop infections. This condition is inherited as an autosomal dominant gene, although an identical deficiency may be acquired as a result of tubular damage.

Congenital Nephrotic Syndrome

This rare condition has an autosomal recessive pattern of inheritance. It was originally described in Finland, but has subsequently been shown to occur in other countries. The microcystic appearance of the kidneys arises from dilatation of the proximal tubules and Bowman's capsule. A defect in glycosaminoglycan synthesis has been suggested, which would correlate with the abnormal ultrastructural appearance of the glomerular basement membrane and the development of nephrotic syndrome due to excessive proteinuria.

These patients are particularly vulnerable to pneumococcal infection. Congenital nephrotic syndrome can be predicted in utero by the detection of high levels of alpha-fetoprotein in the amniotic fluid and maternal blood. There is no treatment for this condition, but the lesion does not recur in a transplanted kidney.

Al port's Disease

Alport's disease is recognised clinically by the triad of:

- nephritis
- deafness
- ocular lesions.

The condition has variable modes of inheritance and is Xlinked in 50% of families. Males are affected more severely and more frequently than females. Renal involvement is heralded by haematuria commencing usually in the first decade, but may be delayed until the twenties, especially in females.

Renal failure by the second decade is the eventual outcome in the majority of males. In contrast, in females renal function may be preserved until the fifth decade. The deafness, which is for high-pitched sounds, is often difficult to demonstrate.

Ocular disease occurs only in severely affected patients and involves dislocation of the lens, cataracts and corneal dystrophy. The pathogenesis of this condition has been clarified by the finding that some patients with Alport's disease lack the Goodpasture antigen. Mutations in the gene coding for the a5 peptide of the collagen IV molecule have been found and could provide the common factor for the glomerular and ocular pathology.

CYSTIC DISEASE

- Cysts may be solitary or multiple, congenital or acquired
- A solitary cyst may simulate a tumour
- Congenital polycystic disease may not present until adult life
- Acquired cysts may be due to renal scarring

Cystic disease of the kidney comprises a heterogeneous group of conditions which are congenital or acquired. Some are an important cause of renal failure. Accurate diagnosis is essential so that, where the disease is genetically transmitted, the appropriate counselling can be given to patients and their relatives.

Cysts in the kidney are classified as:

- simple renal cysts
- autosomal dominant polycystic kidney disease (ADPKD 1)
- autosomal recessive polycystic kidney disease (ARPKD)
- congenital nephrotic syndrome (see above)
- renal dialysis-associated.

In two further conditions the cysts are localised to the cortico-medullary junction and the papillae respectively:

- uraemic medullary cystic disease
- medullary sponge kidney.

Simple Renal Cysts

Simple renal cysts are a common finding both at autopsy and, increasingly, with ultrasound imaging. The incidence increases with age. They may be single or multiple, and vary in size from a few millimetres to several centimetres.

They have a smooth lining, usually contain clear fluid, and do not affect renal function. Occasionally, haemorrhage occurs into a cyst, causing pain. Their principal significance lies in circumstances where the distinction between cyst and tumour has to be made.

Autosomal Dominant Polycystic Kidney Disease (ADPKD)

ADPKD is the primary renal disease in 8% of adult patients in the European Dialysis and Transplantation Registry. The condition is always bilateral; the kidneys are grossly enlarged, each commonly weighing 1000 g or more.

The kidneys are distorted by numerous cysts, from a few millimetres up to almost 100 mm in diameter, with thin bands of renal parenchyma stretched and compressed between them. Most of the cysts contain clear fluid, but previous haemorrhage can result in the contents being brown due to haemosiderin. Microdissection studies have shown that the cysts are formed at all levels of the nephron.

ADPKD is inherited as an autosomal dominant trait with a high degree of penetrance; this is relevant to genetic counselling and screening. Ninety per cent of cases are linked to the a-globin cluster located on the short arm of chromosome 16 (ADPKD 1), the remainder are due to mutations on chromosome 4 (ADPKD 2).

Patients present with this condition at any age from childhood to late adult life. They maintain their renal function until the enlarging cysts press on the adjacent parenchyma, causing ischaemic changes leading to hypertension or renal failure.

There is an association with berry aneurysms of the circle of Willis, a frequent source of an often fatal subarachnoid haemorrhage. Cysts also occur within the liver, pancreas and lungs, but have no functional significance in these organs.

Autosomal Recessive Polycystic Kidney Disease (ARPKD)

Autosomal recessive polycystic kidney disease is a rare condition which has an autosomal recessive pattern of inheritance. There are several subgroups related to the degree of renal involvement, and more than one gene may be involved.

In the *perinatal subgroup,* which accounts for about 10% of patients with ARPKD, some 90% of nephrons are involved. There are severe abnormalities at birth, and the baby either is stillborn or dies of renal failure and respiratory distress soon after birth. The kidneys are usually enlarged and show a characteristic radial pattern of rather fusiform cysts which replace both the medulla and cortex and extend nearly to the capsular surface.

The cysts are dilated collecting ducts. The enlarged kidneys are usually palpable and may impair delivery. *Neonatal, infantile and juvenile subgroups* reflect progressively less severe involvement of the kidney and a longer survival.

All patients with ARPKD have some abnormality of the liver, ranging from bile duct proliferation and cysts, to substantial hepatic fibrosis which will eventually interfere with hepatic function and produce portal hypertension.

Dialysis-associated Cysts

Dialysis-associated cysts occur in the kidneys of patients in chronic renal failure who have received dialysis treatment for some years. The kidneys, which are severely scarred by the original disease prompting dialysis treatment, contain multiple small cysts throughout the cortex and medulla.

The cysts are often associated with oxalate crystals and are thought to arise as a result of obstruction of the tubules by interstitial fibrosis or by the crystals.

Uraemic Medullary Cystic Disease

Uraemic medullary cystic disease (UMCD) complex, or nephronophthisis, is a recently recognised group of conditions accounting for 20-

25% of chronic renal failure in children and adolescents. In many cases there is a family history; there is one subgroup showing recessive inheritance and another in which the inheritance is dominant.

There is also an association with retinitis pigmentosa. The affected kidneys show numerous cysts at the cortico-medullary junction with interstitial fibrosis and thickened tubular basement membranes.

Medullary Sponge Kidney

Medullary sponge kidney results from dilated collecting ducts in the medulla, causing cysts mainly in the papillae. It is usually bilateral, but may be unilateral. Renal function is usually normal but calculi may form in the cysts, causing pain and infection.

GLOMERULAR DISEASE

The introduction of percutaneous renal biopsy in the mid-1950s greatly improved knowledge about renal disease by allowing the abnormalities to be studied as they evolved. Before this, kidneys were studied mostly at postmortem, but the changes were so advanced that they essentially represented end-stage disease.

Immunofluorescence confirmed that many glomerular diseases are due to immunological reactions (e.g. immune complex deposition). Similarly, electron microscopy enabled visualisation of abnormalities that were undetectable with the light microscope. All of these techniques are used in the assessment of renal biopsies.

Classification

- Glomerular disease may be classified by aetiology, immunological reaction or histological pattern
- Aetiological classification includes immunological and non-immunological injury
- immunological injury may be due to anti-glomerular basement membrane antibody (anti-GBM) or to immune complex deposition
- In immune complex glomerular injury, antigens may be derived from bacteria, parasites, drugs, etc.
- Histological classification is based on the reaction of the glomerulus to injury (e.g. proliferative, membranous thickening)
- Histological features assist in the identification of aetiology and in prognostic and therapeutic decisions

Classification of glomerular disease usually presents major difficulties for students of renal disease. As with many aspects of human disease, it is impossible to provide a satisfactory classification of glomerular disease on the basis of one set of features. There are three parallel and complementary classifications:

- aetiological
- immunological
- morphological.

Clinicopathologically, diseases affecting the glomeruli are best grouped initially into two broad categories:

- *primary glomerular* lesions-in which the kidney is the prime target
- *secondary glomerular lesions-in* which the glomerular injury is secondary to events elsewhere in the body.

Either of these may involve:

- *immunological reactions* involving either
  - glomerular antigens (e.g. anti-glomerular basement membrane glomerulonephritis), or
  - non-glomerular antigens (e.g. immune complex glomerulonephritis)
- *non-immunological disorders* (e.g. diabetes mellitus); in most cases, the glomerular injury is secondary.

Nomenclature of Glomerular Injury

Glomeruli show a limited range of reactions to injury. The following nomenclature is used to describe the pattern of injury:

- *diffuse:* a lesion affecting all glomeruli
- *focal:* a lesion involving some glomeruli, but leaving others unaffected
- *global:* affecting the whole glomerulus
- *segmental:* affecting only part of the glomerulus.

Additional terms are used to describe the character of the light microscopic changes within the glomeruli:

- *proliferative:* increased numbers of cells within the glomerulus; due to proliferation of indigenous cells and to recruitment of polymorphs and macrophages from the circulation as a consequence of activation of the complement cascade
- *membranous change:* the peripheral loops are thickened due to basement membrane expansion
- *membrano-proliferative:* a combination of the two preceding features, often with accentuation of the lobular architecture

- *crescentic:* florid proliferation of cells including macrophages lining Bowman's capsule, often compressing the glomerulus.

Recognition of these changes and the use of this nomenclature have important clinical implications; for example, when crescents are present in >80% of glomeruli, this condition is said to be *crescentic nephritis,* associated with the clinical condition of *rapidly progressive glomerulonephritis,* and heralds a poor prognosis for renal function unless it is treated quickly and vigorously.

Morphology alone gives little indication of the precise nature of the underlying or primary abnormality. Similar morphological features occur in entirely different conditions. To establish as accurate a diagnosis as possible, both immunological and ultrastructural features need to be taken into account. Even so, we remain dismally ignorant of the initiating agent in the majority of cases of glomerular injury.

Clinical Presentations

Patients with glomerular disease usually present with one of five possible conditions:

1. *Recurrent painless haematuria* which varies considerably in degree, ranging from macroscopic haematuria to that which may be detected only at a medical examination due to:
   - exercise haematuria
   - mesangial IgA nephropathy (Berger's disease)
   - Henoch-Schonlein purpura
   - bacterial endocarditis
   - systemic lupus erythematosus (SLE)
   - vasculitis-polyarteritis.
2. *Asymptomatic proteinuria,* varying in severity, and detected at a routine or insurance medical examination due to:
   - Henoch-Schonlein purpura
   - SLE
   - polyarteritis
   - bacterial endocarditis
   - shunt nephritis
   - focal segmental glomerulosclerosis
   - mesangiocapillary glomerulonephritis (MCGN).
3. *Acute nephritis,* characterised by haematuria, oliguria and hypertension. Loin pain and headache may be present and the patient will often feel unwell. In post-infective cases the

relation to the preceding infection can usually be ascertained. This may be due to:

- post-streptococcal glomerulonephritis
- idiopathic rapidly progressive glomerulonephritis (RPGN)
- post-infectious RPGN
- Goodpasture's syndrome (anti-glomerular basement membrane disease)
- SLE
- polyarteritis
- Wegener's granulomatosis
- Henoch-Schonlein purpura
- essential cryoglobulinaemia.

4. Nephrotic syndrome, characterised by heavy proteinuria and, as a consequence, hypoalbuminaemia which leads to severe oedema: there is also hypercholesterolaemia. This may be due to:

   a. primary glomerular diseases
      - minimal change disease
      - membranous glomerulonephritis
      - membrano-proliferative GN (mesangiocapillary GN)
      - focal glomerulosclerosis
      - mesangial IgA nephropathy
      - bacterial endocarditis
      - shunt nephritis

   b. secondary glomerular disease
      - SLE
      - Henoch-Schonlein purpura
      - immune complex disease related to tumours, e.g. carcinoma of bronchus, lymphomas
      - diabetes mellitus
      - amyloid
      - drugs, e.g. penicillamine, gold, 'street heroin', phenytoin, captopril
      - infections-malaria, syphilis, leprosy, hepatitis B
      - cardiovascular-constrictive pericarditis
      - bee sting allergy

   c. inherited disease

- congenital nephrotic syndrome (Finnish type).

5. *Chronic renal failure is* characterised by elevated blood urea (uraemia) and vague features including anaemia, nausea, vomiting, gastrointestinal bleeding and itching; there is often polyuria and nocturia.

   The gradual loss of nephrons leads initially to a reduction in renal reserve, so that a relatively minor insult, such as an episode of diarrhoea and vomiting, will reveal renal impairment in an otherwise healthy patient.

   Patients with established chronic renal failure fall into two groups: those with known renal disease which has caused gradual parenchymal destruction, and those who present de novo, the initial disease having been undetected in its active stage.

   Some clinical features of chronic renal failure (CRF) reflect the important functions of the kidney. Clearly waste products accumulate as a result of the failure of the kidney to filter the blood.

   Anaemia results from failure to produce erythropoietin by the damaged kidney in addition to chronic blood loss and haemolysis. Genetically engineered erythropoietin is now available to patients, ameliorating this aspect of CRF.

   Chronic bone disease (renal osteodystrophy) is present in patients with CRE This is very similar to rickets because the conversion of the vitamin D molecule is impaired in the damaged kidney and this in turn reduces intestinal absorption of calcium, resulting in stimulation of parathyroid secretion. This in turn is exacerbated by the phosphate retention which accompanies CRE Renal osteodystrophy can be treated with the active metabolite of vitamin D, 1-alpha-hydroxycholecalciferol. Renin production is increased whenever renal scarring occurs, and contributes to the hypertension found in CRF.

It is important to remember that there is considerable overlap of the conditions within these clinical states. Several diseases, therefore, may give rise to the same clinical picture; conversely, many diseases fall into more than one of the presenting clinical conditions.

All patients presenting with these features must be investigated thoroughly. In most cases this will include a renal biopsy so that the pathological basis of the disease can be established. This is vital because some conditions require prompt and specific treatment. In contrast, there are other conditions for which there is no effective treatment.

It is just as important to establish the correct diagnosis in these patients, thereby avoiding a course of useless and potentially harmful therapy, as the drugs used to treat renal disease cause serious side-effects.

Mechanisms of Glomerular Damage

Glomeruli can be damaged by immunological or nonimmunological mechanisms.

Immune Glomerular Injury

Immunological damage accounts for most human glomerular disease. There are two mechanisms:

- nephrotoxic antibody, as in anti-glomerular basement membrane (anti-GBM) disease
- immune complex deposition.

The resulting disease is referred to as *glomerulonephritis,* or as glomerulopathy. White patients who possess the human leukocyte antigen (HLA) DR3 appear to be susceptible to developing membranous glomerulonephritis; similarly the possession of HLA-DR2 is observed in 80% of patients with Goodpasture's syndrome, and the presence of B8 confers a worse prognosis.

Current understanding of the involvement of the major histocompatibility complex (MHC) and HLA antigens in antigen presentation is beginning to rationalise this association, which will be clarified as more is learned of the interrelationships of these molecules.

Nephrotoxic Antibody

Anti-GBM disease occurs when the individual forms an IgG antibody against an antigenic glycoprotein within the glomerular basement membrane. The antibody binds to the antigen a3 chain epitope in the collagenase-resistant component of collagen IV located in the lamina densa; this binding is revealed by the linear pattern seen after immunofluorescent staining for IgG.

The binding of IgG to the basement membrane antigen activates the complement cascade; polymorphs are attracted and a florid proliferative glomerulonephritis results. Anti-GBM disease is an uncommon cause of glomerulonephritis. It occurs in *Goodpasture's syndrome,* in which the glomerulonephritis is associated with pulmonary haemorrhages, because the antigen is also present in alveolar basement membrane. Clinical and histological features of anti-GBM disease are discussed below.

Immune Complex Deposition

The kidney is probably one of the routes by which immune complexes are normally cleared from the body. Experimentally, immune complex glomerulonephritis occurs in a proportion of animals given intravenous protein from another species, as part of the so-called serum sickness reaction.

The glomeruli are vulnerable to the deposition of immune complexes because they filter large volumes of blood (Fig. 21.7). Immune complex deposition occurs following:

- passive entrapment, leading to mesangial and possibly subendothelial deposits
- binding to a native component of the glomerular wall, leading to subepithelial deposits by in situ formation
- binding to non-glomerular antigens which have been previously 'planted' and subsequent formation in situ.

The concept of in situ formation has been developed by studies of an animal model known as Heymann nephritis or autologous immune complex (AIC) nephritis. These animals develop antibodies to a 330 kD glycoprotein (megalin) occurring in the clathrin-coated endocytotic pits found on the microvilli of tubular epithelial cells and glomerular epithelial cells now known as the Heymann nephritis antigenic complex (HNAC).

The immune complexes once formed are capped and shed from the epithelial cell surface to form discrete subepithelial deposits. These activate complement with the formation of C5b-9 (the membrane attack complex) which is transported across the epithelial cell to be extruded into the urinary space. The complement components are thus separated from the blood and cause no inflammatory reaction.

The histological picture is very similar to that of membranous glomerulonephritis in humans with a granular pattern of IgG corresponding to the subepithelial deposits. These deposits then undergo a dynamic process of remodelling and modification leading to either enlargement or elimination.

The *planted antigen* involves an extrinsic antigen bound to the basement membrane by means which are not immunological. For example, cationic molecules have been isolated from streptococci and may play a part in poststreptococcal glomerulonephritis. Similarly, in systemic lupus erythematosus (SLE) the antigen is DNA, in which the DNAnucleosome complexes interact with negatively charged sites and will therefore bind to the basement membrane.

Circulating antibody subsequently forms complexes in situ with the now fixed planted antigen within the basement membrane.

The deposition of immune complexes can be visualised ultrastructurally and immunohistochemically as granular deposits within the peripheral glomerular loops or in the mesangium.

The two aspects of in situ formation are not mutually exclusive and both mechanisms may work together.

The role of complement in the elimination of complexes, both within the glomerulus and systemically, should be emphasised. Immune complexes are known to be attached to circulating erythrocytes and other cells by a receptor for C3b known as complement receptor 1 (CR1).

In this way the complexes can be further modified and subsequently eliminated by the monocyte-macrophage system. This protective role is highlighted by the tendency of patients with complement deficiencies to develop glomerulonephritis.

Cell-mediated Glomerular Damage

T-cells participate in glomerular damage independently of immunoglobulin, shown experimentally in birds in which the antibody response was ablated. Mononuclear cells characterised these lesions and T-cells release chemokines such as macrophage chemoattractant protein-1 (MCP-1) and macrophage migration inhibitory factor (MIT) relevant in the recruitment of macrophages which act as the effector cell. Macrophages feature in crescentic nephritis.

Further experimental work adds credibility to the concept of cellular immune mechanisms in glomerular disease and there is some evidence for T-cell subset interactions in glomerulonephritis, although this is still poorly understood in most clinical contexts.

Participation by Glomerular Cells

As indicated in the section on normal structure and function, the indigenous glomerular cells have been shown to produce a variety of cytokines and to relate to the coagulation cascade. In cell culture and experimental studies, upregulation of many of the inflammatory cytokines and their receptors have been demonstrated.

Some of these cytokines stimulate the production of extracellular matrix material (ECM) by the glomerular cells, and autocrine and paracrine effects have been proposed. Inhibition of the mesangial proteases by some of the cytokines impairs remodelling of the excess ECM and thus contributes to the development of glomerulosclerosis.

Currently the entire spectrum of proinflammatory and synthetic cytokines has been identified. A more complete understanding depends on the clarification of the precise interrelationships of these substances and the surrounding cells. Blocking of cytokine receptors may offer therapeutic opportunities.

Mediators of Non-inflammatory Glomerular Damage

These lead to marked functional (proteinuria) and structural (epithelial foot process effacement) changes without inflammation necrosis or proliferation. They are relevant to minimal change disease and focal segmental glomerulosclerosis (FSGS). They also feature in membranous glomerulonephritis.

Circulating glomerular permeability factors are postulated following passive transfer of proteinuria to rats by non-immunoglobulin factors derived from the serum of patients with minimal change disease and FSGS. These factors, derived from T-cells, target the epithelial cells, evidenced by the foot process effacement.

The proteins nephrin and CD2AP associated with the slit-pore diaphragm of the epithelial cell are implicated, as monoclonal antibodies to nephrin induce a minimal change-like injury in experimental rats; also, altered nephrin expression occurs in experimental nephrotic syndrome and in minimal change disease.

Mediators of Inflammatory Glomerular Damage

When immune reactants become localised within the glomerular basement membrane, there is activation of the complement cascade and release of vasoactive substances. These are the mediators of acute inflammation, and they are responsible for the damage to the basement membrane, altering its properties to result in some of the urinary abnormalities observed clinically. These substances are as follows:

- *Complement* has a major role in the inflammatory process in glomerulonephritis. The classical pathway is activated by immune complexes fixed within the glomeruli. This process attracts neutrophil polymorphs, increases vascular permeability, and causes membrane damage.
- *Nephritic factors* (NeF-AP and NeF-CP) are immunoglobulins which bind to and inactivate inhibitors of the converting enzymes of the complement cascade. Consequently, the breakdown of C3 continues unchecked, resulting in the depletion of C3 from the plasma, a situation termed hypocomplem-entaemia.

- *Polymorphonuclear leukocytes* are attracted by the chemotactic influence of C5a. The polymorphs bind to the complexes by their C3 and Fc receptors.

  However, they are unable to phagocytose the complexes, which are fixed, and as a result release their lysosomal enzymes in the vicinity of the complexes, augmenting the damage to the glomerular basement membrane.
- *Reactive oxygen species (ROS)* derived from recruited leukocytes and native glomerular cells influence enzymes and their inhibitors with enhanced degradation of the glomerular basement membrane.

  They also enhance neutrophil binding by endothelial cells and, by influencing arachidonic acid metabolism, promote thrombus formation within the glomerulus. ROS have been demonstrated in both immune complex and anti-GBM glomerulonephritis.
- *Clotting factors* also mediate glomerular damage. Fibrin is commonly found in glomerulonephritis. Fibrin entraps platelets which, because of their C3 and Fc receptors, form microthrombi, degranulate and release their vasoactive peptides, thus increasing vascular permeability.

Not every mediator is involved in every case. Permutations of mediators are common and account for the range of histological patterns in glomerulonephritis.

PRIMARY GLOMERULAR DISEASES

Anti-glomerular Basement Membrane Disease

Anti-glomerular basement membrane (anti-GBM) disease occurs predominantly in young men. The mechanism of this disease is discussed above. The usual presenting feature is rapidly progressive renal failure, but occasional patients have haematuria and proteinuria, or nephrotic syndrome.

Haemoptysis may be present. The prognosis is poor without treatment, but the introduction of plasma exchange (plasmapheresis) has substantially improved the outlook, particularly in patients treated early.

Histologically, the characteristic lesion is a focal and segmental glomerulonephritis. With increasing severity, segmental necrosis with fibrin deposition, and a florid crescentic glomerulonephritis occur.

Immune-Complex-Mediated Lesions

Immune-complex-mediated glomerular injury (for mechanism, see above) results in a variety of glomerular reactions depending on the nature of the complexes.

Diffuse Proliferative Glomerulonephritis

Acute diffuse proliferative glomerulonephritis is one of the patterns of glomerular damage associated with a postinfective aetiology. It is usually an acute lesion following a transient infection. For many years it has been associated with a preceding 13-haemolytic streptococcal infection (poststreptococcal glomerulonephritis).

However, acute proliferative glomerulonephritis is associated with a variety of other causative organisms and conditions including:

- staphylococci
- meningococci
- pneumococci
- viruses
- malaria
- toxoplasmosis
- schistosomiasis.

Only for convenience, therefore, is post-streptococcal glomerulonephritis discussed as an example below, keeping in mind that this type of lesion is not unique to a streptococcal aetiology.

Post-streptococcal Glomerulonephritis

3-Haemolytic streptococci of Lancefield group A cause the post-streptococcal glomerulonephritis reaction; within that group, Griffith's subtypes 12, 4 and 1 are nephritogenic. The primary infection usually causes pharyngitis but may also involve the middle ear or skin.

There are considerable geographical differences in the incidence and severity of post-streptococcal glomerulonephritis throughout the world; for example, it is the commonest renal disease in India, but its incidence is falling in the UK.

Clinical features

Post-streptococcal glomerulonephritis affects all ages, but children are more commonly affected, with the onset of malaise, fever and nausea 7-14 days after a sore throat. There is oliguria (a significant reduction in urine volume), and the urine is dark or 'smoky' due to the presence of microscopic haematuria.

Facial oedema, often periorbital, and a mild degree of hypertension are apparent on examination. A raised anti-streptolysin 0 (ASO) titre and a significant reduction in complement (C3) levels are present. A raised blood urea indicates mild renal impairment. Urine analysis confirms the presence of haematuria, together with white cells and casts, and reveals a variable degree of proteinuria.

The kidneys are swollen by oedema, with scattered petechiae beneath the capsule and internally.

Histological features

The glomeruli are distended and hypercellular. All of the glomeruli are involved, hence the use of the term 'diffuse'. The increase in cellularity is due to the proliferation and swelling of mesangial, endothelial and epithelial cells, together with a variable infiltration of polymorphonuclear leukocytes.

Some glomeruli may show proliferation of cells lining Bowman's capsule to form a crescent; the presence of crescents in 80% or more of the glomeruli indicates a rapidly progressive disease and heralds a poor prognosis. There is usually interstitial oedema and a variable inflammatory cell infiltrate.

The tubules contain red cell casts and the tubular epithelial cells may show degenerative changes. Using immunofluorescence techniques, granular deposits of IgG and C3 are identified on the peripheral basement membranes and within the mesangium. The precise streptococcal antigen is not yet known; several antigens, some of which are cationic, have been demonstrated in the glomeruli in this condition.

Ultrastructurally, electrondense deposits situated beneath the epithelial cells on the outer aspect of the basement membrane are the principal feature. These are termed subepithelial deposits, and are often referred to as 'humps' or 'lumpy deposits'; they correspond to the granular IgG and C3 demonstrated by the immunological studies. There is usually a mild degree of foot process effacement or fusion.

Prognosis

This is good in children, but only 60% of adults recover fully. Patients with acute post-streptococcal glomerulonephritis are usually treated conservatively, and renal biopsy does not feature in the management unless the anticipated improvement fails to occur.

In most cases the characteristic morphological changes will have resolved by 6-8 weeks after the onset of the illness. All that remains is mild mesangial hypercellularity, which may persist for many months or even years. The relationship between poststreptococcal glomerulonephritis and subsequent chronic glomerulonephritis remains controversial.

Focal Proliferative Glomerulonephritis

'Focal' implies uneven involvement of the glomeruli with some affected and others normal. In addition, involvement of only parts of individual glomeruli is common, and the term 'segmental' is also appropriate. Thus, focal and segmental lesions are often found together. A focal glomerulonephritis is a fairly common pattern of reaction which is found in a variety of systemic diseases including:

- systemic lupus erythematosus
- Henoch-Schonlein purpura
- infective endocarditis
- microscopic polyarteritis
- Goodpasture's syndrome
- Wegener's granulomatosis.

Some of these conditions are immunologically mediated, and a possible explanation for the focal involvement is that it reflects an overloading of the mesangium's capacity to clear immune complexes.

Complexes, unable to be removed from some of the glomerular tufts, accumulate and activate the complement cascade, causing localised inflammation within that part of the glomerulus. Use of the unqualified term 'focal glomerulonephritis' is not helpful clinically.

The immunological and ultrastructural profile of the glomerular lesion in the renal biopsy must be ascertained so that a more precise diagnosis can be made in each case. There is one significant condition having a focal pattern that affects the kidney primarily: IgA disease. IgA deposition also occurs systemically, giving rise to Henoch-Schonlein purpura, a systemic vasculitis with involvement of the kidney.

IgA Disease

IgA disease is now recognised as the major cause of chronic renal failure and insufficiency throughout the world. The features include:

- children and young adults affected
- episodic haematuria coinciding with upper respiratory tract infections
- mild proteinuria, very occasionally nephrotic syndrome
- hypertension
- raised serum IgA levels.

Aetiology

Little is known of the aetiological factors but reports indicate a geographical localisation, with the highest incidence in the Asia-Pacific area. High levels of circulating IgA are usually present and a possible relationship with diseases in which mucosal immunity is disturbed has been proposed.

There is a weak association with HLADR4, but most attention has been directed to finding factors which will cause an excess of IgA; viruses and food proteins have been incriminated. The prognosis is good in young patients with IgA disease, but not as good in adults.

Adverse clinical prognostic indicators in addition to age are renal impairment at presentation, persistent nephrotic-range proteinuria, and hypertension.

Histological features

A wide spectrum of changes is seen histologically. A mild focal mesangial proliferation, with IgA and C3 located in the mesangium in all of the glomeruli with corresponding electron-dense paramesangial deposits, is associated with a good prognosis.

In contrast, at the other end of the spectrum, a mesangiocapillary pattern, sometimes with segmental necrosis, is associated with a more rapid deterioration of renal function. IgA disease is often accompanied by a brisk interstitial inflammatory component, and established interstitial fibrosis represents an ominous histological feature.

Membranous Glomerulonephritis

Membranous glomerulonephritis (MGN), a chronic immunecomplex-mediated disorder, has a distinctive histology but many causes.

Aetiology

A small proportion of cases have identifiable causes, as follows, and are best termed secondary membranous glomerulopathies:

- infective-syphilis, malaria, hepatitis B
- drugs-penicillamine, gold, mercury, heroin
- tumours-lymphomas, melanomas, carcinoma of the bronchus.

These patients are important to identify because the renal lesions may subside when the causative factor is treated or removed. Patients with systemic lupus erythematosus (SLE) form another important group; approximately 10% have MGN. However, approximately 85% of patients with MGN have no identifiable cause and their disease is said to be idiopathic. The pathogenesis of these cases is still under debate.

Clinical Features and Prognosis

MGN affects all age groups, but adults are affected more commonly, with the highest incidence in the fifth to seventh decades. Males are affected more frequently than females. The presenting feature is usually proteinuria or nephrotic syndrome.

Hypertension features at some time in the clinical course in about half of the patients. The majority of cases are unresponsive to steroids; they progress, over a variable and unpredictable period of between 2 and 20 years, to renal failure due to glomerulosclerosis.

The prognosis in children is much better, however, particularly when there is proteinuria alone. In these cases, only 10% develop renal failure, and 50% remit. The prognosis in cases secondary to treatable antecedent causes is excellent.

Histological features

Capillary wall thickening without proliferation or inflammation featuring characteristic spikes is present in all glomeruli (Fig. 21.10). Immunopathological studies show granular deposits of IgG and C3 in the thickened capillary walls.

Electron microscopy reveals the immune complexes deposited on the outer aspect of the basement membrane beneath the epithelial cells. As the disease progresses, new basement membrane, composed of laminin together with the 0 and a4 chains of type IV collagen, encircles the deposits.

These undergo degradation and lysis in the thickened capillary walls. Eventually the affected glomeruli become sclerosed. Thrombosis of the renal vein may complicate MGN, reflecting the increased coagulability of the blood in this condition.

Membrano-Proliferative Glomerulonephritis

Membrano-proliferative glomerulonephritis (MPGN) alternatively named *mesangiocapillary glomerulonephritis* (MCGN) includes both proliferation and membrane thickening. The lobular architecture of the glomerulus is also accentuated. Since the first description in 1965, two main types have been recognised.

Type I MPGN

Type I MPGN is a chronic immune-complex-mediated lesion, with subendothelial deposits and paramesangial deposits. This lesion is further subdivided into those:

- with mixed cryoglobulinaemia-70-90% have hepatitis C
- without cryoglobulinaemia occurs in:
  - a wide range of conditions including infections, tumours, collagen vascular diseases (SLE), hereditary and aquired complement deficiencies, drug reactions and genetic diso-

rders (e.g. sickle cell disease)

— a small number of patients remaining when all of the other causes have been excluded-termed 'idiopathic MPGN'.

The majority of patients present with nephrotic syndrome, but some have haematuria. A persistently low serum complement C3 (hypocomplementaemia) is present in twothirds of patients. The clinical course is one of progressive deterioration over 10 or more years. A third, rare variant related to immune complex deposition is also described.

Type II MPGN

Type II MPGN is characterised by markedly thickened capillary walls expanded by discontinuous linear deposition of C3. Ultrastructurally, large electron-dense ribbon-like deposits give rise to the preferable, alternative name-dense *deposit disease* (DDD).

DDD may follow an infection, but the lesion is now thought to be due to a basic abnormality in either the synthesis or degradation of the basement membrane itself. The activation of complement via the alternative pathway and the presence of C3NeF are regarded as secondary phenomena.

Crescentic Glomerulonephritis

Crescentic glomerulonephritis-rapidly progressive glomerulonephritis (RPGN)-is a manifestation of severe glomerular injury characterised by the presence of cellular crescents that eventually compress the glomeruli.

Blood and cells gain access to Bowman's space with the formation of fibrin leading to the influx of macrophages and T-cells from the interstitium with the release of inflammatory kinins, which cause the proliferation of macrophages, epithelial cells and interstitial fibroblasts to form the crescent. Three categories have been described:

- due to anti-GBM antibody but without pulmonary haemorrhage
- immune-complex-mediated-represents a heterogeneous group in which crescentic nephritis complicates a known form of glomerulonephritis, e.g. IgA, MCGN, lupus nephritis, etc.
- 'pauci-immune' necrotising GN does not involve demonstrable immunoglobulin or ultrastructural deposits and accounts for 50-70% of patients with primary RPGN; 75-90% of these patients demonstrate a positive ANCA test and 'renal microscopic vasculitis' suggests a relationship with systemic vasculitis. The pathogenesis of this condition remains the subject of controversy, but the lesion may be attributable to cellmediated glomerular damage.

Clinical features

The salient clinical feature is rapid deterioration, with loss of useful renal function within a matter of weeks. Some patients improve if treated vigorously with immunosuppression and plasma exchange (plasmapheresis). Nevertheless, there is a high risk of permanent scarring of the kidney with the likelihood of subsequent hypertension.

Minimal Change Disease

Minimal change disease is also known as *lipoid nephrosis,* a name which reflects the presence of fat in the renal tubular epithelial cells and is the most noticeable feature light microscopically, glomerular changes being absent or minimal; the diagnostic loss of epithelial foot processes is evident only by electron microscopy.

Pathogenesis

This is still not clear, but there is evidence for circulating factors, some derived from T cells, which target glomerular epithelial cell antigens, e.g. nephrin.

Clinical features and prognosis

Minimal change disease affects all ages, but is much more common in children, with a peak incidence between the ages of 2 and 4 years and with a male preponderance. In a few patients it follows an upper respiratory infection or prophylactic immunisation.

Nephrotic syndrome responsive to steroid therapy is the classical presentation. The prognosis in children is good with no permanent renal damage, but in adults the outlook is variable.

Focal Glomerulosclerosis

Focal segmental glomerulosclerosis (FSGS) is an important disease; it is the cause of nephrotic syndrome in some 10% of children and 15% of adults. The pathogenesis is unknown, but circulating permeability factors are again suggested: many experts regard it as part of a spectrum including minimal change disease, implying progression from one to the other.

Segmental sclerosis is seen in a variety of other diseases (e.g. IgA nephropathy, diabetes and reflux nephropathy), but these cases lack the distinctive immunopathological and ultrastructural features of focal glomerulosclerosis.

Clinical features

Focal segmental glomerulosclerosis presents with nephrotic syndrome or alternatively heavy proteinuria. Renal failure ensues within 10 years in most cases. FSGS tends to recur in transplanted kidneys.

SECONDARY GLOMERULAR DISEASES

- Many systemic disorders can result in glomerular damage
- Immune complexes in autoimmune disease (e.g. SLE) can damage basement membranes
- Diabetes mellitus may be complicated by glomerulopathy and renal papillary necrosis
- Glomerular vascular lesions can result from systemic vasculitis and hypertension

Secondary glomerular disease implies renal damage occurring as part of a systemic condition. These systemic conditions may be:

- immune-complex-mediated
- metabolic
- vascular.

Immune-Complexmedlated Conditions

Immune-complex-mediated systemic conditions which may involve renal damage include:

- systemic lupus erythematosus
- Henoch-Schonlein purpura
- infective endocarditis.

Systemic Lupus Erythematosus

Systemic lupus erythematosus (SLE) is a systemic condition affecting multiple organs, including the skin, joints, serosal membranes, heart and lungs. The kidneys are involved in about 70% of cases. The glomerular lesions, found in descending order of frequency, are:

- diffuse proliferative glomerulonephritis
- focal proliferative glomerulonephritis
- membranous glomerulonephritis.

Patients with membranous changes have heavy proteinuria or the nephrotic syndrome.

Henoch-Schonlein Purpura

Henoch-Schonlein purpura is a systemic vasculitis affecting the skin, joints, intestine and kidneys, and occurs most commonly in childhood. A purpuric rash typically affects the extensor aspects of the arms and legs and the buttocks.

Joint pains, and abdominal pain with or without intestinal haemorrhage, are also present. The proportion of patients with renal involvement is difficult to assess, but it may be the majority. Significant renal damage occurs in over one-third of cases, ranging from proteinuria, possibly with nephrotic syndrome, to rapidly progressive glomerulonephritis.

There is good evidence to suggest an immune complex aetiology. A preceding respiratory infection is noted in about one-third of cases, but there is no association with any specific organism.

Infective Endocarditis

Renal complications of infective endocarditis are:

- infarcts due to embolic vegetations from the heart valves
- focal and segmental glomerulonephritis ('focal embolic nephritis')
- diffuse proliferative glomerulonephritis.

The last two complications are almost certainly due to immune complex deposition.

In cases with a focal and segmental glomerulonephritis the kidney shows multiple haemorrhagic foci throughout the cortex and beneath the capsule; it is one of the causes of a 'flea-bitten' kidney. The renal lesions subside when the bacterial source of the antigen is removed by intensive antibiotic therapy.

Metabolic Conditions

Metabolic conditions which may involve renal damage include:

- diabetes mellitus
- renal amyloidosis
- multiple myeloma.

Diabetes Mellitus

Diabetes mellitus is associated with damage involving both large and small vessels throughout the body. The presence of severe atheroma involving the renal artery may cause renal ischaemic lesions and hypertension.

Involvement of the microcirculation, in addition to causing lesions in the retina, nerves and skin, significantly affects the kidneys, leading to glomerulopathy, arteriolar hyalinosis, and tubulointerstitial lesions. The combination of changes that occur in individual cases is varied and often referred to collectively as diabetic nephropathy.

Diabetic glomerulopathy

Glomerular disease in diabetics causes proteinuria, which becomes heavier as the disease progresses, leading to nephrotic syndrome and chronic renal failure. Approximately 10% of all diabetics die in renal failure. However, when patients developing diabetes in childhood (usually insulindependent) are considered separately, death from renal failure occurs in approximately 50% of cases.

This correlates with the fact that renal disease occurs more often, and is more severe, when the onset of diabetes is early in life; glomerulosclerosis eventually occurs in these cases.

Pathogenesis

The pathogenesis of the basement membrane changes is not fully understood. All the features point to a basement membrane which is more leaky than normal. The changes include:

- glomerular hypertrophy
- ECM expansion and mesangial cell hypertrophy
- basement membrane thickening
- a deficiency of proteoglycans, such as heparan sulphate, which are responsible for the polyanionic nature of the membrane.

Factors which appear to mediate these changes are:

- hyperglycaemia
- hyperfiltration due to increased glomerular blood flow in diabetes
- non-enzymic glycosylation of proteins; this occurs in hyperglycaemia and may alter the polyanionic state of the basement membrane and also the physicochemical properties of the circulating proteins
- growth factors
- cytokines.

Both systemic and glomerular hypertension have been shown to accelerate the changes of diabetic nephropathy. Control of systemic blood pressure is an important aspect of the management of the diabetic patient.

Histologically, three types of glomerular lesion occur, representing a continuous spectrum of increasing severity:

- Capillary wall thickening is the initial change.
- The addition of mesangial matrix expansion to the capillary thickening eventually encroaches on the capillaries, and is termed diffuse glomerulosclerosis.
- The nodular expansion of the mesangium at the tips of the glomerular lobules is very characteristic of diabetes, and is

known as nodular glomerulosclerosis or KimmelstielWilson lesion.

The glomerular changes are accompanied by arteriolar hyalinosis affecting both the afferent and efferent arterioles.

Renal Papillary Necrosis

Renal papillary necrosis is frequently seen in diabetics with acute pyelonephritis. The blood supply to the renal papillae via the vasa recta is tenuous, and the vasculopathy together with the effects of the inflammation result in ischaemia of the papillae, which become infarcted. The necrotic papillae may then become detached and either cause an obstruction or are passed in the urine.

Renal Amyloidosis

Renal involvement is present in 80-90% of cases of secondary amyloidosis. The affected patients have heavy proteinuria or the nephrotic syndrome. Renal involvement is the presenting feature in over 50% of patients, and leads inevitably to chronic renal failure, with extensive glomerulosclerosis within 1-2 years.

Multiple Myeloma

Renal damage occurs frequently in patients with multiple myeloma. Renal failure may be the presenting feature. The most significant lesions are tubulo-interstitial, characterised by proteinaceous casts to which there is a giant cell reaction.

Glomerular involvement is uncommon in myeloma, but includes amyloid infiltration in about 10% of cases and the deposition of monoclonal cryoglobulin in a smaller proportion.

Vascular Damage

Glomerular diseases due to vascular damage include:

- polyarteritis nodosa
- Wegener's granulomatosis
- Haemolytic-uraemic syndrome
- idiopathic thrombocytopenic purpura
- disseminated intravascular coagulation.

Thus, the group includes glomerular damage in systemic vasculitis (polyarteritis and Wegener's granulomatosis) and in thrombotic microangiopathies (haemolytic-uraemic syndrome, idiopathic thrombocytopenic purpura and disseminated intravascular coagulation). The glomerular lesions in systemic vasculitis are usually characterised by segmental necrosis, sometimes with crescents.

Circulating auto-antibodies against neutrophil cytoplasmic antigens (ANCA) have been described in these patients. Two patterns are found:

- cytoplasmic (C-) ANCA reacts with proteinase 3
- perinuclear (P-) ANCA reacts with myeloperoxidase.

The majority of patients with Wegener's granulomatosis react with C-ANCA. Patients with microscopic polyarteritis react with P-ANCA but the reaction is less specific. In thrombotic microangiopathies the glomerular capillaries contain fibrin or platelets or both.

Polyarteritis Nodosa

Polyarteritis nodosa involves medium to small arteries throughout the body. Involvement of renal vessels results in haematuria and loin pain due to renal infarcts, often with hypertension developing later.

Microscopic polyarteritis (also referred to as hypersensitivity angiitis) contrasts with the classical (nodosa) form in that smaller arteries, arterioles, capillaries and venules are damaged. Renal involvement presents not infrequently as rapidly progressive renal failure. Untreated patients die within a few months to years, but there is a good response to immunosuppressive therapy.

Wegener's Granulomatosis

Wegener's granulomatosis is a rare necrotising vasculitis affecting the nose and upper respiratory tract in addition to the kidneys. It occurs more commonly in males in their fourth and fifth decades, although it can occur at any age. The clinical indicators of renal involvement vary from microscopic haematuria to rapidly progressive renal failure.

If the condition remains untreated, progressive renal impairment is inevitable, but cyclophosphamide induces a remission in the majority of patients, with complete resolution of the glomerular lesions if treated early enough.

Haemolytic-uraemic Syndrome

Haemolytic-uraemic syndrome (HUS) is a complex condition in which there is:

- acute nephropathy
- haemolysis
- thrombocytopenia.

Fibrin strands are deposited in small vessels, including the glomerular capillaries. The resultant mesh, through which the blood has to pass, deforms the erythrocytes ('helmet' and 'burr' cells) and platelets with subsequent destruction. This process is microangiopathic haemolysis.

There are three subgroups of HUS:

- childhood
- adult
- secondary.

Childhood HUS

Childhood HUS carries a much better prognosis than that occurring in adults. There is often a prodromal episode of diarrhoea or a flu-like illness which lasts 5-15 days. There is a sudden onset of oliguria, with haematuria and occasionally melaena.

There is increasing anaemia. Approximately half the patients develop hypertension. The pathogenesis is uncertain, but geographical variations point to a specific infective agent; verotoxin-producing *Escherichia coli* are thought to be responsible in some cases.

Adult HUS

Adult HUS is more frequently fatal and is seen in a variety of situations:

- pregnancy-sometimes occurring post partum, even several months after delivery
- oestrogen therapy-occurring in women taking contraceptive pills and, rarely, in men treated with oestrogens for prostatic carcinoma
- infections, e.g. typhoid, viruses and shigellosis.

Secondary HUS

Secondary HUS occurs as a complication of:

- malignant hypertension
- progressive systemic sclerosis
- systemic lupus erythematosus
- transplant rejection.

Clinically and morphologically, secondary HUS is identical with the other types.

Histological features of HUS

The glomeruli contain thrombi within the capillary lumen, and there is segmental endothelial and mesangial swelling. The capillary walls are thickened.

Arterioles and small arteries show fibrin and erythrocytes in the walls, often with thrombosis. Cortical necrosis can result when there is extensive arterial thrombosis.

Idiopathic Thrombocytopenic Purpura

Idiopathic thrombocytopenic purpura (ITP) occurs predominantly in women, mostly under 40 years. There are neurological symptoms together with haemolytic anaemia and thrombocytopenia. Renal involvement is seen in approximately half the patients and is manifested by proteinuria, microscopic haematuria and renal impairment.

Histological features

Eosinophilic granular platelet thrombi are identified in glomerular capillaries, afferent arterioles and interlobular arteries.

Disseminated Intravascular Coagulation

Disseminated intravascular coagulation is a systemic problem involving generalised endothelial damage. The most common cause is a Gram-negative septicaemia, analogous to the experimental generalised Shwartzman reaction. Fibrin thrombi fill the lumina of glomerular capillaries, afferent arterioles and small arteries, causing severe renal impairment.

RENAL DISEASE IN ASSOCIATION WITH SPECIFIC INFECTIONS

Leprosy

Several forms of immune complex glomerulonephritis and secondary amyloid in addition to interstitial lesions are recognised. The true incidence of renal disease in patients with leprosy is not known.

Parasitic Diseases

Malaria

The two major forms of malaria involve the kidneys in quite different ways. *Plasmodium falciparum* gives rise to a very brief and insignificant immune complex lesion followed by severe acute tubular necrosis.

In contrast, *Plasmodium malariae* (quartan malaria) gives rise to a high incidence of nephrotic syndrome in endemic areas such as Nigeria and Uganda. The glomerulonephritis is immune complex related, severe and progressive, and is characterised by basement membrane changes and mesangial sclerosis.

Schistosomiasis

The main effects of schistosomiasis are manifest in the hepatobiliary system and lower urinary tract. An immune complex glomerulonephritis is reported in association with *S. mansoni* when there is hepatobiliary disease. The antigens demonstrable within the glomerular deposits derive from the gut of the adult worm. Some cases are shown to involve both *Salmonella* endotoxins, which activate complement, and schistosomal antigens in the deposits.

Filariasis

Filariasis is associated with glomerulonephritis. Patients with *Wuchereria bancrofti* develop a proliferative glomerulonephritis. This contrasts with *Onchocerca volvulus,* which gives rise to nephrotic syndrome due to a range of glomerular lesions including minimal change through to a sclerosing glomerulopathy. Patients with loa-loa develop membranous lesions together with a sclerosing glomerulopathy.

Viral Infections

Viral infections involving the kidney are becoming increasingly important. They involve the glomeruli and interstitium by a variety of mechanisms, some of which are as yet unknown.

Hepatitis B antigenaemia is associated with a membranous or a membrano-proliferative glomerulonephritis, particularly in children in Asia. Disappearance of the HBe antigenaemia and conversion to the HBe-antibody state, in most but not all cases, corresponds to remission of the renal lesion.

A systemic vasculitis manifest as polyarteritis nodosa is more a feature in Western countries. Hepatitis C is associated with mesangiocapillary glomerulonephritis with or without cryoglobulinaemia.

HIV-associated glomerulopathy occurs before the development of AIDS and is therefore distinct from any infective aspects of the latter disease. The renal lesions include a focal segmental glomerulosclerosis (FSGS) which features a characteristic collapse of the glomerular capillaries.

In addition there is severe interstitial fibrosis and inflammation which is disproportionate to the glomerular lesion. The atrophic tubules appear as microcysts. IgM and C3 are present, and abundant clusters of microtubules termed tubuloreticular inclusions are found in endothelial cells.

While these are characteristic they are not pathognomonic, as they are seen in many retrovirus diseases as well as in lupus nephritis. Black races are particularly susceptible and the progress in children is slower than in adults.

Polyomavirus-induced nephropathy is endemic and causes disease in immunocompromised individuals. The two polyoma viruses known (BK and JC) share 70% of their sequence homology with SV40 virus. They have been implicated in a variety of conditions including GuillainBarre syndrome, hepatitis, and SLE. BK virus displays tropism for the urogenital epithelium and causes interstitial nephritis in HIV-infected patients and renal transplants.

It is an important cause of graft failure, which has become more prevalent with the use of tacrolimus and microphenolate. It is imperative to differentiate the changes histologically from rejection because increasing immunosuppression will exacerbate the viral lesion and accelerate graft loss. Urinary cytology assists in the diagnosis of polyomavirus nephropathy by the recognition of cells containing large basophilic intranuclear inclusions, so-called 'decoy' cells.

Epstein-Barr (EB) virus induces B-cell proliferation and transformation by engaging proteins of the tumour necrosis factor (TNF) receptor family of the host. In the context of chronic immunosuppression, post-transplant lymphoproliferative diseases (PTLD) result because the T-cells are suppressed, which is thought to remove a restraining influence on EBV-infected B cells. The PTLD spectrum includes:

- a benign polyclonal proliferation analogous to infectious mononucleosis (55%)
- polyclonal B-cell proliferation with early malignant transformation (30%)
- monoclonal B-cell mostly high-grade malignant lymphoma, with a high proportion showing extranodal involvement (15%).

RENAL TRANSPLANTATION

Patients in chronic renal failure, who in the past would have died, are now effectively maintained on either peritoneal dialysis or haemodialysis, both of which place restrictions on the patient's lifestyle.

For young and otherwise fit patients with domestic and occupational responsibilities, renal transplantation offers freedom from the restrictions of regular dialysis and has transformed the quality of their lives.

The transplanted kidney may be rejected. Rejection may be rapid or slow in onset, and is designated hyperacute, acute or chronic.

Hyperacute Rejection

Hyperacute rejection is due to preformed complementfixing antibodies in the blood of the recipient. The immune damage is directed at the endothelial cells of the graft, and the speed of onset is related to the antibody concentration, so that, when high, damage occurs within minutes or hours, compared with 1-2 days when levels are low. In some cases the reaction is immediate, and is apparent to the surgeon on establishing a flow of blood through the graft: the kidney becomes flaccid, cyanosed and mottled, suggesting intrarenal vasoconstriction. Thrombi form in arterioles and glomeruli, and cortical infarcts occur as a result of vascular thrombosis.

Acute Rejection

Acute rejection may occur at any time from a few days to months or years after transplantation, and involves both cellular and humoral immunity. Acute vascular rejection is evinced by a necrotising vasculitis with immunoglobulin, complement and fibrin in the vessel wall. Superimposed thrombosis may lead to infarction.

Cellular rejection is characterised by a mononuclear cell infiltrate, interstitial oedema and haemorrhage together with a tubulitis. Class I MHC molecules present peptide antigens to CD8-positive T-cells, while class II MHC molecules present peptides derived from extracellular proteins to CD4-positive T-cells. Both of these T-cell types feature in the interstitial infiltrate of a cellular rejection.

Chronic Rejection

Chronic rejection is an important cause of failure of grafts months or years after transplantation. Vascular changes dominate, resulting in ischaemic changes in the renal parenchyma. There is progressive interstitial fibrosis and tubular atrophy. Delayed graft function, episodes of acute rejection, hypertension, recurrent or de novo renal disease and hypertriglyceridaemia are all associated with an increased risk of graft loss.

DISEASES AFFECTING BLOOD VESSELS

In addition to the conditions mentioned above, the renal vasculature may be damaged in:

- progressive systemic sclerosis (scleroderma)
- systemic hypertension.

Renal Infarction

Two mechanisms of infarction are recognised:

- embolic infarction
- diffuse cortical necrosis.

Embolic Infarction

Most renal infarcts result from embolisation of:

- *atheromatous material,* responsible for the small subcapsular pits in benign-phase hypertension

- *thrombotic material* arising from the left side of the heart
- *bacterial vegetations* from infective endocarditis.

Many renal infarcts are clinically silent, but some result in haematuria and loin pain.

Renal infarcts are pale or white, and have a characteristic wedge shape with the apex directed towards the hilum.

Diffuse Cortical Necrosis

Diffuse cortical necrosis is a rare condition complicating pregnancy or trauma associated with severe haemorrhage or severe sepsis. Profound hypotension occurs in these situations, but there is considerable controversy relating to the pathogenesis of this condition.

Vasoconstriction is important because infarction can be avoided by the use of angiotensin antagonists. Diffuse cortical necrosis is a cause of acute anuric renal failure. The prognosis is poor when the infarction is generalised, but is less ominous when the infarction is focal.

Macroscopically, the appearance is striking: the external surface bears irregular yellowish areas with intervening congestion and haemorrhage. The cut surface shows the infarction to be confined to the cortex.

RENAL DISEASE IN PREGNANCY

The kidneys undergo morphological and functional changes during pregnancy. Some of these changes have a bearing on the renal response to disease and are relevant in the context of interpreting function tests.

Renal impairment, whatever the cause, that is present at the beginning of pregnancy has important implications because the risks to both the mother and fetus are significant. The risk of deteriorating renal function and hypertension is increased, and there is a rise in fetal morbidity and mortality.

Infection

Infection is the most frequent urinary tract abnormality in pregnant women and is usually detected on routine testing of the urine during antenatal care. Asymptomatic bacteriuria occurs in up to 10% of pregnant women, and there is good evidence to suggest that such patients run a high risk of developing acute pyelonephritis.

Prompt diagnosis and early treatment are therefore essential. Renal abnormalities such as the coarse polar scarring of vesicoureteric reflux are detected radiologically in a high proportion of these patients. In addition, physiological changes occur in the smooth muscle cells of the lower urinary tract in pregnancy, with slower ureteric peristaltic activity and pelvi-ureteric dilatation. This leads to stasis which, combined with infection, particularly with ureasplitting organisms, predisposes to stone formation; existing stones may enlarge considerably during pregnancy.

Hypertension

Hypertension is an important development in the pregnant patient. The patient may have latent essential hypertension or may have intercurrent renal disease. Alternatively, a condition peculiar to pregnancy called pre-eclampsia or eclampsia may be present.

Pre-eclampsia is a condition characterised by hypertension, proteinuria and oedema; *eclampsia* supervenes when fits occur. In severe cases the glomeruli are large and relatively bloodless due to marked swelling of the endothelial and mesangial cells. Arteries and arterioles display endothelial swelling and myo-intimal proliferation.

The tubules and interstitium are relatively normal. The vascular and glomerular lesions are reversible when the hypertension has been corrected. However, disseminated intravascular coagulation is frequently superimposed during the course of pre-eclampsia, and when fibrinoid necrosis of the arterioles has occurred then persistent hypertension may ensue.

TUBULO-INTERSTITIAL DISORDERS

In tubulo-interstitial conditions there is damage to the tubular epithelial cells and the interstitium. These disorders account for a significant proportion of patients presenting with impaired renal function.

Infections of the kidney affect the tubules and the interstitium, and may present as acute renal failure if there are complications such as tubular or papillary necrosis. These are discussed in a later section because of their clinical importance as a separate entity.

Acute tubular epithelial cell damage causes the condition known as acute tubular necrosis.

Acute Tubular Necrosis

- Important cause of acute renal failure
- May be due to toxic or haemodynamic causes (e.g. shock)
- Regeneration of renal tubular epithelium often permits clinical recovery

Acute tubular necrosis (ATN) is a very important cause of acute renal failure; patients often present with extreme oliguria (less than 100 ml of urine each 24 h). The importance of ATN is that it is fully recoverable if the patient is given adequate supportive fluid and electrolyte therapy.

Following the initial oliguria due to tubular obstruction by swollen and necrotic epithelial cells, there is a later diuretic phase due to the loss of urinary concentration. In the oliguric phase, hyperkalaemia with the risk of cardiac arrhythmias presents a serious threat to life.

This situation contrasts with hypokalaemia which can occur in the early diuretic phase. The histological features range from sublethal cell injury to necrosis of the epithelial cells.

The principal causes of acute tubular necrosis are:

- ischaemia
- toxins.

Ischaemic ATN

Ischaemic ATN follows a variety of clinical situations, such as trauma, burns, and infections in which the patient becomes shocked. Profound hypotension is usually responsible for the hypoperfusion of the peritubular circulation.

The kidneys are pale and swollen. Histology reveals epithelial cell injury along the entire length of the tubules; the cells are flattened and vacuolated. Inflammatory cells pack the vasa recta in response to the necrotic cells; the interstitium is oedematous.

Casts occur frequently in the distal tubules and collecting ducts; they are composed of cellular debris and protein, including Tamm-Horsfall protein. In the case of ATN resulting from a crush injury, myoglobin is present in the casts. Following a mismatched blood transfusion haemoglobin would be present.

Toxic ATN

Toxic ATN results from a wide variety of substances:

- *heavy metals* (lead, mercury, arsenic, gold, chromium, bismuth and uranium)
- *organic solvents* (carbon tetrachloride, chloroform)
- *glycols* (ethylene glycol, propylene glycol, dioxane and diethylene glycol)
- *therapeutic* substances (antibiotics-methicillin, sulphonamides, polymyxin, cephalosporins; nonsteroidal anti-inflammatory drugs; mercurial diuretics; anaesthetics-methoxyflurane)

- iodinated radiographic contrast medium
- phenol
- pesticides
- paraquat.

The kidneys are swollen and red. Histologically, there is often marked vacuolation of the tubular epithelial cytoplasm. The damage is characteristically restricted to the proximal tubular cells, those of the distal tubule being spared.

This situation contrasts with the picture in ischaemic ATN in which the tubular cells along the entire length of the tubule are affected. Recovery is indicated in biopsies by the presence of mitotic figures within the flattened cells.

Interstitial Nephritis

Interstitial nephritis is a term used for a heterogeneous group of conditions which have morphological and clinical features in common, but have a wide range of causes. The common morphology is an inflammatory reaction composed mainly of T-cells in the intertubular (interstitial) connective tissue.

The pathogenesis in many instances is not understood. Classification is therefore based mainly on aetiological factors:

- *toxins* heavy metals (e.g. lead, gold, mercury), or drugs (e.g. gentamicin, cephaloridine, ciclosporin)
- immunological
- metabolic-u rate, etc.
- physical-obstruction
- *neoplastic* myeloma.

Acute Interstitial Nephritis

With acute interstitial nephritis there is acute onset of renal failure; a careful history should be taken to exclude exposure to one of the known substances which can damage the kidney.

There is considerable overlap between the many substances which cause acute toxic tubular necrosis and acute interstitial nephritis. Histologically, there is interstitial oedema, together with a mononuclear cell infiltrate, and evidence of tubular degeneration.

Chronic Interstitial Nephritis

Patients with chronic interstitial nephritis present ın chronic renal failure, and establishing a cause is often very difficult. Histologically, there is marked interstitial fibrosis and tubular atrophy with a variable cellular infiltrate.

Analgesic Nephropathy

Analgesic nephropathy is a well-known adverse reaction to analgesics. It occurs worldwide but shows areas of high incidence, first described in 1953 in Switzerland. Epidemiological and experimental research has shown that the chronic ingestion of large quantities of aspirin combined with phenacetin is particularly harmful.

The phenacetin produces a metabolite which binds to the cellular proteins, depleting cellular glutathione, and is thus toxic. The aspirin is thought to induce papillary ischaemia by inhibiting the synthesis of vasodilatory prostaglandins.

The toxic and ischaemic effects, therefore, are thought to be synergistic to produce, initially, selective damage and, subsequently, necrosis of the papillae.

Transitional cell carcinomas of the renal pelvis and ureter occur more frequently in patients with analgesic nephropathy.

Lesions Associated with Metabolic Disorders

A variety of metabolic diseases and disturbances affect the tubules and interstitium. These include:

- hypokalaemia
- mate nephropathy
- *hypercalcaemia*
- oxalosis.

Hypokalaemic Nephropathy

Persistently low plasma levels of potassium occur in:

- chronic diarrhoea
- hyperaldosteronism, either primary or secondary
- chronic abuse of laxatives or diuretics.

Hypokalaemia causes coarse vacuolation of the tubular epithelial cells principally in the proximal tubules, but in severe states those of the distal tubules are also involved; the medullary tubules are spared.

Urate (gouty) Nephropathy

Renal damage due to elevated levels of uric acid in the blood occurs in gout. Additionally, patients with chronic renal damage due to pyelonephritis or glomerulonephritis have impaired filtration and reduced tubular secretion of uric acid; this leads to retention of uric acid and its subsequent deposition in the kidney. Uric acid crystallises in an acid environment such as that found in the distal tubules, collecting ducts and interstitium of the papillae.

Acute Urate Nephropathy

Acute urate nephropathy presents as acute renal failure and is seen principally in patients with myeloproliferative diseases. It is often precipitated by chemotherapy, when extensive breakdown of cells releases vast quantities of nucleic acids.

The cut surface of affected kidneys displays yellow streaks within the medulla due to precipitation of urate crystals filling the tubular lumina; this precipitation causes obstruction and tubular dilatation.

Chronic Urate Nephropathy

Chronic urate nephropathy is more insidious and occurs in patients with persistently elevated uric acid levels, as in gout. The crystals in the tubular lumina cause chronic obstruction and tubulo-interstitial nephritis in the cortex, which becomes atrophic and thinned.

Urate stones may occur in both acute and chronic nephropathy, and there is an increased incidence of pyelonephritis.

Hypercalcaemic Nephropathy (Nephrocalcinosis)

Calcium deposition in the kidneys occurs when there is hypercalcaemia: this is 'metastatic' calcification. The onset of renal symptoms is insidious; the tubular disturbance results in an inability to concentrate urine, with consequent polyuria often causing the patient to complain of nocturia.

The kidney is often scarred and focally calcified. The cut surface of the kidneys reveals stones within the pelvicalyceal system, and linear white streaks and flecks. There is interstitial fibrosis, a non-specific inflammatory infiltrate and tubular atrophy in relation to the calcification.

Oxalate Nephropathy

Calcium oxalate deposition occurs systemically in the tissues when blood levels are high. Increased urinary excretion of oxalate also occurs and the kidneys may be damaged. Hyperoxalaemia and the resulting hyperoxaluria are either primary or secondary.

The primary form is due to deficiencies of hepatic enzymes, which are concerned with the decarboxylation of glyoxylate, which accumulates and is oxidised by an alternative pathway to oxalate. Secondary hyperoxaluria is seen in poisoning with ethylene glycol (anti-freeze), or the anaesthetic agent methoxyflurane, and in pyridoxine (vitamin B_6) deficiency.

Oxalate deposition is also seen in the kidneys in a variety of chronic renal disorders. In advanced cases, the kidneys are small, granular and scarred, the thinned cortex reflecting the fibrosis and tubular disruption that occurs with the deposition of oxalate. Stones are often present in the pelvis and calyceal system.

Lesions Due to Physical Agents

Radiation Nephritis

The renal tubular cells are sensitive to radiation, and care must be taken to avoid injury to the kidneys during therapeutic irradiation to the upper abdomen. Affected patients present with hypertension and renal insufficiency.

Histologically, there is glomerulosclerosis, marked vascular changes, and interstitial fibrosis. The tubules are lined by atypical epithelial cells and display characteristic thick multilayered basement membranes.

Obstructive Uropathy

Obstructive uropathy is an important cause of interstitial nephritis. The causes of urinary tract obstruction include:

- *congenital anomalies* (uretero-pelvic stenosis, vesicoureteric reflux)
- *tumours* (carcinoma of the bladder and prostate)
- *hyperplastic lesions* (benign prostatic hyperplasia)
- calculi.

Clinical features

The signs, symptoms and prognosis depend on the level of the obstruction. Thus, a renal calculus or a fragment of sloughed papilla will cause renal colic, whereas obstruction due to carcinoma of the bladder or benign prostatic hyperplasia will be accompanied by bladder symptoms.

Acute obstruction in the lower urinary tract will result in anuria and pain, and if not relieved is incompatible with survival. Partial, and particularly unilateral, obstruction is much more insidious. There are few symptoms, the condition remaining unnoticed for many years in some patients.

There is usually polyuria and nocturia. Poor urinary concentration, tubular acidosis and salt wasting can sometimes be demonstrated in the early stages, all of which are expressions of the tubular epithelial cell damage that occurs. Systemic hypertension is common in these patients.

Pathogenesis

The pelvis and calyceal system become dilated due to back pressure; the dilatation is mild in cases of acute obstruction. The peristaltic activity of the ureters is increased in obstruction, which raises the intrapelvic pressure, which in turn is transmitted into the renal parenchyma. Initially, the filtrate formed is reabsorbed through lymphatic and vascular channels.

The continued rapid rise in pressure, however, reduces glomerular and medullary blood flow and eventually impairs glomerular filtration. Gross dilatation occurs as a result of prolonged back pressure. The kidney becomes a dilated sac-like structure: this is *hydronephrosis*.

Pyelonephritis

- A common and important cause of renal disease
- Causative bacteria may reach the kidneys either through the blood (as in septicaemia) or by reflux of contaminated urine from the bladder
- Acute pyelonephritis is characterised by pus in the tubules and by abscess formation
- Chronic pyelonephritis is characterised by coarse scarring and contraction of the kidneys

Pyelonephritis is an infection in the kidney which may arise by haematogenous or retrograde ureteric routes. Due to their rich blood supply, the kidneys are often involved in severe systemic infections by direct spread of organisms through septicaemia. The commonest infecting organisms are bacteria.

Urinary tract infections are common within the community, second only to upper respiratory infections. However, not all urinary tract infections are associated with pyelonephritis; organisms can gain access to the kidney only if there is vesico-ureteric reflux.

The incidence of pyelonephritis parallels that of obstructive uropathy. In infancy, boys are mainly affected because of anatomical abnormalities. From puberty to middle age females show the highest incidence, related to urethral trauma and pregnancy.

After 40 years, prostatic disease provides an obstructive aetiology in ageing men. Other factors include instrumentation (e.g. catheterisation, cystoscopy) and diabetes mellitus.

The clinical distinction between acute and chronic pyelonephritis is quite clear.

Acute Pyelonephritis

Acute pyelonephritis is due to infection of the kidney by pyogenic organisms. It presents with malaise and fever, and pain and tenderness in the loins is not uncommon. Dysuria and urgency of micturition indicate an associated infection in the lower urinary tract. The finding of pus cells in the urine (pyuria) is helpful, but the finding of white cell casts provides unequivocal evidence of pyelonephritis.

Urine culture in suspected cases is imperative, but bacteriuria is regarded as significant only when in excess of 10^5 cultureforming units/ml; this result eliminates cases of extraneous bacterial contamination.

Pathogenesis

The pathogenesis of acute pyelonephritis is either:

- haematogenous spread
- retrograde ureteric spread.

Haematogenous spread can occur in a patient with infective endocarditis or bacteraemia from other sources; the spectrum of organisms can be wide, including bacteria, fungi, rickettsia and viruses. Previous renal damage or structural abnormality predisposes to organisms localising in the kidney.

More commonly, pyelonephritis results from organisms gaining access from the lower urinary tract, known as an ascending infection, in association with reflux of urine. In these cases the infecting organisms are Gram-negative bacilli (e.g. *E. coli, Proteus spp.* and *Enterobacter)* from the patient's faecal flora.

This occurs frequently in young women; predisposing factors include the short urethra, urethral trauma during sexual intercourse, and pregnancy. Instrumentation of the urinary tract in both sexes increases both the incidence and the variety of infecting organisms.

Morphology

Acute pyelonephritis is characterised by either abscesses throughout the cortex and medulla, or wedge-shaped confluent areas of suppuration. The minute abscesses are randomly distributed when the infection is blood-borne, but tend to be located at the upper and lower poles when associated with urinary reflux.

A lower urinary tract infection may be associated with inflammation of the pelvic and calyceal mucosa, and pus may be present in the pelvis. Histology reveals intratubular polymorphs together with interstitial oedema and inflammation.

These white cell 'granular' casts pass into the bladder and are evident on microscopy of the urine. With healing, fibrosis occurs in the interstitium and the inflammatory infiltrate becomes dominated by lymphocytes and plasma cells.

Complications

Three important complications may develop in acute pyelonephritis:

- *Renal papillary necrosis. As* a result of the inflammation, the medullary blood supply is compromised and renal papillary necrosis may ensue, particularly in diabetics or where there is obstruction.
- *Pyonephrosis.* This arises when there is complete obstruction high in the urinary tract near the kidney. The stagnant fluid in the pelvis and calyceal system suppurates. Eventually, the kidney becomes grossly distended with pus.
- *Perinephric abscess.* When the infection breaches the renal capsule and extends into the perirenal tissues, it gives rise to a perinephric abscess.

Chronic Pyelonephritis

Chronic pyelonephritis occurs in association with *vesicoureteric reflux* (VUR), which commences either early in life due to congenital lesions or with obstruction developing during adulthood.

Vesico-ureteric reflux enables organisms to gain access to the kidney from the bladder. The primary abnormality is the angle at which the terminal ureteric segment traverses the bladder wall. Normally the course taken is oblique, at an acute angle to the mucosal surface, so that contraction of the bladder wall during micturition closes the ureteric orifice.

In patients with VUR, the terminal portion is short and orientated at approximately 90° to the mucosal surface; contraction of the bladder tends to hold the ureteric orifice open and facilitates reflux of urine.

Pathogenesis

Reflux of urine into the kidney during micturition raises the intrapelvic and intracalyceal pressure, but intraparenchymal reflux remains the crucial factor for development of pyelonephritis. In cases prone to intraparenchymal reflux, the renal papillae' are flattened rather than conical, and the terminal ducts open on to the surface at right angles.

This situation facilitates reflux into the collecting ducts when the intrapelvic pressure is high, in contrast to the oblique angle of opening of the ducts in non-refluxing papillae. Refluxing papillae tend to be situated at the poles of the kidney, and it is in these areas that the pyelonephritic damage is predominantly seen. The presence of infection accelerates scarring due to reflux.

Morphology

The macroscopic appearance of pyelonephritis associated with chronic reflux is so characteristic as to be diagnostic. Deep irregular scars are seen towards the poles of the kidney.

Involvement may be unilateral, or if bilateral is characteristically asymmetrical. There is a distinctive relationship between the scarred areas and the underlying deformed and dilated calyces.

Microscopically there is interstitial fibrosis with atrophic and dilated tubules containing eosinophilic casts, giving the appearance of 'thyroidisation' of the kidney, so-called because of the resemblance to thyroid histology.

Xanthogranulomatous Pyelonephritis

Xanthogranulomatous pyelonephritis is an uncommon condition which develops in patients with chronic pyelonephritis and is associated with *Proteus* and E. coli infection and intrapelvic stones.

Clinicopathological features

A renal mass is present in the majority of cases; it may distort the external surface of the kidney and resemble a neoplasm. The cut surface shows a yellowish mass surrounding distorted calyces, and small abscesses are often seen in the adjacent areas.

Histologically, foamy macrophages dominate the lesion and are admixed with a varied population of inflammatory cells. The clinical significance of this lesion relates to the potential confusion with renal cell carcinoma, and the risk of fistulae.

Renal Tuberculosis

The kidneys can be affected by tuberculosis as part of generalised miliary spread from an active tuberculous lesion elsewhere (usually in the lungs); the kidneys become dotted with numerous minute white granulomas.

Solitary tuberculous lesions occur in the kidneys of adults. These may or may not be associated with other active tuberculous lesions elsewhere; they may represent reactivation of a dormant lesion. The kidney contains an irregular white mass filled with caseous material.

This arises within the renal parenchyma but may eventually rupture into the calyceal system, leaving an open, ragged cavity and enabling tubercle bacilli to seed along the ureter and into the bladder.

Severe and longstanding tuberculosis may produce a tuberculous pyelonephrosis with complete destruction of the kidney. 'Sterile' pyuria is an important feature in renal tuberculosis and should stimulate an active search for the acid-alcohol-fast bacilli in the urine.

Viral Infections

Virus infection of the kidney is probably a common occurrence. Tubular and glomerular involvement has been demonstrated in cases of measles, mumps, herpes zoster, influenza and other viral infections.

Nevertheless, viruses do not appear to be involved in pyelonephritis. Cytomegalovirus, which gives characteristic cytoplasmic and intranuclear acidophilic inclusions in the tubular cells, is very common but appears to cause little damage under normal circumstances.

URINARY CALCULI

Urinary calculi (stones) occur in 1-5% of the population in the UK, mainly those over 30 years, and with a male preponderance. They may form anywhere in the urinary tract, but the commonest site is within the renal pelvis. They present as:

- renal colic, an exquisitely painful symptom due to the passage of a small stone along the ureter
- a dull ache in the loins
- recurrent and intractable urinary tract infection.

Calculi form in the urine either because substances are in such an excess that they precipitate, or because other factors affecting solubility are upset. Factors influencing stone formation include the pH of the urine, which can be influenced by both bacterial activity and metabolic factors.

Substances in the urine normally inhibit precipitation of crystals, notably pyrophosphates and citrates. The mucoproteins in the urine are thought to provide the organic nidus on which the crystals focus.

Classification

Calculi are classified according to their composition. The categories are:

- calcium oxalate, often mixed with calcium phosphate and uric acid (75-80% of all calculi)
- triple (struvite) stones composed of magnesium ammonium phosphate (15%); these form the large staghorn' calculi
- uric acid stones (6%)
- calculi in cystinuria and oxalosis (1%).

Only 10% of patients with *calcium-containing stones* have hyperparathyroidism or some other cause of hypercalcaemia. However, most have increased levels of calcium in the urine, which is attributable to a defect in the tubular reabsorption.

In the remaining patients, with idiopathic hypercalciuria, no known cause has been identified. The association of uric acid with calcium stones is probably because urates can initiate precipitation of oxalate from solution.

Magnesium ammonium phosphate stones are particularly associated with urinary tract infections with bacteria, such as *Proteus,* which are able to break down urea to form ammonia.

The alkaline conditions thus produced, together with sluggish flow, cause precipitation of these salts and large staghorn calculi form a cast of the pelvicalyceal system. Staghorn calculi remain in the pelvis for many years and may cause irritation, with subsequent squamous metaplasia or in some cases squamous carcinoma.

Uric acid stones occur in patients with gout. Uric acid precipitates in acid urine. The stones are radiolucent.

TUMOURS OF THE KIDNEY

- Benign tumours (e.g. fibroma, adenoma) infrequently cause clinical problems
- Malignant tumours are renal cell carcinoma (hypernephroma), Wilms' tumour (nephroblastoma) and transitional cell carcinoma
- Renal cell carcinoma often presents with metastases (occult primary)
- Malignant tumours present with pain and/or haematuria

Primary tumours and metastases occur in the kidneys, but metastases are less frequent than would be expected in view of the generous blood supply of the kidneys.

Benign Renal Tumours

Renal Fibroma

The commonest benign renal tumour is the renal fibroma or *renomedullary interstitial cell tumour.* This tumour is usually an incidental finding at autopsy with no clinical significance. Renal fibromas are firm white nodules, usually less than 10 mm in diameter, situated in the medulla or in the papillae and composed of spindle cells tending to surround the adjacent tubules.

Benign Cortical Adenoma

Benign cortical adenomas are discrete yellowish-grey nodules, usually less than 20 mm in diameter, situated in the cortex of the kidney. They are not uncommon, being discovered in up to 20% of autopsies.

Histologically, there is nothing to distinguish the adenoma from a renal tubular carcinoma; both are composed of large clear cells with small nuclei.

The distinction is often made only by size: those below 30 mm in diameter are regarded as benign. This distinction is entirely arbitrary and unreliable, as an early carcinoma may not have achieved the 30 mm threshold. Malignancy may develop in cortical adenomas.

Oncocytoma

Oncocytoma is a subtype of adenoma in which the granular cytoplasm, attributable to abundant large and distorted mitochondria, is the most prominent feature. Oncocytomas occasionally attain a considerable size and thus are easily confused with renal cell carcinomas.

Other Benign Tumours

Benign tumours can arise from any cell type within the kidney. Few cause clinical problems, other than *haemangiomas* which may bleed, thus causing pain or predisposing to severe blood loss in the event of trauma.

A rare *tumour of the juxtaglomerular cells* produces renin and is a cause of hypertension in young patients. *Angiomyolipoma is* an intrarenal mass composed of a mixture of blood vessels, muscle and mature fat. The lesion is not a true tumour, but is best regarded as a hamartoma.

The clinical importance of this lesion lies in the association with tuberous sclerosis, an inherited disorder involving the central nervous system, skin and other viscera.

Malignant Renal Tumours

The clinically important malignant tumours of the kidney are:

- renal cell carcinoma (hypernephroma)
- Wilms' tumour (nephroblastoma)
- transitional cell carcinoma of the renal pelvis.

Renal Cell Carcinoma

Renal cell carcinoma (*hypernephroma, Grawitz tumour*) is the commonest primary kidney tumour in adults, but it accounts for only 1-3% of all visceral tumours. It occurs most frequently over the age of 50 years; there is a male preponderance.

The common presenting clinical features of haematuria, loin pain and a mass are late manifestations and account for the relatively poor prognosis. In patients with no evidence of metastasis at presentation, the 5-year survival may be as high as 70%, but it falls to 15-20% when the renal vein is involved or there is extension into the perinephric fat.

Aetiology

There is an increased incidence of renal carcinoma in those who smoke tobacco. There is no evidence to suggest any other known aetiological agents to be relevant in humans. A genetic predisposition is indicated by the strong association with von Hippel-Lindau disease, a rare hereditary condition.

The behaviour of these tumours is very difficult to predict. Hypernephromas are not uncommonly associated with paraneoplastic manifestations, including:

- hypercalcaemia
- hypertension
- polycythaemia.

Additionally, some cases develop an eosinophilia or leukaemoid reaction in the blood, and a small proportion of patients develop amyloidosis.

Morphology

Macroscopically, the kidney is distorted by a large bossellated tumour which most often occurs in the upper pole. The cut surface reveals a solid yellowish-grey tumour with areas of haemorrhage and necrosis. Hypernephromas are sometimes cystic; this can present diagnostic problems.

The margins of the tumour are usually well demarcated, but some breach the renal capsule and invade the perinephric fat. Extension into the renal vein is sometimes seen grossly; occasionally, a solid mass of tumour extends into the inferior vena cava and, rarely, into the right atrium.

Histologically, renal cell carcinomas are composed of either clear or granular cells. The small nuclei belie the malignant nature of this tumour. The clear cytoplasm is due to glycogen and fat; the similarity to adrenal cortical cells is responsible for the name 'hypernephroma', as these tumours were originally thought to arise from embryonic adrenal rests!

Wilms' Tumour

Wilms' tumour is the commonest intra-abdominal tumour in children under the age of 10 years; the peak incidence is between the ages of 1 and 4 years, and the sexes are equally involved. The most common presentation is with an abdominal mass. Haematuria, hypertension, abdominal pain and intestinal obstruction may also be the initial clinical features.

The tumour is aggressive and rapidly growing; spread to the lungs is identified in a high proportion of cases at the time of diagnosis. Aggressive therapy involving radiotherapy, chemotherapy and surgery has greatly improved the prognosis in these cases.

Morphology

Macroscopically the tumour is often large, and frequently extends beyond the capsule into the perinephric fat and even into the root of the mesentery. The cut surface is variegated and reflects the component tissues seen histologically.

Areas of haemorrhagic necrosis are common, merging with solid tumour composed of firm white tissue, together with cartilaginous and mutinous areas. Histologically, both epithelial and mesenchymal tissues are seen, the tumour being derived from the mesonephric mesoderm.

There are poorly developed glomeruli and tubules in a spindle cell stroma. Striated muscle is frequently present in these tumours together with myxoid fibrous tissue, cartilage, bone and fat, thus creating a rather bizarre mixture.

Carcinoma of the Renal Pelvis

While the majority of renal tumours in adults are renal cell carcinomas, the greater proportion of those remaining (5-10%) are transitional cell carcinomas arising from the urothelium of the renal pelvis. As they project into the pelvicalyceal cavity, they present early with haematuria or obstruction.

They frequently infiltrate the wall of the pelvis and may involve the renal vein. The prognosis is not good, especially for those patients with poorly differentiated tumours, and multiple tumours are not uncommon in the ureters and bladder.

Aetiology

There is an association with analgesic abuse and exposure to aniline dyes used in the dye, rubber, plastics and gas industries. A few patients have been reported with transitional cell carcinoma many years following the use of Thorotrast, an a-emitter, in retrograde pyelography.

Clinicopathological features

These are fronded transitional cell neoplasms, identical to their counterparts in the ureter and urinary bladder. It is not uncommon to find multiple transitional cell tumours throughout the urinary tract, suggesting a urothelial field change.

The papillary form of the tumours results in fragments breaking off from the tips of the fronds; atypical tumour cells can be detected in the urine, making these lesions particularly amenable to cytological diagnosis and screening.

In the presence of pelvic stones the urothelium may undergo squamous metaplasia. Squamous carcinoma is known to be associated with calculi and chronic infection, but may also arise de novo from the transitional epithelium. Macroscopically, these tumours are usually flat and infiltrative, and carry a poor prognosis.

URETERS

Normal Structure and Function

The ureters form in continuity with the calyceal system and collecting ducts from an outgrowth of the Wolffian duct. Urine is conveyed to the bladder by peristaltic activity; this activity is reduced in pregnancy, predisposing to stasis and infection. The lumen is lined by urothelium; the muscle layer is predominantly circular with a thin, inner longitudinal layer, and is invested in a fibrous adventitia. The ureteric orifice is slit-like, and the course of the terminal part of the ureter through the bladder wall is oblique to form a valve.

Congenital Lesions

Congenital lesions include *double* or *bifid ureters* which may be associated with structural abnormalities of the pelvicalyceal system. These usually have no consequences for renal function. However, a congenitally short terminal segment of the ureter, which is not oblique, results in vesico-ureteric reflux, an important cause of renal infection and scarring.

Hydroureter is dilatation and often tortuosity of the ureter; this condition may occur as a congenital lesion, when it is thought to reflect a neuromuscular defect. The most frequent causes of hydroureter in the adult are low urinary obstruction and pregnancy.

Inflammation

The ureter may become inflamed due to a urinary tract infection, and chronic inflammation may supervene. In some patients with chronic inflammation, a condition called *ureteritis cystica* develops, in which epithelial cell nests become trapped by fibrosis and subsequently develop into thin-walled cysts.

Obstruction

Obstruction of the ureter is the most frequent problem requiring clinical attention. Acute ureteric obstruction causes intense pain known as renal colic. The consequences of chronic ureteric obstruction are hydroureter and hydronephrosis. In both acute and chronic ureteric obstruction there is an increased risk of ascending infection, causing pyelonephritis.

Ureteric obstruction may be either intrinsic or extrinsic. *Intrinsic lesions* are within the ureteric wall or lumen; the most common is a urinary calculus. Calculi become impacted where the ureter is normally narrowed, that is at the pelvi-ureteric junction, where it crosses the iliac artery, and where it enters the bladder.

Strictures may be congenital, when they occur at the pelvi-ureteric junction or in the transmural terminal segment of the ureter. Acquired strictures occur as a result of trauma and involvement by adjacent inflammatory conditions such as diverticulitis and salpingitis. Severe haematuria may cause obstruction due to blood clot.

Extrinsic factors cause pressure from without, and include tumours of the rectum, prostate and bladder. Aberrant renal arteries may compress the ureter. Retroperitoneal fibrosis causes narrowing and medial deviation of the ureters and may either be due to drugs, such as methysergide, or be idiopathic.

Primary tumours of the ureter are usually transitional cell carcinomas. They may be multiple and are associated with urothelial tumours in the urinary pelvis and bladder.

BLADDER

Normal Structure and Function

The urinary bladder is a cavity lined by transitional cell epithelium-the *urothelium,* surrounded by connective tissue—the lamina *propria,* and smooth muscle. Histologically, the normal bladder urothelium is 7-8 cells thick and has three zones: basal, intermediate and a highly specialised surface layer.

The smooth muscle is arranged in bundles which interlace rather than form defined layers. Urine drains into the bladder from the kidneys, via the ureters, for storage until a convenient time and place is found for its discharge through the urethra.

The bladder responds to obstruction to the outflow by undergoing muscular hypertrophy. The proximity of the bladder to the genital tract in females, to the prostate in males, and to the bowel in both sexes, means that it is often invaded by tumours arising in these other organs.

Diverticula

Diverticula are outpouchings of the bladder mucosa. Bladder diverticula are either congenital or acquired. They are clinically important because urinary stasis within them predisposes to calculus formation and infection.

Congenital diverticula are usually solitary. They arise from either a localised developmental defect in the muscle or urinary obstruction during fetal life.

Acquired diverticula are small and multiple. They are most often associated with outflow obstruction, and the high incidence in elderly males correlates with prostatic enlargement. They occur between the bands of hypertrophic muscle, known as trabeculae, which form in response to obstruction.

Congenital Lesions

Exstrophy of the bladder is a serious developmental defect affecting the anterior abdominal wall, bladder and, in some cases, the symphysis pubis. The bladder opens directly on to the external surface of the lower abdomen. Infection and pyelonephritis, together with a predisposition to adenocarcinoma, are important sequelae.

Vesico-ureteric reflux (VUR) is an important consequence of a developmental abnormality of the terminal part of the ureter, which appears to correct itself as the patient matures. However, during early childhood reflux occurs, which results in substantial scarring of the renal parenchyma. This condition is an important cause of renal impairment and infection in adult life (p. 581).

Persistence of the urachus may be partial or complete. Retention of the entire structure results in a fistula connecting the bladder with the skin at the umbilicus. Partial retention results in a diverticulum arising from the dome of the bladder. Alternatively the central area may persist and present as a cyst. Adenocarcinomas develop in these urachal remnants.

Cystitis

Inflammation of the bladder (cystitis) is a common occurrence as part of a urinary tract infection.

Aetiology

The causative organism is usually derived from the patient's faecal flora. Unusual organisms do occur: for example, *Candida* is seen in patients on prolonged antibiotic therapy, and tuberculous cystitis almost always reflects tuberculosis elsewhere in the urinary tract. Radiation and trauma due to instrumentation cause cystitis, which is often sterile.

Clinical features

Cystitis presents with frequency, lower abdominal pain and dysuria (scalding or burning pain on micturition), and occasionally haematuria.

In some patients there is general malaise and pyrexia. Cystitis usually responds readily to treatment. However, its clinical importance lies in the predisposition to pyelonephritis, a serious complication.

Pathological forms

Several different forms of cystitis occur, each expressing increasing severity. The initial hyperaemia may be excessive, causing *haemorrhagic cystitis*. When there are areas of yellow fibrinous exudate, *exudative cystitis* is present.

In some patients, the exudate is mixed with necrotic mucosa, and the term *membranous cystitis* applies. Finally, ischaemia results in black necrotic mucosa, which is termed *gangrenous cystitis*.

When chroniç cystitis is due to urea-splitting organisms, the alkalinity of the urine encourages precipitation of calcium ammonium phosphate crystals on the surface of the bladder and as calculi in the lumen.

Cystitis *cystica* occurs as a result of nests of urothelial cells becoming trapped in inflammatory fibrous tissue in patients with chronic cystitis. Sometimes these cells undergo glandular metaplasia; this is *cystitis glandularis*. The presence of lymphoid follicles in the lamina propria of patients with chronic cystitis is termed *cystitis follicularis*.

Malakoplakia is an uncommon variant of importance because it can mimic a tumour. Broad flat yellow plaques form in the mucosa, which may subsequently ulcerate. The plaques comprise a mixture of chronic inflammatory cells, including characteristic macrophages; these contain calcified granules known as Michaelis-Gutmann bodies. The granules are composed of bacterial debris, and they are thought to reflect defective macrophage function.

Tuberculous cystitis nearly always implies tuberculosis elsewhere in the renal tract. The organisms enter the mucosa from the urine and stimulate the usual granulomatous response, causing small tubercles which subsequently ulcerate. The tubercles form around the ureteric orifices and in the region of the bladder base. Eventually the bladder wall may become thickened, contracted and fibrous, and lined by caseous material.

Schistosomiasis also causes a granulomatous cystitis, in which the parasites are demonstrable, and is notable for the increased risk of squamous cell carcinoma.

Obstruction

Obstruction to the urinary outflow from the bladder has serious repercussions on the kidneys as well as causing changes in the bladder wall. Most cases are due to:

- prostatic disease in elderly men
- prolapse in elderly women, when part of the bladder protrudes into the vagina, producing a pouch
- calculi
- bladder tumours (see below)
- urethral strictures
- neurological damage.

The bladder wall becomes thickened due to hypertrophy of the muscle bundles, causing the characteristic interlacing ridges-trabeculae-between which small diverticula may develop.

Bladder Calculi

Diverticula, obstruction and inflammation are all important in the development of stones within the bladder. Alternatively, calculi may be passed down the ureter from the kidney.

Bladder stones may be asymptomatic, but eventual chronic irritation and infection lead to frequency, urgency, dysuria and sometimes haematuria. There is an increased risk of bladder carcinoma; this is often of squamous type arising from metaplastic squamous epithelium.

Fistulae

Fistulae between the bladder and adjacent structures occur as a result of:

- invasion by a malignant neoplasm
- radiation necrosis
- inflammatory bowel lesions (diverticulitis of the colon, Crohn's disease)
- surgical complications.

Vesico-vaginal and vesico-uterine fistulae, presenting with urine draining through the vagina, result from carcinoma of the cervix and uterus respectively. Vesico-enteric fistulae cause turbid urine with bacterial contamination and inflammation, and in some cases faecal material in the urine.

Tumours of the Bladder

- Most bladder tumours are transitional cell carcinomas
- Squamous cell carcinomas and adenocarcinomas are less common
- Sarcomas are rare

- Aetiological factors for transitional cell carcinoma include smoking and occupational exposure to dyes
- Aetiological factors for squamous cell carcinoma include calculi and schistosomiasis

Epithelial tumours of the bladder are common; sarcomas are relatively rare. The majority are transitional cell carcinomas; a small proportion are squamous. Adenocarcinoma of the bladder is uncommon.

Aetiology

The strong association of bladder tumours with certain chemicals has resulted in measures in industrial processes to reduce the level of risk to the employees. Bladder carcinogens include some dyes in textiles and printing, and reagents in the rubber, cable and plastics industries.

The carcinogenic substances are intermediate metabolites of aniline compounds; these are excreted in combination with glucuronic acid and are subsequently released in the bladder by the action of β-glucuronidase, which is facilitated by the acidity of the urine.

An increased incidence of urothelial tumours is also seen in heavy smokers and analgesic abusers. Schistosomiasis is an important cause of squamous cell carcinoma of the bladder.

Transitional Cell Carcinoma

Transitional cell carcinomas arise from the urothelium and are frequently multiple. The multifocal origin suggests that the entire urothelium may be unstable as a result of exposure to a carcinogen. Carcinoma is often preceded by dysplasia.

Painless haematuria is the commonest presenting feature, with dysuria, frequency and urgency occurring in some patients. When the tumour is near a ureteric orifice, obstruction causes unilateral pyelonephritis or hydronephrosis. Many of these tumours are papillary and tumour cells are frequently shed into the urine, where they can be detected by cytology.

Morphology

Most bladder tumours are papillary, the delicate fronds of which are best appreciated cystoscopically. The fronds are covered by an abnormally thick layer of urothelium, with atypical cytological features. In some lesions, the cells closely resemble normal urothelium and there is no evidence of invasion.

With increasing cytological abnormalities, however, the likelihood of invasion of the lamina propria increases. When the deep muscle of the bladder wall is invaded, the tumour becomes fixed clinically. Poorly differentiated transitional cell carcinomas are solid, usually invasive, and display severe cytological atypia.

A significant proportion of transitional cell carcinomas show microscopic foci of squamous or, more rarely, glandular metaplasia. Such areas form a substantial part of the tumour in about 5% of transitional carcinomas, which are then termed mixed tumours.

Staging and grading

Transitional cell carcinomas are graded I-III according to the degree of cytological atypia; this is a guide to prognosis. Staging is also used to judge prognosis; the TNM system is used. There is good correlation between grade and stage, as the majority of papillary growths are grade I and are non-invasive. In contrast, grade III lesions are usually flat, ulcerated and invasive, and carry a poor prognosis.

Carcinoma in situ

Carcinoma in situ of the urothelium is often found as a multifocal change in areas between tumours, and in some bladders in which no obvious tumours are present. It is a precursor of invasive carcinoma.

Squamous cell carcinoma

Squamous cell carcinomas arise from metaplastic squamous epithelium; this change occurs most often in association with calculi and with schistosomiasis. They are usually solid invasive tumours. The prognosis is not as good as for transitional carcinoma, but depends on the grade and stage of the individual tumour.

A similar histological appearance is produced by involvement of the bladder by a squamous carcinoma of the cervix; this sometimes causes diagnostic confusion.

Adenocarcinoma

Adenocarcinoma of the bladder is uncommon. It can arise from:

- urachal remnants at the bladder apex
- cystitis cystica
- glandular metaplasia in a transitional carcinoma
- periurethral and periprostatic glands.

Mesenchymal Tumours

Benign and malignant mesenchymal tumours occur in the bladder, but uncommonly. Benign tumours reflect the range of cell types in the wall:

- leiomyoma
- rhabdomyoma

- haemangioma
- neurofibroma.

Malignant mesenchymal tumours are usually rhabdomyosarcomas and occur in both adults and children. The appearance in the two groups is distinctive and merits comment. Rhabdomyosarcomas in adults occur in patients over 40 years, and are usually solid growths, histologically resembling the rhabdomyosarcoma seen in striated muscle.

In children, the tumours are large and composed of polypoid clusters resembling bunches of grapes, typical of a sarcoma botryoides or embryonal rhabdomyosarcoma.

Secondary Tumours

Secondary tumours of the bladder usually occur by direct extension, most often from the cervix, prostate or rectum. Haematogenous and lymphatic spread may occur from carcinomas in distant primary sites, e.g. lung.

INDEX

A

B

C

D

E

J

K

L

M

N

O